D0611210

# MORE ENGLISH DIARIES

BY THE SAME AUTHOR

ENGLISH DIARIES
SCOTTISH AND IRISH DIARIES
THE CAMEL AND THE NEEDLE'S EYE
THE DECLINE OF ARISTOCRACY
DEMOCRACY AND DIPLOMACY
WARS AND TREATIES (1815–1914)
A CONFLICT OF OPINION (a discussion on the Failure of the Church)
RELIGION IN POLITICS
NOW IS THE TIME (an appeal for Peace)
THE PRIORY AND MANOR OF LYNCHMERE AND SHULBREDE

---

WITH DOROTHEA PONSONBY

REBELS AND REFORMERS

# MORE ENGLISH DIARIES

## FURTHER REVIEWS OF DIARIES FROM THE SIXTEENTH TO THE NINETEENTH CENTURY WITH AN INTRODUCTION ON DIARY READING

BY

ARTHUR PONSONBY, M.P.

O! that I could persuade all my fellow mortals to journalize! If they were to begin in earnest they would be so delighted as to be unable to discontinue. It would insensibly lead their minds into a train of thinking attentively, and I trust I may add, that it would conduce to their acting circumspectly.

WILLIAM JONES

METHUEN & CO. LTD.
36 ESSEX STREET W.C.
LONDON

*First Published in 1927*

PRINTED IN GREAT BRITAIN

# PREFACE

OVER three years have elapsed since the appearance of *English Diaries*. The reception given to the book encouraged me to pursue the study and a further instalment is presented in this volume.

I have adopted the same method as in the previous volume in dealing with the diaries separately and chronologically. But this time I have commented on the smaller diaries in the introduction instead of detaching each for a short notice. I have limited my exploration to diaries published up to 1925, but I am fully aware that the whole ground is not yet covered. I am doubtful, moreover, if it ever can be. Even since 1925 a number of noteworthy diaries have been published and an increasing interest is being taken in this form of literature.

My thanks are very specially due to those who have been kind enough to lend me unpublished manuscript diaries. An acknowledgment to the possessor of the manuscript is made in each case. Some forty manuscript diaries have been examined. My chief difficulty has again been to *find* the diaries, and I am grateful to many friends who have given me hints and suggestions in my quest, and also to Miss C. Bower Alcock for her assistance in research work. In a few cases in which I have quoted from recently published books I have obtained the consent of the publishers for using the extracts in this volume. I have again to thank Sir Charles Strachey for his careful and helpful revision of the proofs.

A. P.

SHULBREDE PRIORY
SUSSEX
1927

# CONTENTS

# MORE ENGLISH DIARIES

# MORE ENGLISH DIARIES

## INTRODUCTION
## ON
## DIARY READING
### WITH NOTES ON MINOR ENGLISH DIARIES

AS I think I may with some certainty claim to have read more diaries than any of my contemporaries it will not be regarded as presumption on my part if I attempt to give the impressions received from this peculiar form of reading. In the Introduction to *English Diaries* an analysis was given of the method and motive of diarists, their tricks and peculiar characteristics. Since the publication of that volume, having absorbed a still larger number of diaries, I may approach the subject rather more from the opposite angle of the reader in order not to cover the same ground.

A reader of many diaries

In case the claim I make may be taken to mean that I have actually read every diary from cover to cover, it must be explained that this would be impossible. Most published diaries are in themselves incomplete. I have not been to Golden Square and read the whole vast manuscript of Crabb Robinson's diary, I have had no access to the archives of Windsor Castle to go through the 100 volumes of Queen Victoria's diary, I have not sat for weeks in the British Museum going through the original MS. of Greville, and even in the case of published diaries I must acknowledge that a conscientious perusal of every line of the eight volumes of Wesley's diary, for instance, was a task I attempted but failed to execute and one or two other works of great length daunted me. However, in the case of the smaller diaries there has

Impossibility of reading entire manuscripts

been no difficulty in reading all that is available. And many manuscript diaries, in spite of the obstacle of handwriting, I have read with special care in my quest for possible literary, historical or psychological treasures in the dust, such for instance as the talk with Buonaparte in Kershaw's [1] time-stained notebook and the life story of William Jones.[2] I will not substitute the word "perusal" for "read" as it seems to imply desultory skipping, whereas I have in all cases had to keep a very vigilant eye for quotable and characteristic passages. The word "examined" is perhaps more accurate and I may claim that given my purpose my examination has been thorough.

Diary reading

I believe that Mr. Gladstone when kept waiting used to pray. I have used all such intervals during the last few years in reading diaries. I have kept one in my pocket, I have put one in my bag when travelling and I have had one ready in any house or library where I was likely to find myself for any length of time. They are better than novels, more accurate than histories, and even at times more dramatic than plays. Divide them up how you will into ancient and modern, social, political, travel, or personal, introspective or objective, within each category there is infinite variety with just the slender but very distinct link that all these men and women have felt impelled to keep a book in which periodically to write down something about themselves.

Of course there is an immense amount of dross. My eye has, however, got sufficiently sharpened to prevent me wasting much time. One entry—even quite bald—could very often give a clue; and in the case of printed diaries passages from the editor's preface have sometimes saved me the trouble of burrowing further into a diary, specially in the case of social diaries where affectionate and sentimentally-minded descendants have rescued the effusions of grand- or great-grandparents from oblivion.

Attractive entries

On the other hand, a single entry or a few lines by their peculiarity or originality have made me resolve not to miss a line in all of the diary that is available. Here are some examples of passages which when they caught my eye made me eager to read more:

[1] See p. 185. [2] See p. 119.

LADY HOBY
to refresh myself being dull I plaied and sang to the Alpharion.

THOMAS ISCHAM
Father had a cough and stone. We attacked the fifth proposition of Euclid.

ANTHONY WOOD
The melancholy, malitious and peevish woman slighted me and rose in the middle of dinner from the table.

ELIZABETH FREKE [1]
The voylence of this my Fall struck outt my Cheek Teeth that strong as they weer, Fell out of my mouth—Roots and all.

THOMAS ROMNEY
I find my spirits the lowest I ever remember owing to domestic matters displeasing me most sadly.

FORD MADOX BROWN
Wasted one and a half hours cleaning a damned pipe.

Whereas entries such as "the dear Duchess of Gloucester is at death's door" or "better news from Siam" did not whet my appetite.

Old diaries

I must confess a preference for old diaries over the more modern, not only because there is naturally an enhanced interest in a document that is centuries old, but also because in the older records there is an un-selfconscious sincerity, a formless spontaneity, which is absent from the more elaborate social and political records of modern times.

Diaries of obscure people

I must further confess a still stronger preference for the diaries of obscure people over the diaries of celebrities. The percentage of what I may call good diaries among the former is far higher than among the latter. One can enjoy Thomas Turner,[2] William Jones, George Ridpath and James Woodforde without having to keep the *Dictionary of National Biography* and a peerage at one's elbow. It is probably because their range is restricted that these diarists excel. Great events and great people are only interesting to read about if the writer can introduce them quite naturally into his record. Nearly always, unfortunately, there is a strain and effort with regard to the introduction of the great people and an inevitable incompetence to deal with the great events. So far do I carry this preference which is the outcome of a very comprehensive study that when I hear of the publication of

[1] *Scottish and Irish Diaries*, p. 120.
[2] Now published, edited by Mrs. Charles Lamb.

the diary of a celebrity my heart sinks ; but when I get wind of the appearance of the diary of some one I have never heard of I am in hot pursuit.

James Woodforde and Lord Bertie

A specific illustration may be given in two diaries which have been published in recent years. The diary of an eighteenth-century parson, James Woodforde,[1] whose name was quite unknown, and the diary of Lord Bertie, the British Ambassador, in the very world centre of affairs during the greatest war that has ever been waged. The former redolent of atmosphere, intimacy and charm depicts utterly unimportant incidents of village life and is a delight to read, not because it has any literary merit, but because it is the punctual record of events well within the range and comprehension of a humble mind. The latter deals with the greatest men of the moment and world affairs of a magnitude too great for any pen to depict and is quite unreadable. Lord Bertie was a very amusing man, but he had no conception of how to write a diary, nor did he realize that in attempting what he did he was trying to accomplish something beyond human power. The result is bald, dull, pompous and glaringly inadequate.

No diary negligible

However, I have never been able to cast aside a diary and dismiss it at once as unworthy of notice. A few which I shall mention later are notable for their baldness, badness or pretentiousness, and a good many are too scrappy to count. But in most diaries there is some feature which deserves special notice, a peculiar method, an incident well related, a curious thought, an unusual trick or some salient characteristic which takes one by surprise. It took me some time to grasp Thomas Hollis's strange hallucinations, and when I found Colonel Peter Hawker the sportsman playing Bach I was delighted. Trivialities are never to be despised ; when a man writes down what soap he uses you listen to him all the more attentively when he describes what creed he believes in.

Introspection

I certainly like the introspective note to be present in a diary. The egotist may be expected by revelations, self-analysis and even morbidity to arrest one's attention. As a rule introspection is more common in youth than in middle age. In long diaries it is in the earlier volumes that the passages of self-analysis occur. The middle-aged man gen-

[1] See p. 92.

erally thinks it futile to continue this method, partly because he tends to become rather less interested in himself and partly because he is reluctant to show that his attempts at self-correction have been in vain. I believe that even Barbellion, had he lived to middle age, would as time passed have become more and more objective in his writing. But there is a fascination in self-regardant, self-absorbed youth and the resolution to drop what may appear to the older writer to be a childish habit does not improve the later volumes of a diary.

**Self-portraiture**

When there is a deliberate attempt at self-portraiture one must be prepared for disappointment. The difficulty in this is not language but perspective. The eye turned inwards somehow loses its focus. For this reason those who have deliberately attempted self-portraiture, while they may produce an interesting psychological study, do not succeed in presenting a likeness. On the other hand, when there is no intentional attempt at self-portraiture but a faithful register is kept of thoughts and feelings as well as incidents, however much the diary may be filled with contradictions, illusive mysteries, inconsistencies and repetitions, the personality of the writer will emerge in a realistic photograph. In self-portraiture, which of course is more common in autobiography than in diary, the canvas is vanity, the paint self-deception, consequently the result may either be idealization or caricature. These self-painted pictures, however, remain and posterity for all time will accept them as correct. But a student of diaries knows how the unguarded, perhaps incompleted, sentence may give a strikingly vivid impression of the personality behind, while laboured introspection does nothing of the kind.

**The beginning of diary writing**

The evolution of diary writing is interesting. There were no doubt early attempts which have disappeared. The latter half of the sixteenth century gives us our first few. On one side punctual keeping of accounts led to more than actual sales and purchases being recorded and gradually daily events crept in. John Dee,[1] one of the earliest, was a magician and scribbled events on his calendar which appeared to him of occult importance. But Thomas Coningsby [2] and the two

[1] *English Diaries*, p. 61.
[2] *Ibid.*, p. 68.

early women, Lady Hoby [1] and Anne Clifford,[2] whose diaries are reviewed in this volume, appear to jump into the correct daily diary method, although it seems unlikely that they were copying any model. On another side religious discipline acted as a strong incentive and this continues till modern times.

Religion and piety

To this religious motive we owe the immense number of diaries given up to self-disparagement, repentance, prayer and supplication. The Puritans, the Covenanters and the Quakers were taught by means of diaries to watch themselves, correct themselves, to mark out their course of life, and to note any deflections from the straight path. If praying in the pages of a diary (Viscountess Mordaunt [3] did literally nothing else), if abject humility and violent self-depreciation constituted saintliness, we should be able to point to a large number of diarists who ought to be canonized. But it must be frankly confessed that this kind of diary is very difficult to read. Piety is an extraordinarily unattractive virtue, if it be a virtue at all, except in the mythical romance of early saints. There is a snare in repeated supplication and a fallacy in the belief that repentance in words or writing is of any value. But in some people a belief in the efficacy of grovelling is ingrained.

Self-deception

After a careful perusal of these diaries, some of which by wearisome iteration of catch phrases in what may truly be described as religious jargon, are almost impossible to wade through, I am forced to the conclusion that those who indulged in this form of diary writing did themselves a great deal more harm than good. They found relief in the mere writing and mistook written confessions of their supposed wickedness for self-correction. They felt better when they got up from their writing, but they deceived themselves because they had done nothing. I am inclined to think that the diarist who sincerely rates his powers and his character very low is too painfully impressed with his defects to write about them, at any rate at any length. Whereas self-depreciation comes easily to those who regard mere expressions of penitence as a virtue. However, while Pharisaism, wherever it intrudes, can be condemned, it would be unfair not to recognize a note of sincerity in many of these outpourings.

[1] See p. 43. [2] See p. 49. [3] See p. 71.

Curiously enough, " might have done's " and " might have said's " hardly appear in diaries, however much the writer may be addicted to self-disparagement. The truth is that *l'esprit de l'escalier* attacks the mind but is too annoying and provoking for record by the pen. Diarists do not want any more than other people for ever to be reminded of these small failures and lost opportunities, however much the memory of them may disturb the still watches of the night. Misgivings

It seems clear that the morbid dwelling on unexplained and undescribed faults, sins and vices so frequent in this kind of diary must be attributed in most cases to the inevitable presence of the lusts of the flesh and the sensual aberrations which in different temperaments and in different ways must always crop up and disturb the even tenor and routine of the most humdrum as well as of the most exciting life. To pursue " Satan " in this particular guise becomes an occupation involving recapitulation in the mind, if not on the page, of the secret lapses. When self-disparagement reaches the savage pitch—it does in the case of Lord Wariston[1]—then it becomes entertaining. But when it takes the anæmic and milder form, as in the case of Mary Rich [2] or John Marsden,[3] it is inexpressibly tiresome. We can skip it in William Jones because there is so much else to entertain us. Secret faults

I have been fortunate, since *English Diaries* was published, in having been allowed to peruse a considerable number of manuscript diaries which have never been printed. The worn, dogeared pages of old notebooks can conjure up a personality and indeed a whole life better than any printed page. If there is a more or less complete series of volumes the handwriting itself tells its tale. The careful beginning, the hurried scrawl on busy days, the change in mood and method, the almost sudden consciousness of the advance of old age (as when William Jones and Macready study themselves one morning in the looking-glass), and sometimes the scrawl of senility before the blank pages begin. The books seem hardly inanimate; they breathe life. Manuscript diaries

They vary from pocket size to folio size. I have seen Henry White's huge volumes and I have studied a little book which Variety in diary books

[1] See *Scottish and Irish Diaries*, p. 34.
[2] *Ibid.*, p. 116. [3] See p. 140.

required a magnifying glass. Elizabeth Freke had large books which her husband gave her, knowing her weakness. John Marsden's varied in size, although the handwriting throughout is wonderfully tidy and regular. Lady Pechell had a nice fat quarto book, and Thomas Hollis had four vellum-bound massive volumes. Modest but methodical writers will buy their standard diary book and continue each year to buy a similar printed volume for their entries. Some of the older specimens of these books are nicely bound in leather and contain a great deal of useful information. *The Universal Cash Book and Newcastle Pocket Diary* used by an eighteenth-century diarist contains lists of important people, epitomes of various Acts of Parliament, lists of horse-races, fairs, etc., tables of various sorts, including "A window Cess table" and "Regulation of the Flys which arrive at Newcastle." There is also a very nice little diary book, with leather flap and strings, which was kept by a Chichester man during a journey to America. What he wrote unfortunately is of no sort of interest, but the little book, *Kearsley's Gentleman and Tradesman's Pocket Ledger for the year* 1791, is packed with information and in addition to the usual lists and tables, contains "Useful Hints to Persons going from the Country to London" and "Cautions to Strangers in walking the Streets of London." One Hint and one Caution must be quoted :

> Sedulously avoid all overtures or familiarity from strangers in coffee houses or out of them be their dress and address ever so genteel.

> If you walk with an umbrella and meet a similar machine lower yours in time lest you break it or get entangled with the other.

There are instances of no book being used but just sheets of paper. This was the case with Charles Russell,[1] the foreman riveter in East Africa, to whom it probably never occurred to keep a diary at all till he began writing his absolutely unique record.

Effect of diary reading on a Diarist

Much Diary reading may have a disturbing effect on a diarist. Among the readers of my first volume, *English*

[1] See p. 234.

*Diaries*, was one, himself a diary writer, on whom the perusal of so many diaries had a strange effect. I will give his impression in his own words : "I have kept a diary for thirty years and more, scribbling down in it events and incidents, impressions and confessions just as they came into my head. After reading so many diaries of other people as well as the analysis of their motive, their object, their peculiarities, and more especially their consciousness of an eye eventually perusing their record, I have been set thinking. I have become self-conscious. What hitherto I did without a thought I now do with hesitation and even misgiving. Why do I write ? Who will read ? am I honest ? am I writing myself up ? These questions which never occurred to me before are now constantly present in my mind in setting down the most trivial event and restrain me when I feel inclined to expand into self-analysis or confession. My diary writing has in fact been spoilt although the habit remains." I asked him what his original motive was in keeping a diary. He said he was abroad, no one suggested it to him, but he felt inclined to write about what he saw and what he did. Once started the habit remained.

**A diarist's ignorance of the morrow**

In reading diaries there is one peculiar charm, one valuable element which not only differentiates daily diary writing from any other form of writing but gives it a peculiar apprehensive suspense and excitement which cannot be found elsewhere in literature. This arises from the simple fact that the writer as he writes does not know what is going to happen. A writer of history or of fiction knows, a biographer knows, even an autobiographer knows. But the diarist is utterly ignorant of what the morrow will bring. When he relates the proceedings in a dispute, speculates as to the issue of public events, records an adventure of some days' duration or notes his apprehensions with regard to his wife's confinement, he is quite in the dark as to the culmination of the events. This quality, which reflects so exactly the uncertainty of life, may be produced by a word, a sentence, a paragraph or a page. But however it is done, one is made to feel the daily doubt and misgiving which beset us all as to what the future will bring. John Mitchel's [1] adventures before his escape is a dramatic

[1] *Scottish and Irish Diaries*, p. 184.

example. Such an adventure written by a man who knew as he wrote that he eventually succeeded or failed could have nothing like the same effect.

Bogus diaries

Some time has had to be wasted over bogus diaries. There is the diary of Lady Adolie, a carefully prepared fake of a sixteenth-century diary over which much trouble appears to have been taken, although it is little known. Traces of a diary which had been publicly referred to as that of Elizabeth Woodville led to much correspondence. It was probably an extract from some work of fiction, but was never run to earth. Then there was the *Diary of an Ennuyée*, by Mrs. Jameson, which had to be read before it was discovered that fictional matter had been introduced. This may have given it literary interest but rendered it as a diary absolutely valueless. The fact that bogus diaries appear shows that the diary form of writing attracts. But considering how many genuine ones exist and also that a diary's authenticity is an absolute *sine qua non* in estimating its value, it is surprising that anyone should think it worth while to forge them.

Inaccessible diaries

There has been continued difficulty in finding and unearthing diaries. Some, although their existence is known, prove inaccessible. For instance, the Rev. R. C. Fillingham began to write when he was eleven years old, in 1871, after reading the *Moonstone*, in which several of the characters are given to the habit. He continued all his life till he died in 1908. The 186 volumes, written in a very small hand, have been deposited in Merton College, Oxford, but are not accessible.

John Richards

I have also missed what appears to be a good diary kept by John Richards, Lord of the Manor of Warmwell in Dorset, who lived in the reign of William III. A meagre reference to it [1] set me in search of the MS., or the copious extracts which were printed in some local Dorsetshire paper about eighty years ago, but in vain. Richards apparently gave very full details of his life and plenty of gossip, noting trivial incidents such as his tiffs with the parson.

This morning passing by Flower's house Mr. Bound peept over

[1] Paper in *Dorset Natural History and Antiquarian Field Club*, Vol. XXVIII.

**the hedg by the Tower and sneeringly ask$^{t}$ me how I did. I looking upon him reply$^{d}$ 'Oh be y$^{u}$ there: never the better of y$^{u}$,' and so left him.**

When referring to his wife he always wrote in Italian. Unfortunately only one extract remains in translation.

**Having kept myself for two days strange she said to me in the morning if I did not mind my manners in a short time, she declared etc upon which insolence losing all patience I burnt my will before her eyes.**

**Records which are not diaries**

There are records which cannot be brought into the category of diaries, but some of which nevertheless have personal references. I was obliged to reject a very intimate study written by a man between his wife's death and her funeral. It was a psychological curiosity but not a diary. The so-called diary of the Rev. J. Ward, vicar of Stratford (1648–78), the manuscript of which rests in the Library of the Medical Society of London, is a collection of memoranda and anecdotes. The manuscript is known because it contains a mention of Shakespeare. It was transcribed by Charles Severn in 1839. *The Diary of Colour Serjeant Calladine*, 1793–1837, is a lively autobiography founded on a diary. A regimental record of the doings of the Royal Dragoons from 1811 to 1816, compiled largely by Captain Trafford,[1] although not a personal diary, is an extremely entertaining day to day chronicle, full of racy humour and good character sketches. A personal touch is given to it by the natural tone of the writer and the entries are interspersed with rather broad jokes. Henry Silver kept a regular account of *Punch* dinners in the time of Thackeray. This interesting manuscript I have been allowed to examine by the courtesy of the Proprietors of *Punch*, but I found I should not be justified in adding it to a collection of personal diaries.

**A diary of servants' faults**

Richard Sackville, Earl of Dorset, kept a "Diary of servants' faults"[2] (1660–1670), out of which it is impossible to resist quoting a page.

[1] Examined by kind permission of Brig.-General E. Makins, M.P., C.B., D.S.O.

[2] From *Knole and the Sackvilles*, by V. Sackville West.

| | £ s d |
|---|---|
| Henry Mattock for scolding to extremity on Sunday without cause | 3*d* |
| William Loe for running out of doors from Morning till Midnight without leave | 2 |
| Richard Meadowes, for being absent when my Lord came home late and making a heedless excuse | 6 |
| Henry Mattock, for not doing what he is bidden | 1*s* |
| And 3*d* a day till he does from this day | |
| Henry Mattock, for disposing of my cast linen without order | 3*d* |
| Robert terrell, for giving away my money | 6*d* |
| Henry Mattock for speaking against going to Knole | 6*d* |

Isaac Fletcher

If Isaac Fletcher [1] had allowed himself more room he might have left a good diary because he was a regular and methodical writer. But the spaces in the *Newcastle Pocket Diary* are less than an inch for each day, so he could never write more than four lines. There are twenty-six volumes of the diary, beginning in 1756 and ending in 1761. He was a Quaker and "Statesman" or yeoman farmer in Cumberland: he also acted as an Attorney. Two of his great-grandchildren were M.P.'s for Cockermouth. The brief entries in the diary concern his business, his movements, purchases, family matters and his attendance at "meeting" with very frequently a word or two on the weather. He wrote punctually on the day and if he was ill he left a blank; occasionally he notes public events and "Nothing remarkable" occurs when he feels unable even to fill the short space. There is interest in the diary as a family record, but the entries are too meagre to call for attention.

Zachary Macaulay

There is no question as to the merit of Zachary Macaulay's journal in Sierra Leone (1796–98), but it was definitely undertaken in order to furnish Mr. Henry Thornton, the Chairman of the Court of Directors of the Sierra Leone Company, with a daily report of all that transpired during Macaulay's sojourn in the colony and cannot be classed as a private diary but rather as a remarkable official chronicle.

In the region of collections of anecdotes and special notes, through which the personality of the writer hardly emerges and which contain few if any personal entries, two good instances may be mentioned.

[1] Volumes of the Diary kindly lent by Mrs. Hickson, a descendant of the diarist.

Between 1705 and 1735 Thomas Hearn, the Oxford Antiquary, filled 145 small quarto note-books, one of which he always kept in his pocket. He jotted down matters of antiquarian interest, literary extracts and anecdotes of Oxford. He is not to be compared with Anthony Wood, but some of his entries are quaint. As, for instance, this description of Bath:

Thomas Hearn

> There is nothing at Bath but gaiety and ludicrous diversions so that even at London there is much more privacy and retirement than at Bath, specially since at Bath all people will be acquainted with one, whether one will or no.

Six volumes of *The Farington Diary* have recently been issued. It is a rich mine of anecdote and curious information. Farington, a mediocre artist, was an indefatigable collector of gossip, conversations, titbits of information and records of what other people said about other people. He was the Grant Duff of his day, except that he did not himself come into contact with most of the people about whom he wrote. A little reading of this sort of thing goes a very long way.

*The Farington Diary*

Travel diaries abound because quite a number of people only keep diaries when they travel. An early one is Sir John Glanville's journal [1] of The Voyage to Cadiz in 1625. It is of considerable historical interest, but entirely public in its character.

Travel diaries

A few others of this type to which I have not devoted special separate reviews may be mentioned.

Henry Reeve, the father of the editor of *Greville's Memoirs*, kept a diary of travel in 1805–6.[2] It is a well-written description of events in Vienna and Berlin. He has a talk with Haydn, who calls England "the first and best country in the world." He hears Beethoven conduct "at the pianoforte" the first performance of *Fidelio*; and he gives a detailed account of the appearance of Napoleon, whom he sees at Schonbrunn and by whom he is greatly impressed. He hears Fichte lecture, but declares "the nonsense was incomprehensible"; and he has a zoological conversation with Humboldt. His record is entirely objective

Henry Reeve

[1] Camden Society, 1883.

[2] *Journal of a Residence at Vienna & Berlin in the eventful Winter* 1805–6. Published by his son in 1877. By Henry Reeve, M.D.

M. K. S. Frith

Descriptions of adventure have value when they are written at the moment, such as the foundering of a ship on the sands and the dangers of a complete wreck related by the Rev. M. K. S. Frith on his voyage from Bermuda in 1859.[1] He also kept a diary as Vicar of Allestree between 1862–69, relating the incidents of the day. He wrote on separate sheets, some of which are written over across.

Mrs. Trench

Mrs. Richard Trench's diary of a visit to Germany in 1799–1800 is not without interest. She had a flowing pen and gives a very unflattering description of Nelson and Lady Hamilton at Dresden. But there is little else that calls for comment.

Lady Franklin and Mrs. Sherwood

Travel diaries are often woven into biographies. This was done with Jane Lady Franklin's diary and also with Mrs. Sherwood's (the authoress of *The Fairchild Family*), who was a voluminous diary writer. From her diary Mrs. Sherwood compiled an autobiography of fifteen manuscript volumes, which was published in 1854. Captain Sherwood, her husband, also kept a journal. From all this material *The Life and Times of Mrs. Sherwood*, edited by F. J. Harvey Darton, was published in 1910.

Whaley Armitage

Whaley Armitage[2] of Moraston, Herefordshire, kept a careful journal of the grand tour he made in 1790 and 1791. He merely notes the sights he sees and the people he meets and indulges in no reflections. One gathers that he is a man of considerable erudition, delighting in a close examination of museums, etc. There is a good deal of dry statistical information with regard to the dimensions of buildings and monuments. After a while he finds it too fatiguing to note everything he observes and he writes:

> I propose leaving off giving any particulars in this Journal of the different articles which I see in any Churches etc. as it takes up some time and I find I but imperfectly sketch what may be found at large in the description of ancient and Modern Rome which I have.

If only travel diarists would all realize that guide-books give far better descriptions than they do!

[1] Original MS. kindly lent by Mr. H. E. Milliken of Malvern.

[2] The original manuscript is in the custody of Miss Armitage of Ross. By the courtesy of Mr. J. C. Hurle, of Bridgwater, a typed copy has been examined.

In Paris he attends meetings of the National Assembly and sees the King and Queen. But his observations are not very illuminating. He thinks Louis XVI "very like the late Dr. Smith of Hatton Street."

There is hardly a personal reference of any sort except on one occasion when he writes with pardonable pride of his own erudition :

> We talked a great deal about mathematics and the Classics and they seemed delighted to meet with one who knew something about each. In mathematics I quite distanced them when we came to fluxions and Newton.

The tour was undertaken shortly after he had taken his degree at Cambridge.

**John Fox**

Not only the grand tour and travels abroad have inspired people with a desire to write down their experiences, but there are instances of diaries kept for journeys in England. John Fox, a London solicitor,[1] who was of a literary turn of mind and published many articles on literary subjects, although he was not a regular diarist, always kept a full record of his walking tours between 1819 and 1843. The distinguishing feature of these journals is that Fox combines with description and appreciation of the country he passes through and the sights he sees entertaining comments about the strangers he meets and his adventures in inns. When he tells us of the hole in his boot, the food at the inn, the altercations with innkeepers, and the appearance and talk of fellow-travellers, he carries the reader with him on his walk and gives colour and atmosphere to what might otherwise be a rather dull recital of facts.

On starting out for a tour in Derbyshire in 1839, "I began as usual with a quarrel," he writes, and proceeds to describe at some length a row he had in the coach. No one can describe a quarrel without incidentally giving some description of themselves. So we see something of Fox himself at the very start and feel inclined to travel on with him. In the same way he tells us of his exasperation when he wants to make an early start at not finding his boots at his door. "I rang

[1] The manuscript is in the possession of the diarist's son, Sir John C. Fox, who has kindly allowed these extracts to be made.

my bell and holloaed and roared and stamped." He talks to his guides and finds out about wages and prices. He does not complain of excessive charges when he says:

> I came back hungry enough I and the dog (who had a round) ate 5 rounds of buttered toast and I had 2 eggs and first rate tea and cream for all of which I paid 1/–

When he arrives at an inn without luggage and the timid landlady asks for payment before lodging him he puts down the whole dialogue. What he asks her to give him shows how determined he was to be comfortable:

> I want a bed, a fire in my bedroom half a pint of sherry, half a pint of very cold water, a lemon two lumps of sugar, some biscuits and some fruit if you have any.

And he gives her a sovereign to change. He excuses her for suspecting him and writes:

> I care as little as anybody about looking like a thief. My dress is of the shabbiest and my poor father used to say when I was so dressed "John you look like a thief."

There is always a word or two about the people he comes across:

> I met about 17 or 18 good vulgar Manchester and Dublin men and their wives with a son and a flippant daughter or two. There seemed to be but one south country man a wanderer and an idler of some place near London a dark bilious eyed man with some likeness to Lord Denman. . . . I was surprised to see the havock which ladies who had dined at 4 made with the cold meat.

His descriptions of scenery are good and he shows real appreciation and enthusiasm as when he begins "and now I made the most delightful journey that ever I made in my life." He is never a bore, but he does not succeed more than any other diarist in making actual travel notes really interesting. But like many others probably, he was just writing to remind himself in later life of his pleasant expeditions:

> I sat up until one o'clock writing up my silly journal which I like to keep because hereafter though I cannot describe it will help me to remember and to see again some of those very beautiful scenes which I am amidst.

Alfred Dolman's travel notes [1] in Africa are brief and matter of fact but not without importance from the point of view of mid-nineteenth century exploration in Africa.

Alfred Dolman

A couple of purely military diaries need only be mentioned. Lieut.-Colonel William Tomkinson [2] wrote a military record of the Peninsula and Waterloo campaigns and General Cavalié Mercer [3] kept a journal during the Waterloo campaign. I must also dismiss a few politicians with brief references. Circumstances may be very favourable for an interesting diary and yet the author is incapable of taking advantage of them.

Military diaries

Henry Sidney, Earl of Romney,[4] who was closely concerned in the intrigues to bring William III over to England and was Minister in Holland, kept a diary. If this diary is taken in conjunction with his correspondence (more especially the letters to him from Lady Sunderland, Sir William Temple, Lord Halifax, etc.) and read consecutively, a good deal of historical interest will be found in the narrative. But the diary itself is disappointing. Thomas Burton, who was M.P. for Westmorland, 1656–59, kept a Parliamentary diary. Although it is only a record of speeches and proceedings, it has a certain personal colour, showing he only wrote of what he actually saw and heard. But it is nothing like Egmont or Greville.

Politica diaries

Gathorne Hardy, afterwards Lord Cranbrook,[5] was a punctual diary writer. He began in 1840 and kept it up till 1906, when he was 92. It is a voluminous but colourless chronicle of late nineteenth-century politics. Although it contains a good deal of the personal element and expressions of his own opinions, hopes, fears and ambitions, it is wonderfully dull. The contrast of this diary and Lord Shaftesbury's affords a good illustration of the inevitable conclusion one comes to in reading diaries that the personality of the writer, not the subject matter of the diary, is what counts.

[1] *In the Footsteps of Livingstone.* Being the Diaries and Travel Notes made by Alfred Dolman. Ed. by John Irving. 1924.

[2] *Diary of a Cavalry Officer.* Ed. by James Tomkinson. 1894.

[3] *General Cavalié Mercer's Journal of the Waterloo Campaign.* Published in 1870.

[4] *Diary of the Time of Charles II.* By Hubt Henry Sidney. Edited by R. W. Blencoe. 2 vols., 1843.

[5] *Gathorne Gathorne Hardy, 1st Earl of Cranbrook.* A memoir, ed. by A. E. Gathorne Hardy. 2 vols., 1910.

Other diaries

There are a few diaries which need only be mentioned. Public and local events were noted by William Whiteway of Dorsetshire [1] between 1618 and 1634. *A Cavalier's Note Book*, written by William Blundell of Crosly Hall between 1659 and 1679, contains a few dated entries, but it is chiefly a commonplace book devoted to striking events intermingled with aphorisms. William Warcup,[2] nephew of Speaker Lenthall, wrote elaborately about the Popish Plot and other intrigues in the late seventeenth century, and the fact that his diary contains cross references shows that he himself found it useful. John Allen,[3] a Quaker brewer of Wapping, kept business memoranda in 1777 into which slip a few family notes. Peter Walkden,[4] a Dissenting Minister, kept a diary of which two volumes (1725 and 1729) were rescued from being burnt as rubbish. He explains it was " Done to be a mirror to view my life and actions in that I may know how to walk." The elaborate indexes show he consulted it frequently. It is not all religious; he pays some attention to his agricultural and farming pursuits. Mary Hamilton,[5] who was a favourite at Court and knew many famous people towards the end of the eighteenth century, recorded the gossip of the time, but there is nothing much in it. Lady Shelburne's semi-political and semi-social diary is stiff and dry. A manuscript diary belonging to Frances Lady Kinnaird,[6] daughter of the 3rd Lord Bessborough, is quite a good example of the habit of social diary-keeping which was common in the mid-nineteenth century and has family interest. Maria Hare's early nineteenth-century diary, which is fully quoted in Augustus Hare's *Memorials of a Quiet Life*, is only a commonplace record of events interspersed with religious reflections and heartsearchings.

Minor diaries

There are minor diaries which, while they have not been separately reviewed, cannot be passed over without some comment, as in various ways they have points of interest.

Edward Burghall

Edward Burghall, the Vicar of Acton in Cheshire, kept a

[1] *Dorset Natural History and Antiquarian Field Club*. Vol. XIII.

[2] *English Historical Review*, No. 158, April, 1925.

[3] *Leaves from the Past*. Ed. by Clement Young Sturge.

[4] Extracts from the *Diary of Rev. Peter Walkden*, with notes by William Dobson. 1866.

[5] *Mary Hamilton at Court and at Home*. E. & F. Anson. 1925.

[6] Kindly lent by Sir Herbert Ogilvy, Bart., her grandson.

peculiar diary[1] between 1628 and 1633. He calls it "Providence Improved" and it consists of very brief entries at first —only one or two in each year, but he expands it later when he gives rather fuller accounts of incidents in the civil war. For the first twelve years the diary is simply a catalogue of crimes of violence, murder, adultery, suicide and drunkenness and epidemics interspersed with admonitions against the perpetrators of the crimes.

This year Doctor Lamb the conjuror a debauched vile wretch coming from the playhouse was slain by certain sailors and apprentices in London.

William Syme of Alpraham having the end of his nose bitten off by John Astbrook of Banbury in a drunken fray this year lost also one of his eyes in a mad quarrel by William Witter of Tarporley who was also an adulterer.

He describes supernatural happenings to illustrate the judgment which overtakes the wicked. But it is certainly a curious illustration of the relish taken in other people's misfortunes, as in the earlier part of the diary he thinks hardly anything else worth recording. His recital of incidents during the civil war are not worth quoting.

Sir Humphrey Mildmay

Sir Humphrey Mildmay, who was born in 1592 and was High Sheriff of Essex in 1636, kept a diary between 1636 and 1666[2] which is well worth a passing notice. Lawsuits and drinking bouts are the chief subjects referred to, but he also records his ordinary pursuits:

We all went a Maying to Hyde Park to see the Ladyes.

To Maldon I am going to the Bayley's feaste there I was and mett with base company and rascally saucy ministers.

There are entries about executions as well as music and mirth and card playing. Sir Humphrey was evidently a bit of a Don Juan:

To Mr. Maine's to supper where I laughed and kissed the wenches exceedingly.

---

[1] A transcript of the MS. is given in *Cheshire: its Historical and Literary Assoc^ns^*. By T. Vortington Barlow. 1855.

[2] Brit. Mus. Harl. MS. 454, quoted in a brief Memoir of the Mildmay family by Lieut.-Colonel St. John Mildmay, 1913.

Early up to be gonne, a heavy Parteinge, the wenches cried to lose their Danceinge, I spent my money freely.

He had a good many quarrels with his wife. Here is one with an amicable ending:

Soon after dinner my woeman and I did fall out ill favoredly and so we both continued sullen till worthily I did acknowledge the error to be mine, when all became well againe and we to supper and bedd.

He gives a sidelight on his religious views:

Not to Church, the covenant being hot, and I none of the tribe.

After one of the feastings he goes home "well smitten with wine" and he refers to "my ordinary trade of drinking" and also to "fuddling at a tavern." There are a few short entries about the Rebellion. Sir Humphrey strikes one as having a cheerful dashing disposition and writes his entries with freedom and a rather humorous bite.

Peter Briggins

A few quotations must be given from a good diary kept by Peter Briggins [1] in the early eighteenth century. Peter Briggins was a prosperous merchant and exemplary Quaker. His diary extends from 1703 to 1716, although some volumes are missing, and records his daily pursuits and gives weather notes:

1703 . . . to Hornsy and fished about 2 hours and only caught about 8 minnows and stone roaches and so to Hibery Barn with my Wife and Bro and our two elder children met us and so we got home about 6—a fine pleasant day.

fair pleasant weather and Morefields very full of rude people flinging at Cocks.

His children's education and health occupy much of his attention and he often mentions public events:

1713. Last night a Messenger came with ye treaty of Peace signed by ye French and ye Confederates except ye Emperor and ye Mob was very Rude and broak ye windows of those y[t] put not out candles—but we escaped.

He describes the great frost of 1715 when the Thames was frozen over:

[1] *The Eliot Papers*, No. 11, compiled from Family Papers by Eliot Howard.

**Afternoon I went to London Bridge and saw booths & shops as farr as ye Temple but they say there is booths to Chelsey and below Bridge from about ye Tower booths & many huts and people crossed over. There was they say 2 Oxes rosted.**

He gives full accounts of discussions in meeting about the solemn affirmation in 1712. If there were more of it, Peter Briggins's diary would be worth special notice.

**Mary Weston**

Another Quaker, Mary Pace,[1] who married Daniel Weston, wrote voluminous journals describing her travels on horseback in England between 1712 and 1757 and also a visit to the American colonies in 1750. She omits all picturesque detail and only records bare facts. John Eliot, her son-in-law, carefully preserved the Journals and copied them into a large folio volume.

**Mrs. Gisborne's manuscript diary**

The small manuscript diary kept by Mrs. Gisborne between 1749 and 1769, is preserved in the Jackson collection in the Sheffield Public Libraries. It is one of those slight records which fascinate me, although most people would claim there was nothing in it. The perusal of the actual manuscript undoubtedly conveyed to me something of the personality of the writer. Mrs. Gisborne's object was only to record the goings and comings of her family and friends, their illnesses, deaths and marriages. Her own pursuits are scarcely mentioned, neither does she express any opinions. The first personal pronoun hardly occurs at all. The fond wife and mother just took out her notebook and recorded when " my dear son Thomas " arrived and went and " My dear daughter Dolly's " or " my dear daughter Hawkin's " movements in one or two lines, sometimes accompanied by brief expressions of gratitude to God. Her husband, James Gisborne, was rector of Staveley, and his journeys, especially to Durham, are punctually set down. On almost every page we find " Dear Mr. Gisborne and his serv$^{t}$ set out for Durham," or " My dear Mr. Gisborne and his serv$^{t}$ came safe and well from Durham." So it goes on till suddenly the announcement comes without any warning: " My Dear Mr. Gisborne died between 3 and 4 o'clock in the morning." On this occasion, it is true, she does devote a few lines to a description of his illness and one or two to the funeral, the account of which ends " I do believe the whole

[1] *Ibid.*

parish were greatly grieved." In the last entry she says a word about her own health and perhaps that is why it is the last entry.

George Crabbe

When one discovers that a man with an interesting and original mind, whose romantic life story and poetic achievements form part of our literary history, was a diarist, it is a great disappointment to find that the diary extracts available are very meagre and not particularly characteristic. This is the case with George Crabbe, the poet. He was not a regular diarist, but his son, who writes his biography, gives quotations from Journals which his father kept on several occasions. While struggling with extreme poverty Crabbe kept, for two months in 1780, a journal dedicated to Mira (Miss Elmy), to whom he was engaged and whom he afterwards married. He called it "The Poet's Journal" and it was only discovered long after his death. In it he describes under dated entries his efforts to gain a living by his pen and his constant disappointments and the discomfort in which he lives. "It is the vilest thing in the world," he writes, "to have but one coat," and this coat gets torn on "a confounded stove's modish ornament." He gets needle and thread and declares in conclusion "but that it is thicker, the elbow is a good one yet." There is often a note of depression and deep humility :

> Heaven and its Host witness to me that my soul is conscious of its own demerit. I deserve nothing. I do nothing but what is worthy reproof.

In the last entry on January 8 he gives a lively account of the Lord George Gordon riots. At the same period he kept a notebook devoted entirely to prayer. Another fragment is a month's daily diary in 1817, when he was in London in very different circumstances from those in which he found himself when he wrote the Poet's Journal. It consists of real little bits of diary jotting, evidently quite private. An unusual peculiarity about it is that when recording events he writes in the historic present. But the entries are very thin and brief.

John Russell

John Russell,[1] who did portraits in pastel at the end of the eighteenth century, kept a diary in Byrom's system of short-

[1] *John Russell.* By George C. Williamson. 1894.

hand which remained for many years undeciphered. He was intensely religious, having been converted "On Sep. 30, 1764, at about half an hour after seven in the evening." His master, Francis Cotes, did not agree with his religious views and disturbs him "with oaths" at his prayers. He cannot "keep calm" in these altercations with his master. In 1767 he is engaged by Lord Montagu to make drawings of Cowdray, but his religious zeal brings him into disfavour and he notes that if Lord Montagu had "known my character before I came as well as he does now, I should not have been welcome to his house." He tries to convert his sitters and his piety is greatly offended by other members of the Royal Academy:

Obliged to fly from the R.A. as they were full of filthy blasphemy.

Gradually the diary becomes exclusively devoted to spiritual matters.

John Burgess

John Burgess, who in addition to being a breeches-maker was a currier, a fellmonger, wool dealer, jacket-maker, stay-maker, glover, harness-maker, rope-maker, grave-digger, gardener, haymaker, bookbinder, carpenter, appraiser and Baptist lay preacher, lived at Ditchling in Sussex and kept a "Jernel" at the end of the eighteenth century before he left to settle in America.[1] A few entries may be quoted which refer to his various pursuits:

Went to Mr. Drawbridges at Lindfield to dinner we had Lege Mutten and Brad pudden for dinner I stop[d] till about 7 o'clock we had some Comfortable Conversation upon morral and religious supjects.

This morning Went to the Jintler with a pr Breeches for Mr. Wood done at 1.7.0 they fit him well the best that he had any before.

Went to Plumpton green for the old Black mares Hide chang[d] my white dog away for the Hide & 1 Bushel Apples etc.

Bo[t] a pr spackeld stockings 2/6 for myself etc.

Bot 2 Shillings worth of Glovers Stamps at Harbens.

Preached upon Psalms 84 and 11 the Lord is a Son & Shield etc.

His grave-digging operations seem to have been occasionally rather gruesome:

[1] Sussex Archæological Society. Vol. XL.

Master Hallet & I did open a Steen Grave where in Mrs Chatfield was buried in ye year 1766. She was 54 years of age we took her Coffin out sat in the meeting House all night we opened it there was Nothing to be seen but a perfect Skilliton she was Grandmother to Miss Sally Matt who is to be buried there to-morrow etc.

There are several entries about digging graves and digging out vaults and accounts of funerals and sermons as well as careful weather notes. Burgess ended most of his entries with "etc." and then a scroll. He may have been illiterate, but he was scrupulously accurate, as is shown by one entry in which he begins:

What I have said a bout bean at Weavelsfield last Thursday was set down rong out of a mistake it was last Wensday I was there.

Considerations of space alone have prevented further comment on this curious diary.

John Taylor

Another man of many pursuits kept a diary. He was an actor, attorney, coroner, lecturer and preacher. But unfortunately John Taylor of Bolton [1] did not begin his diary till he was 33, in 1844, when he was fast becoming rather oppressively religious. In his autobiographical notes he refers to his early experiences as an actor and had he kept a diary for the first half instead of the second half of his life it would probably have been entertaining. But the extracts he gives from the diary he kept after 1844 only record his professional activities as a coroner, local events, a good many notes on his health and a great deal of pious meditation.

Pretentious diaries

Bad grammar, inconsequence and irregularity in no way detract from the merits of a diary. One's pleasure in reading a diary depends on the treatment, the spontaneity, the sincerity, and the powers of selection of its author, and also on the sort of personality we catch sight of behind the screen. There are many dull diaries which do not call for much comment. The unoriginal, unobservant writer cannot perhaps attract us, but at any rate he does not annoy us. There are, however, a few instances of really pretentious diaries written by conventional people with a view to publication. They imagine all the time that they are contributing something important to the history of their times. Lady Knightley of Fawsley, for

[1] *Autobiography of a Lancashire Lawyer*, *John Taylor*. 1883.

instance, wrote sixty volumes, no part of which has any sort of merit. She was no doubt a capable businesslike woman, but she had neither the intelligence nor the imagination to know what was interesting and what was not. She had a remote connection with the Royal Family, whom she visited occasionally, and she was therefore under the impression that what she wrote was important. So it would have been if she had been able to give us amusing gossip, character sketches, or impart to her readers the atmosphere of Balmoral in the 'sixties and 'seventies. But it is all hopelessly commonplace and her lack of perception, her trite comments and pointless remarks produce an unconquerable irritation as one reads the superficial outpourings of her flowing pen. The thing strikes one as a sham. She wrote for publication and took herself very seriously. In order " to improve her journal " she studied amongst other books the diaries of Sir M. Grant Duff and Marie Bashkirtseff ! It certainly was not Bashkirtseff by whom she was captivated, nor did she manage to collect any good stories like Grant Duff. There was just one moment of hope when I read the following sentence : " I wonder whether there is any use in struggling against a growing sense of one's own mental superiority." Unfortunately that was her only effort at self-revelation ; but it is illuminating. The *Court Circular*, intermingled with shallow politics and dull good works, fill the volumes to overflowing and it must fairly be admitted give an excellent portrait of the author. If people find pleasure in writing down this sort of stuff no one should interfere with them. But it is manifestly unkind to publish in cold print the result.

My quarrel is not that these diaries were written but that they were printed. I came across another of a nineteenth-century gentleman whose object quite obviously was to magnify his own importance. All he succeeded in doing was to display his pretentiousness, lack of humour and pomposity. I should not wonder if the diary might not have been saved by some domestic or personal absurdities which the family editor thought it proper to omit.

Sir Algernon West

Lord Bertie's diary has already been mentioned and further comment on it is unnecessary. There are two others of recent date both written by men in the very thick of public affairs.

Sir Algernon West [1] was Gladstone's private secretary, so he was in a very central position. But his political gossip and social notes are entirely devoid of colour or personality. There is not an entry which rises above pointless gossip or the bare recital of political events. A standard of this sort of chronicle has been set by Greville, Creevey, Henry Fox and others and the inevitable comparison relegates a diary such as West's to a lower position than it might have reached had it stood alone.

**Colonel Repington**

Lieut.-Colonel C. à Court Repington's war diary cannot be classified as bad because not only is it well written but it depicts the author and discloses his motive in writing it. One can see at once that he wants to establish for himself a position in high Society and to show his contemporaries how he was at home with smart people and important statesmen. The diary comprises what he himself calls "a rare lot of gossip." The passages about the War are sometimes clever and show the facile pen of the journalist, although of course the crisis was too big for him to represent even in part, and his comments and stories are obviously of not sufficient importance to justify the publication of his book. In addition to the snobbishness and vulgarity of many of the society notes, the whole tone adopted by this officer, who was watching events from the centre in the greatest tragedy which has ever befallen humanity, is depressing in the extreme to any reader who is not a mere gossip-monger. It seems hardly credible that society was as cruelly callous as he paints it. But according to him the round goes on with "the very pleasant dinners," of which lists are punctually given, the bridge parties, the country-house parties where "Bridget kissed me under the mistletoe," interlarded with the would-be serious note: Lady Somebody or other at dinner "impressed on me one night the efficacy of prayer." This is the way he records the effect of the terrible world struggle on society:

> The only visible signs of war are that the men now wear usually short coats and black ties in the evenings, that dinners are shorter and that servants are fewer and less good.

---

[1] *Private Diaries of the Right Hon. Sir Algernon West.* Ed. by H. G. Hutchinson.

Perhaps we are too near the events to judge fairly of a diary of this sort and may be pardoned if we feel inclined to throw it on the dust heap. It is to be hoped, however, that posterity will not take this as an accurate picture and will detect what Col. Repington's real motive was in writing and publishing his record.

**A murderer's diary**

Let us turn from vapidity to tragedy, from the diaries of social and political gossip to the diary of a murderer. Palmer, the Rugeley poisoner, made entries of his engagements in a printed diary. He was in the habit of noting his journeys, business matters and racing engagements. It will be remembered that he earned his living as a bookie towards the end of his career. When at home, and only when at home, he always went to church, and this is duly noted: "Went with Willie to Church," "at Church—Hamilton preached." On the day of the death of his wife in 1854 (whom he had poisoned), he writes:

> My Darling Annie was called to-day by her God to the home of bliss so well deserved.

And on the day of the funeral:

> Saw the last of my dear wife for ever. How desolate life is!

Within a week he was clamouring for the £13,000 insurance and was living with his maid as his mistress. His friend Cook afterwards falls ill. "Sat up with Cook all night," "attending Cook all day," "Cook died at 1 o'clock this morning," "attended a P.M. examination on poor Cook." It was the death of Cook, his last victim, which finally brought him to justice. The motive in making these entries was clearly to put people off the scent should there be any trouble. But it shows that he must always have feared the possibility of detection. There were probably other instances of criminals using their diaries as blinds to their actions, but they are difficult to find. Curiously enough there is almost an exact parallel in Scotland to this diary.[1]

**Stephen Reynolds**

While some have no sympathy whatever with diary writing and therefore never indulge in the practice, there are others whose disposition is drawn strongly to the recording of events,

[1] *Scottish and Irish Diaries*, p. 16.

but they find an outlet other than a diary to satisfy their desire. A good instance of this is Stephen Reynolds. Mr. Harold Wright, who edits his letters,[1] tells us that Reynolds made several unsuccessful attempts to keep a diary, but "the events and experiences of his life were too interesting and momentous, in his eyes, to be locked away in a private record; he felt an irresistible impulse to share his thoughts with a friend." It was therefore in his letters that he wrote his experiences and accounts of all his doings. The few extracts given from his attempts at diary writing are just like his letters, only balder and more formless, but there is one quotation which is particularly interesting because it shows the need he felt—and no doubt there are others like him—of an immediate reader. That curious undetermined aim which often seems to make diary writing a purposeless subjective discharge of feeling or at most a recording of events to be perused by remote posterity is unattractive to those who want to talk over their passing moods immediately with their friends. In Stephen Reynolds's peculiar circumstances this was very natural. Had he lived as a married man among his friends in all probability he would have talked more, written less, worked less and kept a diary, but then he would not have been Stephen Reynolds. On October 16, 1916, after a long entry recording thoughts and events he ends up:

> If I hadn't written this I should have done a letter to Garnett. Perhaps this diary will spare my friends when I am bubbling over. Queer—I'm writing this with an idea in the bottom of my mind of some one seeing it eventually. Is it the practice of writing to be read —or in hope of it?

This statement by one who failed to keep a diary is psychologically interesting because it shows that he had not just the bare "itch to record" but the "itch to relate." That is to say, an immediate audience was to him indispensable. The real diarist does not take this consideration into account at all.

Destruction of a diary

Anthony Trollope furnishes us with the instance of a diarist who not only left off writing but destroyed what he had written. In his autobiography he tells the story: "Early in life at the age of fifteen I had commenced the dangerous habit of

[1] *Letters of Stephen Reynolds*. Ed. by Harold Wright. 1923.

keeping a journal and this I maintained for 10 years. The volumes remained in my possession unregarded—never looked at—till 1870 when I examined them and with many blushes destroyed them. They convicted me of folly, ignorance, indiscretion, idleness, extravagance and conceit. But they had habituated me to the rapid use of pen and ink and taught me how to express myself with facility."

This must have been a good diary if it produced the effect on its author which Trollope describes. Many people do not re-read, they take the risk. No one leaving a diary—a really sincere self-exposure—imagines that they will thereby enhance their reputation. Eminent people will prefer a biographer. But we owe a great debt of gratitude to the many who had no expectations of entering the temple of fame yet kept a record of their thoughts and doings.

**Diaries reviewed**

In the new series of English diaries I am presenting in this volume women are very much to the fore. A single sentence from a diary may suffice to recall a fashion that has vanished. The following gem from a mid-Victorian girl's diary speaks volumes:

> As I entered the ballroom I was faced by a row of curly brown beards—a really beautiful sight.

Lady Hoby, Anne Clifford, Lady Pechell and more especially Dorothy Wordsworth are all good diarists, while Lady Mordaunt and Miss J. are strikingly peculiar. Among the men there may be no Pepys, but there are several the quality of whose records is high and all of them contribute some individual element to the fascinating study.

**Effect of reading diaries**

In reading such a large number of diaries I seemed to have established very close relations with those who have gone before. I am greatly impressed by the ceaseless human effort at self-correction amid the common trials and temptations to which all human beings are subjected. Apart from the attempts at self-aggrandisement in a few and our murderer's subterfuge, I have conceived a great affection for my diarists and am grateful to them for having furnished me with several years of absorbing reading.

# LIST OF DIARIES

## *ARRANGED IN CHRONOLOGICAL ORDER.*

### SIXTEENTH AND SEVENTEENTH CENTURIES

| Name of Diarist. | Occupation. | Date of Diary. | Source. | Page. |
|---|---|---|---|---|
| **Philip Wyot** | Town Clerk . | 1586–1608 | Transcript of original MS. by Philip Incledon (1768), in the possession of Mr. Alfred James. | 37 |
| **Adam Winthrop** | Cloth worker, Lord of Groton Manor, Suffolk | 1586–1617 | Brit. Mus. MS. 37419. The Massachusetts Historical Society (The Wintrop Papers), 1925. | 40 |
| **Margaret Lady Hoby** | Wife of Sir Thomas Posthumus Hoby of Hackness | 1599–1603 | British Mus. MS. Eg. 2614. Transcript in the possession of C. T. Clay (Librarian of the House of Lords). | 43 |
| **Anne Clifford** | Countess of Dorset and Countess of Pembroke | 1603–1619 | *The Diary of Lady Anne Clifford*, ed. by Victoria Sackville West, 1923. | 49 |
| **Walter Powell** | Country gentleman | 1606–1655 | *The Diary of Walter Powell*, ed. by J. A. Bradney. | 56 |
| **The Ishams** | Sir John . .<br>Sir Thomas .<br>Sir Justinian . | 1626<br>1671–1673<br>1704–1730 | *Sir Thomas Isham's Diary*, ed. by Walter Rye. Privately printed 1875. *Transactions of the Royal Historical Society* (Series 3, Vol. 1). | 59 |
| **Sir John Reresby** | Member of Parliament | 1634–1689 | *The Memoirs of Sir John Reresby*, ed. by James Cartwright, 1875. | 64 |

| Name of Diarist. | Occupation. | Date of Diary. | Source. | Page. |
|---|---|---|---|---|
| **Anthony Ashley Cooper, 1st Earl of Shaftesbury** | Statesman . | 1646–1650 | *Life of Anthony Ashley Cooper, 1st Earl of Shaftesbury*, by W. D. Christie, Vol. 1, 1871. | 68 |
| **Viscountess Mordaunt** | | 1656–1678 | *Diarie of the Viscountess Mordaunt*, with preface by Lord Roden (privately printed 1861). | 71 |
| **Anthony Wood** | Antiquary . . | 1657–1695 | *Wood's Life and Times*, ed. by Andrew Clark. Oxford Historical Society, Vols. XIX, XXI, XXVI. | 74 |
| **Sir Richard Newdigate** | Country gentleman | *circ.* 1680–1709 | *Cavalier and Puritan in the Days of the Stuarts*, by Lady Newdigate Newdegate, 1901. | 83 |

EIGHTEENTH CENTURY

| Name of Diarist. | Occupation. | Date of Diary. | Source. | Page. |
|---|---|---|---|---|
| **James Clegg** | Nonconformist Minister and Doctor | 1701–1755 | *Extracts from the Diary and Autobiography of the Rev. James Clegg*, ed. by Henry Kirk, 1899. | 89 |
| **James Woodforde** | Vicar of Weston | 1758–1787 | *The Diary of a Country Parson, The Rev. James Woodforde*, ed. by John Beresford. 2 vols, 1924–26. | 92 |
| **Thomas Hollis** | Antiquary . . | 1759–1770 | Original MS. in the possession of the Antony family. | 101 |
| **Nicholas Cresswell** | of Edale, Derbyshire | 1774–1777 | *The Journal of Nicholas Cresswell* (1925). | 110 |
| **Joseph Mydelton** | Minister . . | 1774–1787 | Original MS. in the possession of Mr. W. M. Myddelton. | 115 |
| **William Jones** | Clergyman. . | 1774–1821 | Original MS. in the possession of Mr. O. F. Christie. | 119 |
| **Henry White** | Rector of Fyfield | 1780–1784 | Original MS. in the possession of Miss Martelli of Bexhill. *Notes on the Parishes of Fyfield, Kimpton, etc.*, by the Rev. R. H. Clutterbuck, F.S.A. | 133 |

| Name of Diarist. | Occupation. | Date of Diary. | Source. | Page. |
|---|---|---|---|---|
| **Samuel Teedon** | Schoolmaster . | 1791–1794 | *The Diary of Samuel Teedon,* ed. by Thomas Wright, 1902. | 137 |
| **John Marsden** | Corn Merchant | 1795–1816 | Original MS. in the possession of Miss G. Gibson. | 140 |
| | | NINETEENTH CENTURY | | |
| **Dorothy Wordsworth** | — | 1798–1828 | *The Journals of Dorothy Wordsworth,* 2 vols., ed. by William Knight, 1897, and 1924. | 147 |
| **Thomas Asline Ward** | One time Master Cutler of Sheffield | 1800–1871 | *Peeps into the Past,* ed. by Alexand. B. Bell. | 158 |
| **Colonel Peter Hawker** | Soldier and sportsman | 1802–1853 | *The Diary of Colonel Peter Hawker,* ed. by Sir Ralph Payne Gallway, 2 vols., 1893. | 162 |
| **Thomas Rumney** | Yeoman farmer | 1805–1806 | *From the Old South Sea House,* ed. by A. W. Rumney (1914), who possesses the original manuscript. | 167 |
| **Katherine Bisshopp** | Lady Pechell . | 1808–1834 | Original MS. in the possession of Mr. Arthur F. Somerset, of Castle Goring, Sussex. | 170 |
| **J. Vine Hall** | Bookseller . . | 1810–1860 | The Author of *The Sinner's Friend.* | 179 |
| **William Kershaw** | Purser in Merchant Service | 1815–1816 | Original MS. presented by Miss le Pelley to the author. | 183 |
| **Henry Edward Fox, 4th Lord Holland** | Diplomatist . | 1818–1830 | *The Journal of the Hon. Henry Edward Fox,* ed. by the Earl of Ilchester, 1923. | 190 |
| **Antony Ashley Cooper, 7th Earl of Shaftesbury** | Statesman . | 1825–1885 | *The Life and Work of the 7th Earl of Shaftesbury,* by Edwin Hodder, 1887. | 195 |
| **Emily Shore** | — | 1831–1839 | *Journal of Emily Shore,* 1891. | 204 |

| Name of Diarist. | Occupation. | Date of Diary. | Source. | Page. |
|---|---|---|---|---|
| **William Charles Macready** | Actor . . . | 1833–1851 | *Diaries of William Charles Macready*, ed. by William Toynbee, 2 vols., 1912. | 210 |
| **Miss J.** | Spinster . . | 1834–1851 | *The Letters of the Duke of Wellington to Miss J.*, ed. by Christine Terhune Herrick, 1924. | 219 |
| **Ford Madox Brown** | Painter. . . | 1847–1858 | *Pre-raphaelite Diaries and Letters*, by William M. Rosetti, 1900. *Ford Madox Brown*, by Ford M. Hueffer, 1896. | 226 |
| **Charles Russell** | Foreman riveter | 1898–1901 | *The Work*, privately printed 1912, with introduction by B. Eastwood. | 234 |
| **Wilfred Blunt** | Country gentleman and traveller | 1888–1913 | *My Diaries*, by Wilfred Scawen Blunt, 1912, 2 vols. | 241 |

# SIXTEENTH AND SEVENTEENTH CENTURIES

## PHILIP WYOT

OBJECTIVE diaries of public events do not often repay very close study, more especially when they are of recent date. The older ones, however, not only gain interest by their age but also from the fact that the compiler of the diary often has an ingenious way of revealing something of his personality by his choice of the events he thinks worthy of record and by his lapses into gossip and personal detail. Philip Wyot, Town Clerk of Barnstaple, kept a notebook *de rebus gestis circa villa de Barnstap*, from 1586 to 1608, in which he noted each year under the particular date the incidents he considered of importance. These include deaths, purely official matters, the price of corn and weather reports. Under the last heading in 1593 we find there was a " long Drieth," and at the end of September the river was frozen over and in 1606 a tremendous flood which is fully described. There is nothing about the Armada, but there are several references to Sir Richard Grenville.

**1586. 16 Ap: S^r Richard Greynvylle sailed over the Barr with his flee-boat and friget.**

**1591. 12 Oct. . . . report came that her Majesty's ship at Sea S^r Richard Greynfield Captaine was taken by the Spaniards after encountering the whole Spanish fleet for 2 daies.**

And there are several accounts of ships bringing in " prices " (prizes). The fear of invasion in 1587 is reflected in the following entry :

The Dearthe of corne yet remains Wheate a/viii[s] yet this countrye is dailey further charged with ammunition and Harness expecting and providinge for Invasions and warrs which maketh to common sort fall into poverty for want of Trade so that div[rs] fall to robbynge and stealyng, the like hath never been seene.

1588. 5 Ships went over the Bar to join Sir F. D. (Francis Drake) at Plymouth.

The entries are comprehensive in the range of subjects with which they deal and are by no means always strictly official as the following selection will show:

Ld Bathe and the Countess his wyfe dyned at the New Mr. Maor's—the Women this year were not bidden wherefore there was much chatteringe among them.

At assizes this year at Exeter before Lord Anderson and Baron Gente one Menarde of Exon had his ears cut off, his nostrils slitte and burnt in the face with a hot Iron w[th] the Lre f.

On account of plague of pestilence assizes held at honyton . . . xvll prisoners executed the most part for murder—plague much at Totness.

xii Nov. dyed Clemente Barton was sometime servante and secretarie to the old S[r] John Chechester K[t] and lived a Batchelor he was accounted a wise man and a good scholar and would buy and have the most part of all Books made whereby he had a great Librarie and was buried in the Guyld at Pynton.

proclamation published forbydding the wearing of Daggs or Pistolles.

Anne Kemyns, Nich[s] Gays daughter and one Davy were all carted about the Towne for their filthie and lascivious Life and the next day being friday they satt all three at the high Cross in the Stocks.

Mr. John Trender Vicar of this Towne inveighed in his Sermonage the Aldermen for not coming to church whom he said were like two fat oxen that they would not hear when X called unto them but drew backwards and drew others from X. the Aldermen were present but unseen and on this and his indecent Behaviour on being questioned for this abuse, he was committed to warde for want of sureties—the E of Bathe next day discharged him—William Collybear sen[r] Alderman who during his office is a Justice was bound over by E of Bath and Mr. H. Ackland to appear at the next Sessions for Behaviour—The like was never heard before it. was all Mr. Ackland's doinge who prevailed on E of Bathe to join him in it.

One John Symons a petie Skolemaster of this Towne not very hardly witted but one of the Anabaptistical and precise Brethren had a child brought to the Church to be christened and called it Doe

Well; the Vicar dislyking it called it John which caused a great murmuring among the Brethren who said it came from the Hebrew word Abdeel.

This yere at the request of Sir Robert Bassett one Sharland a musician was retained by Mr. Maior and his Brethren to go about the Towne about iiii o'clock in the morning with his Waits and is promised viii[L] began on all Saints day and to continue till Candlemas.

Mr. Richard Smyth the hired preacher of this Towne and Jo Smyth preacher of pylton were inhibited to preach in this dioces by reason they wd not wear the Surplice.

Mr. Major and aldermen going upon their search in the Evenyng as usuall found the Vicar Mr. Tynder in John Williams house being a Tipler with other Company and having amongst them a pip with a Taber a little after nyne and because Mr. Tynder w[d] not come down to Mr. Major from ye chamber upon commandment and for other his . . . was commytted to warde where he abode till morning.

This story continues showing that the Vicar was released and "Sunday following he preached ii hours being a cold daye he weryed all his audience." Finally he is "bound over for his good behaviour."

Wyot's record is of great antiquarian interest. The original manuscript was in the possession of William Palmer of Barnstaple in the eighteenth century. A transcript of it was made by Philip Incledon in 1768, who added memoranda written by the Rev. Wood, Vicar of Fremington between 1604 and 1667. These are very brief and not to be compared with Wyot's. Incledon's transcript was bought by Sir William Tite at a sale of books in 1853; and the present possessor is Mr. Alfred James of Cirencester by whose kind permission a copy has been examined and extracts made.

## ADAM WINTHROP

THE diary of Adam Winthrop of Groton in Suffolk has been fully transcribed by Miss Redstone for the Massachusetts Historical Society and published in the Society's volume for 1925. The diary (1586–1610–1617) consists very largely of births and deaths, business entries and accounts, arrival and departure of servants, and there are very few entries which occupy more than two or three lines. The early years are given up almost exclusively to accounts. In 1595 the heading is: "Special matters and observations noted in the Yere of Our Lorde God 1595. By me A. W." Some of these are worth quoting:

> Memorandum that John Raven the same day that he fell sicke went into his yarde and sawe a wrenne strike down a Robin red breast starcke didde which he took up and showed his wife thereof presently.

The swarming of bees and weather changes are recorded as well as public events. In two consecutive entries we find

> My northern branded cowe died of the gurgett being great with Calfe.
>
> Sir J. Puckringe Lord Keper of the Great Seale died of the deadde palsey.

Here are some other "special matters and observations":

> 1595 The XVIIIth daie being S. Lukes day John Hawes rent Mary Pierces peticote and did beate her sister Katherine with a crabtree staffe.
>
> The 27 day my sister Hilles came to my howse for that her husbande had beaten her face and Armes grevously.
>
> 1600 The XXIth day my brother Alibaster camme to my house and toulde me that he made certayne inglishe verses in his sleepe which he recited unto me, and I lent him XLS.

**1603 The VIII day of June olde Doare of th age of LXV yeres maried Margarett Coe the pedders daughter. The XIth day her sister died and the same day I saw a grey conye in my woode yard.**

**The XVth of Marche Mistres Anne Browne was condemned of petit Treason for procuring one Peter Gouldinge to murder her husband Mr. Browne For the which facte the said Peter was hanged and she burned quick at Bury the XIX of Marche.**

**The XXXth of August Johane Bettes my maide did wounde John Wailley my man in the hed with her patten for which she was very sorry.**

**1608 The XIth day of Maye Mr. Cartar preached at Boxford Rom. 6. 12 the same day I had a yong barrowe hog died through bursting.**

Winthrop keeps a careful record of his goings and comings and the arrival and departure of his guests as well as deaths, births and marriages. There are a few health notes such as " I fell sick of a Colde and payne in my left eare " and " I was greeved with collick." He tells us when the cow calved, when a hornet's nest was taken, when " a great pump " was put in, when his lambs die, when he resigns his auditorship in Trinity College, Cambridge, and there are many entries about land and money.

In 1597 he gives a list of the books he had lent. They included: *The Perambulation of Kent*, *Petrarcha his Workes*, *The Defence of the Apologie*, Eusebius and Socrates in English, four volumes of *Lyra* and Googe's *Husbandry*.

In addition to his very elaborate accounts he makes other lists such as " a register of divers persons that have been killed, hanged, or drowned themselves in Suffolk." He had an orderly mind. When trouble arises over his cousin Joshua's wife, Anne, he writes down consecutive dated notes of her " behaviour since she came to dwell in Groton." It is rather difficult to gather what was wrong with the lady except that she was robbed, resented Mrs. Winthrop reproving her for " her expenses in apparell " and when Mrs. Winthrop " did frendly reprove " her for not going to Church on Sunday " she fell out with her in bitter wordes and left the house." Later on " she was cited to appere at Bury " and the following week " she sownded (swooned) and was sicke for greefe." Finally "she went to London in Colchester wagon."

Adam makes very brief one line entries in Hopton's Almanack in 1614 and in Brentnor's Almanack in 1617. They are little more than engagements and deaths, births and marriages, with a few other events such as:

> My sons first fit of his ague.
>
> Brand brak his leg at foteball.
>
> I was powled.[1]
>
> John Plombe being sick made his testament.

These diaries, together with accounts, correspondence, deeds and wills, make a very valuable collection of family papers.

Adam Winthrop died in 1623. His son John, born in 1588, became Governor of Massachusetts. He, like his father, kept a journal, part of which takes the form of reflections on passing events and on abstract subjects. He calls it "Experientia." From his departure from England in 1630 to 1649 he kept a daily record of events—now known as *Winthrop's History of New England.*[2]

The MS. of Adam Winthrop's Diary is in the British Museum (MS. 37419).

[1] *I*.e., had his hair cut.

[2] Other diaries of this family are catalogued in *New England Diaries*, compiled by Harriette M. Forbes, 1923.

# MARGARET LADY HOBY

SIR THOMAS HOBY, who is famous for his translation of Castiglione's book, *The Courtier*, wrote an autobiographical memoir entitled *A Booke of the Travaile and Lief of me Thomas Hoby.* It covers the period 1547 to 1564, but it is in no sense a diary, although in the last eight years there are a few brief entries in each year which concern his domestic life at Bisham Abbey. The rest is an interesting survey of his travels and observations in Italy and Germany. Sir Thomas was an intellectual observer who desires to record, but the diary form had hardly yet been introduced except as a method of chronicling public events. Had he lived a little later he would no doubt have adopted it, as his last entries begin to be more personal. But there are very few of them and they are confined to matters he considered important, as, for instance, his contemplated marriage:

> The XI of Maii I came to London being sent for to set my hand to a recognisance, and retourned again the XIII taking my way to Wimbleton where I communed with Mrs. Elizabeth Cooke in the way of marriage.

There are also one or two health notes such as:

> Upon Christmas Day fell I sick of a sore pleurisie.

In the travel journal there is, of course, much to be learned with regard to his opinions, appreciations and projects of translating *The Courtier*. But his book comes more nearly under the category of autobiography than of diary.[1] Sir Thomas Hoby died in 1566 as Ambassador in France.

[1] It has been fully transcribed in the Camden Miscellany, Vol. X, and there is a good account of him and his work in *Some Authors*, by Sir Walter Raleigh, 1923.

Sir Thomas Hoby's second son, Thomas Posthumus Hoby, was born in 1566 and was godson of Queen Elizabeth. He married in 1596 Margaret, only daughter and heir of Arthur Dakins, of Linton and Hackness.

This lady is the earliest known British woman diarist and indeed one of the earliest diarists, as there are very few to be discovered in the sixteenth century and these with only two or three exceptions simply record public events, but Margaret's diary is one of the first, if not the first, discoverable punctual daily personal record. Her diary and that of Anne Clifford [1] open the question as to whether they are exceptions or whether there were not many diaries of the ladies of three hundred years ago which have been destroyed.

Margaret was the daughter of Arthur Dakins and Thomasine Guy (or Gye) and was born in 1570. She lost two husbands before she married Thomas Posthumus Hoby. In 1591 she married Walter Devereux, brother of the Earl of Essex. He fell in battle. She then married Thomas Sidney, who died in 1595. After this second bereavement we learn from the epitaph to Arthur Dakins at Hackness that "in the 13th month of her single and most solitarye life the said Margaret disposed of herself in Marriage to Sir Thomas Posthumus Hoby Knight," etc. If anything of Margaret can be learned from these three marriages it is that she could not bear living alone and that she was evidently attractive. She kept a diary from 1599 to 1603 fairly regularly. She died in 1633 and her epitaph tells us that "she had lived seven and thirty years and one month with her said husband in mutuall, entire affection to both their extraordinary comfortes; and had finished the woork that God had sent her into this world to performe."

She was no doubt instructed to keep a diary for the sake of religious discipline. Her piety is very pronounced. Not only does she go to church frequently and listen to many sermons, but she has private prayers, writes out sermons, writes notes in her Testament, sings psalms, listens to lectures and nurses the sick. Mr. Rhodes, who seems to have been a sort of resident chaplain, is in constant attendance. But the diary is not exclusively confined to her religious exercises.

[1] See p. 49.

We learn much of her daily occupations. How she gathers "apeles," exercises her "body at bowles a while of which I found good"; is busy "preserving quinces" and damsons, busy in the kitchen, busy dyeing wool, "stilling," "working some fringe," "dressing sores," taking "the aire in my cocsh," out fishing or relining "a sute of blake satan for Mr. Hoby." (She always refers to her husband as Mr. Hoby.)

Her garden was the counter-attraction to her devotions. She writes:

I bestowed to much time in the garden and thereby was worse able to performe spirituall dutes.

Nor does she always feel inclined for religious exertions:

This day I went to church but havinge an indisposition of bodie I proffitted not as I ought.

She has "praier and a lecter" before supper because she says it was more convenient "in regard of mens dullness after meate" and in another place she is "verie emptie" on purpose "that I may be fitter to hear."

A full entry may be given in 1599:

In the morninge I praied privately and wrett notes in my testament till 7 o'clock then I took order for diner and thinges touching the house, after I had breakfast I wrought till dinner time and hard Mr. Rhodes till dinner time, after dinner I walked with Mr. Younge tell 2 o'clock then I went to work . . . after I had praied and taken order for supper walked abroad tell after 5 at which time I retourned to examenation and praier at which time it pleased the Lord to give me sure testimonie of his favor in Christ his name evermore be praised who sendeth not his . . . away; tell super time I was busie in the granerie and after supper and praiers I went to bedd.

She notes illness, but tries to prevent its interfering with her devotions:

after dinner it pleased God for a just punishment to comite my sinnes to send me febling of stomach and paine of my head, that kept me upon my bed tell 5 o'clock.

1599 I took a glester for which cause I kept my chamber tell the afternone then hard one read of ardentous book after supper I conferred with Mr. Maud of feelinge and then after some privat conference between Mr. Rhodes and me and some thing of that concerned us both nearly went to bed.

I not beinge well did heare Mr. Rhodes read of Gyford upon the songe of Sollomon sone after I went to breakfast after dinner I walked about the house, barne and fieldes then I went to take my Beefe then I went to se my honnie ordered.

The frequent references to Mr. Rhodes make one a little nervous, but fortunately he eventually marries.

After a break of several days

I went about diverse thinges in the house with some paine of the tooth aike after talked with an neighboure but beinge in greate paine was forced to use diverse medisons that did little profett for all the next day and all the week after I . . . to goe out of my chamber nor the Lordes day after which was the 9 of March I durst not goe to the church which was much grefe unto me beinge by that meanes deprived of the word and Sacramentes.

1599 I talked with a phisition which I hope the Lord hath provided for me in stead of Doctor Brewer and some other gentlemen; after dinner I had companie of many gentlemen that came to me and Mr. Ffuller my Lord Burley's chaplin who seemed a godly and relegous young man then I went to vesitte my coussin Bouser that lay in and thence returned to supper to the Skidmores; after supper divers gentlemen came in who taried so late that we had no publick praiers.

Her household duties were very varied and there are business entries about paying bills and signing leases and talks with the servants. But she has some relaxation, she walks "in to the fieldes with Mr. Hoby" and pays visits. From "the sarmon" she flits to the kitchen and there is sometimes a little music:

I did write in my sarmon book almost all the afternone I was busie making gingerbread and other thinges.

After diner I dressed up my closite and read and to refresh myselfe beinge dull I plaied and sang to the Alpharion.[1]

There is a note of self-correction in

I had occasion to chide, which I ever take to be a buffett of Satan's malice after I went to the workmen.

A series of short consecutive entries in 1600 runs as follows:

[1] A stringed instrument.

*The* 22 *day* I was busie about sweetmeants ; I talked with Mrs. Ward.

*The* 23 *day* I wrott notes and talked with my maides of good thinges.

*The* 24 *the Lordes day* To the church after talked of the sarmon reed to the good wives then againe to the church.

*The* 25*th day* I went to workinge some fringe.

*The* 26 *day* I did worke som fringe.

*The* 27 *day* I spake with Mr. Ewrie who was so drunke that sone made an end of that I had no reason to stay for and after brake my fast.

*The* 28 *day* I walked with Mr. Hoby and so I dined and bestowed the afternone in goinge about and takinge order for the entertainment of strangers then talked with Mr. Hoby about the abuse offered by Mr. Ewrie and his companie.

Sir Thomas Hoby was M.P. for Scarborough, so his duties took him to London. Sometimes she accompanies him. In London she records going " by water to the friers," going to " a standinge to see the quene come to London " and inspecting the monuments in " the Minster." But she was not comfortable :

After I came to London I was viseted with all my cosine Cookes and went to bed, wher I was more meanly lodged with so great cost than to my remembrance I was ever in my life, and yet I was glad of my brother's house.

Her love of " sarmons " is illustrated by the following :

1601 Lord's day.
I hard Mr. Fuller preach, after dinner came in Mr. Ewry, after I came home Mr. Hoby rede to me a sarmon of Udall and after I lay downe being not well when after a little sleepe Mr. Fuller came in and repeated to us the substance of Mr. Egerton's sarmon.

Occasionally she writes more general reflections :

As through corruption we use not the blissinge of peace as we ought, so are we to expecte new temptations to humble us for our former necclegence and so I have benne this day boffeted for bitter heed.

This day I had temperate prosperitie but found inward corruption to my great griffe.

The diary ends abruptly, which may mean that the rest of it is lost. The style is laconic but informing. A very careful analysis tells one a good deal of Margaret Hoby's pleasant homely life and something of her amiable character.

The MS. is in the British Museum (Eg. 2614). A typed transcript with full notes has been made and is in the possession of Mr. C. T. Clay (Librarian of the House of Lords), who has kindly allowed it to be examined and extracts to be made. It should certainly be published in full.

## LADY ANNE CLIFFORD

OUR second woman diarist, Lady Anne Clifford, wrote only a few years later than Lady Hoby. The life-story of this remarkable lady is fascinating in its picturesque interest largely because she wrote so much about herself. In addition to diaries, of which only a small portion have survived, she wrote biographies of her parents and "a true memorial of the life of me," compiled no doubt from her diaries. All that remains of the actual diaries is a reminiscence written in 1603 and a regular diary for the years 1616, 1617 and 1619, and some day by day entries of the last three months of her life. But even the diary for 1616–19 is a transcript the incompleteness of which is shown not only by the fact that 1618 is omitted, but by such an entry as "I do not remember whether my Lord went to Church" given as the only entry occurring ten days after the last and eight days before the next. It is highly improbable, judging by the rest of the diary, that this was her only remark during a period of eighteen days, but it is quite likely that the transcriber detached this reference to her husband out of other brief and less interesting entries.

In spite of all these drawbacks we have enough of Lady Anne's actual diary to make us rank it very high in the woman's series. A brief note must be given of her career.

Anne, the only surviving child of George, third Earl of Cumberland, a rich and aristocratic adventurer, was born in 1590. In 1609 she married Richard Sackville, who became second Earl of Dorset. He died in 1624 and four years later she married Philip Herbert, fourth Earl of Pembroke. She and her mother fought in continual lawsuits for her father's estates which, in spite of bullying and coercion, she maintained should have descended to her, and in 1643, on the death of her cousin, they did indeed revert to her sole possession. Lord Pembroke died in 1650 and she herself lived to the age of eighty-seven. She resided at fixed times at each one of her six castles and spent much money on building and repairing. She was of a very masterful and tyrannical disposition and ruled over her estates, her vast households and her numerous grandchildren with a rod of iron. "If she will she will you may depend on't; if she won't she won't and there's an end on't" was said of her and also "she knew well how to discourse of all things from predestination to slea silk." It was not till her later days that she fully developed the masterful characteristic for which she became famous. In the interesting introduction to her diary by Victoria Sackville West it is well put that "She was not born to be a wife and a young mother; she was born to be a great-grandmother and a widow."

The earlier diary gives us an insight into her married life with Dorset. It is excellent diary writing, detailed, natural and spontaneous. A series of entries may be given which show the continual wrangle carried on over the question of her inheritance which her husband and others wanted her to renounce.

She goes to the north to consult with her mother, who in all her difficulties was her friend and ally. Dorset sends messengers after her with

> letters to show it was my lord's pleasure that the men and horses should come away without me, so after much falling out betwixt my Lady [her mother] and them, all the folks went away by my Lord's direction and contrary to my will. At night I sent two messengers to my folks to entreat them to stay. For some two nights my mother and I lay together and had much talk about this business.

When she returns

> I had a cold welcome from my Lord.

He goes away and sends a message demanding that the child be sent to London.

> When I considered that it would both make my Lord more angry with me and be worse for the child I resolved to let her go; after I had sent for Mr. Legg and talked with him about that and other matters I wept bitterly.

All this time my Lord was in London where he had all and infinite great resort coming to him. He went much abroad to Cocking and Bowling Alleys to plays and horse races and commended by all the world. I stayed in the country, having many times a sorrowful and heavy heart, and being condemned by most folks because I would not consent to the agreement so as I may truly say like an owl in the desert.

My Lord came down from London my Lord lying in Leslie Chamber and I in my own. My Lord and I after supper had some talk, we fell out and parted for that night.

There were intervals when things went better:

My Lord assured me how kind and good a husband he would be to me.

My Lord and I were never greater friends than at this time. . . .

My Lord brought me down to the coach side where we had a loving and kind parting.

in the afternoon I wrought stich work and my Lord sat and read by me.

We came from London to Knole ; this night my Lord and I had a falling out about the Land.

My Lord sat the most part of the day reading in his closet.

She stood up to the Archbishop of Canterbury, "who sometimes terrifying me and sometimes flattering me" tried to persuade her and then

Upon the 18th being Saturday I went presently after dinner to the Queen to the Drawing Chamber where my Lady Derby told the Queen how my business stood and that I was to go to the King, so she promised me she would do all the good in it she could. When I had stayed but a little while there I was sent for out, my Lord and I going through my Lord Buckingham's chamber, who brought us into the King being in the Drawing Chamber. He put out all those that were there, and My Lord and I kneeled by his chair side, when he persuaded us both to peace and to put the matter wholly into his hands, which my Lord consented to but I beseeched His Majesty to pardon me *for that I would never part from Westmoreland while I lived upon any condition whatever*, sometimes he used fair means and persuasion and sometimes foul means, but I was resolved before, so, as nothing would move me, from the King we went to the Queen's side and brought my Lady St. John to her lodging and so went home.

The King asked us all if we would submit to his judgement in this case, my uncle Cumberland my Coz: Clifford and my Lord answered they would but I would never agree to it without Westmoreland at which the King grew in a great chaff.

My Lord went up to my closet and said how little money I had left contrary to all they had told him, sometimes I had fair words from him and sometimes foul, but I took all patiently and did strive to give him as much content and assurance of my love as I could possibly yet *I told him I would never part with Westmoreland.* After supper because my Lord was sullen and not willing to go into the nursery, I had Mary bring the child to him in my chamber which was the first time she stirred abroad since she was sick.

My Lord supped privately with me in the Drawing Chamber and had much discourse of the manners of the folks at Court.

My Lord and I had much talk about these businesses, he urging me still to go to London to sign and seal but I told him that my promise so far passed to my brother and to all the world that I would never do it whatever become of me and mine.

My Lord told me he was resolved never to move me more in these business because he saw how fully I was bent.

After supper my Lord and I walked before the gate where I told him how good he was to everybody else and how unkind to me.

The "falling out" goes on periodically, she weeps bitterly and is "extremely melancholy" and strives "to sit as merry a face as I could upon a discontented heart," but in spite of all bullying she never gives in, although some of her days must have been very melancholy, such as:

being Whit Sunday we all went to Church but my eyes were so blubbered with weeping that I could scarce look up and in the afternoon we again fell out about Mathew. After supper we play'd at Burley Brake upon the Bowling Green.

The following entries show her general occupations:

Upon the 1st I rose by times in the morning and saw the sun rise.

Upon the 4th I sat in the Drawing room chamber all the day at my work.

Upon the 9th I sat at my work and heard Rivers and Marsh read Montaigne's Essays which book they have read almost this fortnight.

Upon the 12th I made an end of my cushion of Irish stitch, it being my chief help to pass away the time at work.

Upon the 20th I spent most of the day in playing at Tables. All this time since my Lord went away I wore my black taffeta night-gown [evening gown] and a yellow Taffety waistcoat and used to rise betimes in the morning and walk upon the leads and afterwards hear reading.

Upon the 23rd I did string the pearls and diamonds left me by my mother into a necklace.

Upon the 24th Basket set out from London to Brougham Castle to fetch me up. I bought of Mr. Cleburn who came to fetch me a clock and save-Guard (Cloak) of cloth laced with black lace to keep me warm on my journey.

I dined above in my chambers and wore my nightgown because I was not very well which day and yesterday I forgot that it was fish day and ate flesh at both dinners. In the afternoon I played at Glecko with my Lady Gray and lost £27 odd money.

Glecko (gleek) was evidently a favourite game, as on two days she says: "I spent most of my time in playing at Glecko," and another day

I made an end of reading Exodus. After supper I played at Glecko with the Steward as I often do after dinner and supper.

Her solicitude for "the child" (Lady Margaret Sackville, who eventually married the Earl of Thanet) appears in many of the entries:

Thomas Woodgate came from London and brought a squirrel to the Child and my Lord wrote me a letter by which I perceived my Lord was clean out with me and how much mine enemies have wrought against me.

The child had a bitter fit of her ague again insomuch I was fearful of her that I could hardly sleep all night and I beseeched God Almighty to be merciful and spare her life.

The 28th was the first time the child put on a pair of whalebone bodice.

I cut the Child's strings from off her coats and made her use togs alone so as she had two or three falls at first but had no hurt from them.

I began to dress my head with a roll without a wire. I wrote not to my Lord because he wrote not to me since he went away. After supper I went out with the child who rode a pie-bald nag that came out of Westmoreland.

Her notes on clothes are frequent. We find her wearing " a black wrought taffety gown which my Lady St. John's tailor made " or " my plaine green flannel gown " or " my sea water green satin gown and my damask embroidered with gold " " both which gowns the Tailor which was sent from London made fit for me to wear with open ruffs after the French fashion." " My new black mourning nightgown and those white things that Nan Horne made for me." Food is not mentioned to any great extent. She makes " rosemary cakes " and

after supper we went in the coach to Goodwife Syslies and ate so much cheese that it made me sick.

It is a pity we have no diary record of her life with her second husband, Philip Earl of Pembroke, who is described by Dr. Williamson as " violent and contemptible, indeed almost crazy, contemptuous of all culture, careless and cross, false, cruel and cowardly." She was his second wife. In her autobiographical memoir Lady Anne says, " marble pillars of Knole in Kent and Wilton in Wiltshire were to me often times but the gay arbours of anguish."

The diary of her last days is described by Victoria Sackville West in *Knole and the Sackvilles* : " that document of intimacy, autocracy, piety and exactitude carries its entries down to the very day before her death. . . . whether her laundry maids went to Church, whether she pared her finger and toe nails, whether her dog puppied, whether she received letters, whether she washed her feet and legs (this is on the 22nd of Feb., the last occasion being on the 13th of December preceding), whether she kissed the sempstress—all is noted with the same precision and gravity."

One entry may be given :

In the morning did I see Mr. Robert Willison of Penrith paid for a randlet of sack but I was very angry with him because I thought it too dear and I told him I would have no more of him and then he slipped away from me in a good hurry.

On March 21, 1676, the day before she died, she made her last entry.

*The Diary of Lady Anne Clifford* (1923), by Victoria Sackville

West, has an excellent description of her in the introduction. *Knole and the Sackvilles*, by the same author, and *Lady Anne Clifford*, by Dr. George C. Williamson (1922), may also be consulted.

## WALTER POWELL

NOTES of passing events when they are three hundred years old have a special value and interest however brief they may be. A single line shows in a concentrated form what the diarist thinks important at the moment and it may not always be a public matter which he notes. Walter Powell was a country gentleman who lived in the parish of Llanarth and subsequently at Llantilio and Penrhos. He was deputy-steward and receiver of rents to the Earl of Worcester. The entries in his diary are seldom more than one line and in few cases are there more than twenty in one year. In fact it is, as we find by the title he gives it, " a shorte breviat " of some longer record with entries taken from the Church register concerning his family as a preface. He continues his notes from 1606 to 1655, the year when he died, at the age of 74.

The original manuscript is entitled :

a booke of ould remembrances collected by me Walter Powell of the ages of me and my ffrindes and children.
and of other matters happening in my occasions, collected out of my ould Almanacks wch I have filed togeather from yeare to yeare, as in the blanks thereof they are written more at large.
of all wch, this booke is a shorte breviat to be carried about me to helpe my memorie concerning those things and upon all occasions.

The entries mostly concern births, deaths, marriages, movements, payment of rent and debts, business memoranda, with occasional references to public events, and a few more domestic details such as, for instance,

this was the greatest years of ffruite that er' I saw. I made 50 hogsheades of sider of the tieth of both parishes.

There is an entry in 1613 which is rather puzzling :

Mr. Nelson sent a goose to Penros Church that abused the x'p'ning there 8 Augusti.

It was probably Mr. Nelson's method of scoffing at the christening ceremony. Perhaps he remained in the porch and "sent" the goose in.

A manorial custom is noted in the following:

the great comorth to impale and inlarge Lantilio Parke ult'mo Julij.

"Cymorth" was the assistance which tenants had to give to the lord for a certain number of days in the year.

Even marriage entries are sometimes noteworthy:

My daughter Anne m'ied John Watkins, both younge.

They were indeed. We find she was ten and he was twelve.

Here is a casual note of an incident which most diarists would certainly enlarge on at greater length.

Wynter Jones offered to stabb me at Raglan 3 m'cij.

Accidents and illnesses are often noted:

I fell sick of the small pocks for 6 dayes.

My gout began in ye joynt of my great toe.

I fell on my stayres and brake my Ribbe.

My right eye began to faile and I fell sick shortly after and was like to dye at Christmas.

The cateract in my eye appeared ripe my eye was cooched by Anthony Atwood very fairly but yet failed to be a cure because it was spoiled before and then appeared a new cateract to begin to grow in my left eye.

I had the yelow Jaundise.

I tooke phisicke of Mr. Brees.

All the dates with regard to the birth, etc., of his children are of course noted and occasionally a few other remarks:

that day my sone Charles was skalded in the Brawne tubbe.

The following looks like a quarrel:

Served my sonne John with a suppena after he had formerly removed himself out of my house he was to appear in Chauncery 28 November following.

Of the stirring events which were going on in the neighbourhood after 1642 we get just a passing glimpse mixed in with other matters. A few extracts from these years may be given :

**1643. 23. Ap. Monmoth taken a hoobub and Herefford was taken.**

**17 Aug. Siedge began at Gloucester and Margaret Jones that day brought to bedd.**

**1644. Nov. 18. Monmoth retaken p'Rege by Raglan men.**

**27 Nov My da: Margaret and Besse at Johan Prichards by night.**

**28. and this day she ran away to Skenfreth and my knee went out of Joint.**

**1645 19 May. I payed 28[s] at Raglan p' muskett.**

**1646 25 May. I was comitted prison' at Raglan to the Marshall of the Garison, where I remayned close till 8 Junij p'xo.**

**29 May. My house was plundered at Penros by the p'liament forces.**

**3. Junij the siedge at Raglan began.**

**Raglan yealded upp 19 Aug. p'xo.**

**8 Junij I was suffered to come out through the leaguer.**

There is a suspicion of scandal in the following, although it is not very explicit :

**Tho Richard rayled at my wief, teste John Powell of Skenfreth, this was after they thought I had been at Kilpeck with the woman, etc.**

Public events do not occupy many entries or much space :

**1648 30 Jan'ij King Charles beheaded after he had raygned 23 yeares and 10 months wanting 2 dayes.**

Powell's diary is in the possession of Sir Henry Mather Jackson, Bart., and was transcribed, printed and edited with notes in 1907 by J. A. Bradney, F.S.A.

## THE ISHAMS

### SIR JOHN, SIR THOMAS, AND SIR JUSTINIAN

THERE are three early diarists in the Isham family: Sir John, the first baronet (1582–1651), Sir Thomas, the third baronet, his grandson (1657–1681), and Sir Justinian, the fifth baronet, nephew of the latter.

Of Sir John's diary [1] only some pages of travel notes survive, written in 1626. He lays down the following instructions with regard to travel "to suspect all extraordinary and groundless civilities of foureigners," "to sequester yourselfe from ye company of your countreymen as far as may be convenient," and to "especially beware of intrigues with women."

His son, Sir Justinian, was a man of culture and some note. He lived at Lamport Hall, Northamptonshire, and was elected M.P. for the county in 1661. Whether it was that he was a believer in diary writing or because he was looking for some method of encouraging his son's Latin studies is not clear, but at any rate he promised the boy £6 a year if he would write down what happened every day in Latin. Accordingly Thomas, at the age of fourteen, began a Latin diary which he continued from November, 1671 to September, 1673.

In its way it is a unique diary and the matter chosen by the boy is both interesting and amusing. The pity is that in the translation which has been made we cannot get the real language and idiom of the day nor can we have the tone given by archaic spelling. Thomas naturally tells us more about his play than about his work. There are constant entries about catching rabbits, netting partridges, trapping martens and fishing and also about gardening and the planting of trees. He tells anecdotes and always relates the

[1] There is apparently some doubt as to whether this may not be a second Diary by Sir Thomas.

arrival and departure of visitors. We hardly get sufficient of the trivialities which would give us the domestic customs in a great country house of the time for we are interested to learn that in the spring " the paper windows were taken out of the dining-room."

The first entry runs :

" My father taught me the way to draw parallel lines and to divide a straight line."

Sir Justinian was evidently particular about the education of his children. His daughter Mary we learn from the diary spoke Latin fluently. Lamport Hall was much visited, but the behaviour of the guests was not always exemplary :

Mr. Charnock came and being well drunk fell down from table in the midst of the ladies so that no one could refrain from laughing.

And here is more gossip :

We hear that Anthony Cable went from Maidwell to Ketteringham and came home late at night very drunk, and when he tried to kiss his wife, she, being disgusted hit him such a blow with her fist that she nearly felled him to the ground. Mr. Hazelwod hearing of it said there should be a due riding celebration according to custom.[1]

Four full consecutive entries will give a good idea of his doings in 1672 :

This day we went to Northampton for the sake of eating cherries and Mr. Richardson gave us his company. When we arrived the cherries were either over ripe or very filthy from the great rains ; but since we were in the orchard we told the gardener to bring the best fruit for we meant to spend most of the day there. Mother sent Lewis from the garden to summon the man who sold glass dishes but when Mother agreed with him for the price of some of them she ordered him to place them safely in a basket. When Lewis was about to pay him the money the scoundrel said it was less than Mother had agreed to give but when Mother refused to give more he returned to his house with a displeased face.

9. Mr. Jackson the music master who formerly lived with us came here. He had now got a good engagement at Norwich, which brought him in at least £40 per annum. There came with him a gentleman named Stepkins from Sir William Langham's, the like of whom you will scarcely find in all England to play so well upon the fiddle. Sir William Langham came in the afternoon and having staid a short

---

[1] Riding the stang—a punishment for violent and unruly wives.

time went home with Jackson, who was obliged soon after to return here because he had thoughts of returning to London in Fisher's van.

10. Mr. Eyre sen. came with his son John. They slept here because of the rain. Jackson came by promise, and being ready went to the inn; at the same time it chanced that a gentleman arrived and got off his horse, that he might receive him, whom Jackson not only saluted by word but with a kiss and so suffocated him with his foul breath that the gentleman stopped his nose and could hardly refrain from striking Jackson; he however took himself quickly and opportunely off. It was clear the two could not remain in one place and that it was necessary Jackson or the gentleman should depart.

11. Mr. Eyre sen. with his son is gone to Harboro' to meet Mr. Berry and Mr. Wilshire who had lately married wives from Coleorton. John Chapman went part of the way with them to whom Mr. Eyre said that he had eaten too much at Lamport for breakfast and was afraid that he should only be able to eat less venison than he wished, so when about a mile from Harbro' he got off his horse and walked I believe to sharpen his appetite. But oh horror! when he arrived at Harboro he heard that Mr. Berry had arrived the previous day with his wife grandly escorted by a troop of his scholars.

And a series of consecutive short entries towards the end of the same year:

Nov. 22. To-day we made cider.

23. We saw by the "News" that the Poles conquered the Turks. Sharper of Scaldwell found a hare which we hunted and killed after breakfast.

24. One hundred soldiers clothed in red coats, passed through the town on their way to York and stole many hens. Mr. Meridon preached because Mr. Baxter was not well.

25. Father told the men to clean out the spring on the public road.

26. Father and Mother and sisters went to Sir William Hazlewood's but he was not at home.

27. Father had cough and stone. We attacked the fifth proposition of Euclid.

A "sporting" incident:

We went out into the home fields with the small dogs to seek the bitch fox where Toss found a hedgehog. Last night we set a trap and when Robert went to look at it and saw it closed not doubting the fox was inside, he brought the trap home from Blaxley's and when we opened it with many people present expecting the fox, it turned out to be a cat and all were ready to die of laughter.

His father took him and his brother to Oxford in 1673. This is Thomas's description of the Encænia:

To-day they have in the Theatre creations by the Doctors clothed in the most learned sentences and weighty language. There England's sons scatter their jokes and expressions in the midst, seasoned with salt, one of whom in truth handled his jokes so wittily and with such ease that I should have thought he did it from memory had not his eyes been fixed the whole time on his book. And to make all complete the ladies, the other page of human life, were well represented—matrons, virgins, rustics, and gentlewomen, with whom was an old woman who took her nickname from lice, a disgrace to her sex, who, as soon as she was observed by the academics, sent the whole Theatre into a roar of laughter.

The following year, when he was at Christ Church, his father died. After he succeeded to the baronetcy he did not continue to keep a diary. His accounts show that he had a singing master as well as a riding master and played tennis.

Sir Thomas had been made to keep a diary, but Sir Justinian, his nephew, was much more of a real diarist. He was a squire and antiquary who was not attracted by public life. When asked to stand for Northamptonshire he refused, but he went to the election,

Where I found Mr. Wikes canvassing about the town with good success and giving a shilling a piece to the women whose husbands were voters.

His home diaries between 1708 and 1736 have not been transcribed, but quotations from them show that he noted domestic as well as public affairs. There are mentions of hunting, preachers, and his journeys. Going to London he writes:

If there can't be six mares the Coachman must drive with the four.

The trial of Dr. Sacheverell seems to have been very much like a *cause célèbre* of to-day:

All the conversation in town runs upon this trial, the Ladys get up by 4 o'clock in the morning to go to it and all foreign and home news . . . are quite laid aside.

Sir Justinian was a playgoer. In 1712 he writes:

I was at ye Play where there was great disturbance concerning Cibbar whom they hissed and catcall'd off ye stage.

I looked in at ye Playhouse, it being Mrs. Oldfield's benefit night which quickly after was put in a confusion by a Party who espoused

Mrs. Rogers cause and declared against plays by subscription and what by Catcalls and hissing there was such a disturbance that ye Curtain was forced to be let down and ye audience which was very numerous to retire.

His marriage to Mary, daughter of Lisle Hackett, in 1725, is just briefly noted.

In his travel diaries he gives full and elaborate accounts of his tours on the Continent. One extract may be given of his visit to Altranstädt in 1707, when he met Charles XII of Sweden, of whom he gives an excellent description:

Dinner being brought in between 12 and 1 o'clock consisting in several dishes that looked well dressed and butter being set before each cover with which the Swedes usually begin in came the King walking very fast, almost double, and holding his sword. He is a tall thin man, very awkward and ungain, his face is not bad, he hath a large nose, good eyes but something wild in them, his hair is fair, short and staring up on end, his dress was a black crape or some such thing about his neck, a blue coat, with short sleeves and brass buttons, over which was a great leather belt with a sword that reached not a little way hanging to it, his wastcoat and breeches were buff, he had large boots on and to his hat a great brass button which dress with his air makes him look not very considerable. . . . His Majesty being not very well hardly eat anything but sat most part of the time rubbing his hands between his thighs and now and then looking very earnestly on some of those who were to see him dine which were of several degrees; he said not a word except when he called for beer which he did frequently, drinking no wine, but a small sort of beer, when he refused a plate that was offered to him it was by signs and when he took one he snatched it doing everything one would think by springs.

There is also a glimpse of Frederick the Great:

he is very little and crooked but hath something good natured enough in his countenance, he had a red coat on.

Thomas Isham's Latin diary was translated by the Rev. Robert Isham and printed privately, with an introduction and notes by Walter Rye. This volume also contains information about the other Isham diaries and accounts. Justinian's foreign diary is fully quoted with notes in the *Transactions of the Royal Historical Society*, Vol. I (Series 3).

## SIR JOHN RERESBY

THERE can hardly be a better instance of a man writing himself up in the hope of drawing the admiration of posterity than is presented by the Memoirs of Sir John Reresby, Bart., of Thribergh. After giving the family records and story of his early life, the memoirs are founded on dated diary entries, most of which were obviously written at the time although expanded later.

Little or nothing would ever have been heard of Sir John Reresby had he not taken the trouble to describe himself and to give the little touches to the diary record which presents him to posterity as not only an important but a heroic figure. He writes well and the germ of truth which a dated entry written at the time naturally suggests makes the reader inclined to accept it all and as he reads to wonder why the name of this confidant of kings and queens, this courageous and sagacious statesman, is not written larger in the pages of history.

Sir John was born in 1634, educated at Trinity College, Cambridge, became M.P. for Aldborough in 1673, and Governor of York in 1682. He was a time-server and hanger-on of royalty rather than a supporter of the Royalist cause.

The memoirs begin with recollections of early days. After 1660 there are dated entries, and although they are seldom from day to day, they become more frequent in the later years. His method is to summarize periods, sometimes a few days and sometimes a whole month. Even in the dated entries there are obvious signs that he wrote up and added passages when he was compiling his memoirs. The greater part of his record is more or less official and political, but he understood how to lighten his biography by more personal and even trivial comments. For instance, after an account of one of his entertainments in which he described in detail his musicians and wines, he adds:

> Though such remarks as these may seem frivolous to others, yet to posterity of one's own family (for whom this work is chiefly designed) they may appear otherwise, that sort of curiosity being as well pleased with enquiry into less things sometimes as greater.

It is clear here and in several other entries where such expressions occur, as, for instance, "as you will read hereafter," that Reresby wrote for posterity, hoping no doubt that posterity would publish. And posterity did publish, although not till forty-five years after his death. But in the edition which appeared in 1734 there were many alterations and omissions and it was not till 1875 that a full and accurate version of his manuscript appeared in print.

Sir John must have been of a quarrelsome disposition judging by the astonishing number of fights and brawls in which he partook. Of course, he was always in the right and he invariably scored. He draws his sword on the slightest provocation, he boxes people's ears and is continually the centre of street brawls. He throws a glass of wine in some one's face and cudgels a man in Holborn who gave him "very rude words." But we must let Sir John relate some of his escapades in his own language:

> This day in the afternoon I had a quarrel at the King's playhouse upon this occasion. As I sate in the pit a gentleman whose name I afterwards heard to be Mr Symons came and placed himself next me; and not content to rest there after a while desired me to give him my seat or to exchange with him pretending he was to speak to one of his acquaintance on the other side. I had no mind to quit my seat which was better to see than his; besides he having been drinking his manner of asking was not altogether so grateful in so much that I denied it. Hereupon he said I was uncivil and I told him he was a rascal, upon which we were both prepared to strike one another, had not a gentleman that sate near us put his hand between us to prevent it. After a little while when I saw nobody observed us, I whispered him in the ear to follow me out telling him I would stay for him at the out-door.

The fight, however, was prevented by the Captain of the Guard.

At a dinner to the justices at Rotherham a dispute arises between Sir John and a Mr. Jessop, "a known favourer of dissenters," who cast reflections on the proceedings of the justices,

> to which I replied that it was something saucy to arraign so many gentlemen of quality concerned in the commission of the peace for his single opinion. He stood up and retorted with great insolency 'You are very impudent' at which words I took up a leaden standish (he sitting behind a table and at some distance from me) and threw it at his face, where the edge lighting upon his cheek cut it quite through. We after this drew our swords and I went into the middle of the chamber but the company prevented his following of me and afterwards reconciled us.

In 1660 Sir John becomes acquainted with Mistress Brown and finds he has "more inclination for this gentlewoman than any I had seen before." He marries her in 1665. He writes very little about her and there is nothing to suggest that his quarrelsome nature disturbed his domestic life. However, there are of course omissions of any incidents which might reflect discredit on himself in his memoir. She evidently did not share his ambition for public favour judging by the following entry:

> I had a letter from my wife whose fear that a man was less safe for having several commands made her not satisfied with the last the King had done me the honour to bestow upon me; a woman's kindness being sometimes so mistaken as to wish a husband's safety before his honour or preferment. The truth is few things are pursued in the world without hazard and Providence suffers sometimes those men to fall into it the soonest that avoid it the most.

Reresby always notes the praise and congratulation he receives and tells us himself repeatedly how well he discharged the duties entrusted to him, "I had behaved myself in some remarkable concerns with all the diligence and integrity I was able to express." If there is any doubt about other people noticing your superlative qualities it is just as well to get them down yourself in black and white for posterity. We should hardly expect him to disclose any weaknesses he may have had, such as drinking. But once or twice he states the facts:

> One day ten gentlemen came and dined with me at once; that day we made a debauch.

I dined with the Earl of Feversham where me made a more than usual debauch.

Somehow Reresby's Parliamentary and Court gossip is largely devoid of interest, in spite of the spurious air of importance he imparts to it by his style of writing. A number of the entries are concerned only with his personal affairs, his appointments and his projects. His talks with Charles II are sometimes more amusing:

I was at the King's going to bed. There were but four present; and his Majesty being in good humour spent some time upon the subject of showing the cheat of such as pretended to be more holy and devout than others and said they were generally the greatest knaves. He gave us several examples of them and named some eminent men of the present age and some mitred heads which he proved not the best for passing for the most devout and pious. But these were some of them men that the King had no reason to love upon a political account. He was that night two hours putting off his clothes and it was half past one before he went to bed. He seemed extremely free from trouble and care though at times one would have thought he was under a great deal.

When he was at Newmarket with the King, His Majesty's day was arranged as follows:

Walking in the morning till ten o'clock; then he went to the cockpit till dinner time; about three he went to the horse races; at six to the cockpit for an hour; then to the play though the comedians were very indifferent; so to supper; next to the Duchess of Portsmouth's till bedtime; and then to his own apartment to bed.

In the ups and downs of his career Reresby occasionally philosophizes, not without shrewdness:

This confirmed me in the opinion that a middle estate was ever the best not so lowly as to be trodden upon, nor so high as to be in danger to be shaken with the blasts of envy. Not so lazy as not to endeavour to be distinguished in some measure from men of the same rank by one's own industry; nor so ambitious as to sacrifice the ease of this life and the hopes of happiness in the next to climb over the heads of others to a greatness of uncertain continuance.

His last entry is dated a week before his death.

## ANTHONY ASHLEY COOPER
### (First Earl of Shaftesbury)

THE interesting and exciting but turbulent career of the first Lord Shaftesbury, who lived from 1621 to 1683, covers a period of English History when violent party fury raged in public affairs. He took a very prominent part and was the target of much abuse and calumny. We cannot, however, follow him through the varying chances and charges of his public life because the story is told in State Papers, memoirs, and the Journals of Parliament, and the very meagre diary he kept between January, 1645 and July, 1650 only gives the baldest record of facts. Towards the end of his career he began an autobiography which was to constitute a vindication of his actions and opinions. This, however, is only a fragment carried up to the year 1639. He never finished it. In 1645 he wrote a sketch of facts and incidents in his life from his birth to that date; and in the following year he began his diary. This diary he kept merely to record in the briefest possible way births, deaths, domestic incidents, movements, payments and official business. The dated entries only occasionally exceed one or two lines and are not written daily. He had been in command of the Parliamentary forces in Dorset, but during the period of the diary he was not in Parliament but living in comparative retirement. Although these years cover the defeat of the Royalist cause, the execution of the King, and the establishment of a Commonwealth, the diary does not contain a single comment on any of these unusual political events. We get brief notes of quarter-sessions and the Dorsetshire committee:

We ended the sessions. Nine hanged only three burnt in the hand.

We sat in the Shire hall at Dorcester by the ordinance for punishing pressed soldiers that run away of the 15th January last; when three were condemned to die two to run the gantelope (gauntlet) two to be tied neck and heels, one to stand with a rope about his neck.

There are one or two other similar records of punishments.

However brief and businesslike a diarist intends to be his own health cannot escape notice:

I had a nerve and vein cut by Gell and two more, for which I was forced to keep my chamber twelve days.

I fell sick of a tertian ague whereof I had but five fits, through the mercy of the Lord.

His movements are accurately recorded in single sentences and one entry shows him engaged in an occupation which for once is neither military, administrative nor political:

I met my cousin Earle and divers other gentlemen at Brienston bowling green where we bowled all day.

On the day Charles I was executed his entry is: 1648. Jan 30. "I went to Bagshot," and the following day: "I came to London and lodged at Mr. Guidott's in Lincolns Inn Fields."

To his first wife Margaret (daughter of Lord Coventry, the Lord Keeper), whom he married when he was eighteen, there are several references:

We came to Bath where my wife made use of the Cross Bath for to strengthen her against miscarriage.

My wife was delivered at seven o'clock in the evening of a dead maid child; she was within a fortnight of her time.

In July, 1649, she dies and in the middle of the bald, brief, prosaic record Cooper suddenly writes a most touching and charming eulogy of her which with the account of her death is worth quoting in full:

My wife just as she was sitting down to supper, fell suddenly into an apoplectic convulsion fit. She recovered that fit after some time and spake and kissed me and complained only in her head, but fell again in a quarter of an hour and then never came to speak again but continued in fits and slumbers until next day. At noon she died; she was with child the fourth time and within six weeks of her time.

She was a lovely beautiful fair woman, a religious devout Christian, of admirable wit and wisdom beyond any I ever knew, yet the most sweet affectionate and observant wife in the world. Chaste without a suspicion of the most envious to the highest assurance of her husband, of a most noble and bountiful mind, yet very provident in the least things, exceeding all in everything she undertook, housewifery, preserving, works with the needle, cookery, so that her wit and judgment were expressed in all things, free from any pride or forwardness. She was in discourse and counsel far beyond any woman.

It was this entry which so greatly impressed his descendant the famous seventh Earl.

On April 15, 1650, he makes the following brief entry:

I was married to Lady Francis Cecil and removed my lodging to Mr Blake's by Exeter House.

On the following July 10th the diary breaks off abruptly in the middle of an entry and it was never resumed.

The diary is printed in full in an appendix to Vol. I of Mr. W. D. Christie's *Life of Anthony Ashley Cooper*, published in 1871.

# VISCOUNTESS MORDAUNT

PRAYER, although a common, is not always a very welcome interlude to the reader of a diary. But when a diary consists only of prayer and of absolutely nothing else it becomes a curiosity.

Elizabeth Viscountess Mordaunt, who was a granddaughter of Robert Earl of Monmouth and mother of the Earl of Peterborough, celebrated the chief events of her life as well as public occurrences from 1656 to 1678 by writing out a prayer, in her " Diarie," a volume bound in vellum and closed with a silver lock. Except for the headings it would be difficult to gather what occasioned these outbreaks of remorse, penitence and praise. The occasions are various : public, such as the Restoration of the Monarchy, the Fire and the Plague ; or private, such as the birth of her children, the illness of her husband, her children's recovery from small-pox, and even minor ailments of her own as " After the recovery of ye sprane in one fut and illness in ye outher."

Her husband was tried for high treason under the Commonwealth and was acquitted by one vote, Colonel Pride being absent by illness. Others, including Sir Henry Slingsby,[1] who were no more involved than Mordaunt, were condemned to death. The prayer on the occasion of her husband's acquittal is headed

In the yere of our Lorde 1658 on the first of June, my Deare Husband was tryed for his Life by a Corte, calede the Highe Corte of Justis and on the second day of June was cleerd by one voys only, 19 condemning of him and 20 saving of him and the twenty had not prevaled but by Gods emediate Hand, by striking one of the Corte with an illness which forsed him to goe out, in whous absens, the vots wer geven and recorded so that his returne no way preiusdis'd Mr Mordaunt tho in his

[1] See *English Diaries*, p. 76.

thoughts he resolved it (Prid was the person) many outher meracolus blesings wer shod in his preservation for which Blesed be God.

This is followed by two long prayers.

For a while, in 1657, Lady Mordaunt has a more elaborate scheme for her diary in which every day of the week is entered in two columns headed *To returne thanks for* and *To aske perden for.* A few quotations from the second column in this section of the diary may be given, as here we are enabled to see more precisely what it was that troubled the good lady. While it is generally only omitting her devotions or spending her time "eydely" there is something more to be gleaned from this interesting attempt at candour.

Ofended by disputing with my Husband and thereby geving him a truble, having bin weded to my owne opinion, and not yelding, tho I thought my selfe convinced by loking uppon a mane when my harte tould me, it might renue his pashon agane for me which being marryed was unlafull, by not spending this thy Sabethe day so well as I aught to dow; but was drowsy at the evening sermon.

I have sayd one or to things that wer not exactely true. I have omited parte of my devotions today and spent my time in the vanety of discors and cumpany.

I have ofended this day in ometing my pryvet prayrs in the morning; and in eydel discors; and in the vane desirs of being thought handsum; and in thinking ill of outhers my selfe and by being angery at my devotion this evening, O Lord forgeve and acsept and daly increse my repentance.

Having been angry today in my house with Lady P—— and for having been dull at prayrs and for having in returne to a complement told a lye.

. . . I tould a thing to one that might insence her against an outher which were ill tho the thing wer true.

Sufering my illness to slaken my devotion and by spending mor time in reding a foulish play than was spent in thy servis.

O Lord forgeve my having spent this day so long a bed and if I have tould anything of untruthe or to Lady ——'s preiudis, in my relation of her carage to Lady —— forgeve dere Lord and all my secret and past sins.

This days preparation hathe bin very imperfit for I have not bin so greved for my sins as I aught O Lord incres my repentance.

I have ofended my God this day by shortening my prayrs and by telling an untruthe and by being to much plesed with sumthing to ete.

O forgeve derest Lord the ofences of this day, my ometing to returne thee prays for my deare Husband's returne tell now and my telling him sum things that may insence him aganst his mouther.

Forgeve Lorde my keping upe my husband tell his slepynes mayd him neglect his prayrs and my neglecting them to often myselfe.

O my God cure my Husband of this sadnes and make him thine with mor of mekeness but my scins have deserved so ill how dare I expect so good but in mercy of my God ther is Joy everlasting.

In the "thanksgiving" column we find

I bles my God for geving me patient to ber with my Husband when he is in his passionat Humers.

to return thanks for the gret mercy that nether me nor my husband nor any that belongs to me hath reseued any priudice this day and that I have been able to ete mete without being very ill after it.

This treatment of her diary as a daily confessional lasted only seven or eight weeks. The strain was too much. Had she continued we should have learnt a great deal about her. At any rate we can gather that she had a perfect passion for repentance.

The manuscript was discovered behind some books in the library of Dundalk House. Lady Mordaunt's great-grandchild married the first Earl of Roden, to whom Dundalk belonged. It was privately printed in 1861 with a preface by Lord Roden.

# ANTHONY WOOD

AMONGST the immense quantity of material available for the life of Anthony Wood (or as he called himself —Anthony à Wood), the seventeenth-century Oxford Antiquary, there is an autobiography (1632–72) and there are journal notes preserved in an unbroken series in interleaved almanacs from 1657 to 1695, amplified by further notes from a manuscript of his known as the "secretum Antonii." It is with the journal and additional notes that we are concerned here. Wood was a laborious and indefatigable collector of archæological matters and recorder of incidents public and domestic connected with the University of Oxford. He was born at Oxford, entered at Merton College in 1647, lived in rooms opposite the College in Merton Lane practically all his life, died at Oxford in 1695 and was buried in Merton College Chapel. He never married nor was he given any post or reward for his antiquarian researches. His manners seem to have been uncouth and his temper uncertain. He was constantly at cross-purposes with college authorities in his endeavours to examine college registers and muniments. The diary notes show the extraordinary diligence with which he noted in detail every conceivable event remotely connected with Oxford, in addition to his own pursuits, his accounts and his movements. For the historian and antiquary a record of this description is of great value. But the ordinary reader can hardy find sufficient interest in the greater part of Wood's diary to encourage him to plough through several large volumes of it. Nevertheless, there are many personal touches which are intimate and amusing and his accounts of University events are often picturesque. A curious feature of the diary—almost unique it may be said—is the fact that Wood generally, though not invariably, refers to himself in the third person by his initials A. W. He must have done this in order to give his record an impersonal historical air rather than from any desire to avoid the charge of egotism.

Thomas Hearn,[1] his brother antiquary, gives us a little sketch of Wood taking notes for his record:

> Mr Joyner told me Mr Wood used often to come to him and that he told him many stories which he (Mr Wood) penned down in his presence and when anything pleased Mr Wood he would always cry *Hum* upon which Mr Joyner would go on to expatiate.

In addition to his antiquarian interests, bell-ringing was one of his hobbies and he also tells us he had "from his most tender years an extraordinary ravishing delight in music" and "his mind hung after antiquities and musick." He takes lessons on the violin from "Monseur William Jeams" and he has a good deal to say about that instrument:

> The gentlemen in privat meetings which A. W. frequented, play'd three, four and five parts all with viols, as treble-viol, tenor, counter-tenor and bass, with either an organ or virginal or harpsicon joyn'd with them; and they esteemed a violin to be an instrument only belonging to a common fidler, and could not indure that it should come among them for feare of making their meetings to be vaine and fidling. But before the restoration of K. Charles 2 and especially after viols began to be out of fashion and only violins used, as treble-violin, tenor and bass-violin; and thinking according to the French mode would have 24 violins playing before him while he was at meales, as being more airy and brisk than viols.

He records how at a party given by the Warden of Wadham he was induced to play "with and against" Thomas Baltzar from Lubeck "the most famous artist for the violin the world had yet produced." He also frequented musical meetings and "catch-meetings." As for his reading it was naturally mainly of an antiquarian character, but we find him on one occasion absorbed in a book by Dr. John Dee[2] on spiritualism so that "his thoughts were strangely distracted and his mind overwhelmed with melancholy."

Wood often writes about his health, his "tertian ague," the issue in his left leg which was dressed "10 times

[1] See p. 15.
[2] See *English Diaries*, p. 61.

with plaisters of salve" but "by his continual standing at his study and much walking withall, too much of the humour issued out which alwaies after made his left legg and thigh cold, especially in winter time." For more than a month in 1666 there are a series of entries recording day after day the taking of "vomits," "potions," "plaisters" and "clisters." From this attack of ague, he says, "his body was pluck'd downe and much time was lost before he could recover himself and be in a posture to study." He had recourse to vomits too when he was "possessed with great melancholy and distraction." One more of his health troubles may be quoted:

> About two in the morning a terrible fit of the crampe above the ancle and about the lower end of the calf of my left legg occasion'd by either throwing that leg out of bed being hot weather or by over-retching myself. I was then in a sweat.

His deafness too causes him considerable anxiety. He makes occasional notes on public health:

> Beginning of this month colds became verie frequent in Oxon; many sick and huping; colds without coffing or running at the nose only a languidness and faintness. Certainly Oxford is no good aire.

When Wood was allowed access to the University archives he was so delighted and worked so hard that

> his acquaintances took notice of the falling away of his body the fading of his cheeks, the change of redness in them to white etc. Yet he was very cheerful and contented and healthfull, and nothing troubled him more than the intermission of his labours by eating, drinking, sleeping and sometimes by company which he could not avoid.

He had difficulty with some of the college authorities, but in the long run he generally managed to get what he wanted. With Dr. Fell, the Dean of Christ Church, who was responsible for the publication and translation into Latin of Wood's *magnum opus* on the Antiquities of the University of Oxford, he has a very severe quarrel which he relates at length, beginning with a statement that the Dean "set upon me at a very foule rate," and "told me I was a verey uncivill fellow." Wood must have heartily approved Tom Brown's rhyme, "I do not love thee, Doctor Fell." With his sister-in-law Wood's relations were far from happy, as the following two extracts show:

A. W. was dismist from his usual and constant diet, which for many years he had taken in the house where he was borne and then lived by the rudeness and barbarity of a brutish woman.

The melancholy, malitious and peevish woman slighted me and rose in the middle of dinner from the table. My brother Kit asked me whether I would be godfather and give a piece of plate to the childe in her belly. She said she " would first see it rot etc " with an envious eye and teeth.

There are accounts of brawls at cards and rows in the street where " ill-language " is used against him. In 1678 he is suspected of being a papist, his rooms are searched and he is made to take the oath of allegiance. Wood had enemies who spread all sorts of malicious reports about him.

Mr Charlet told me from Mr Martin vice principal of Hart Hall that I had a B at Hedington who heard it reported at the coffey-house. This is now raised to pluck me downe, when my name was up in the gazet for a famous antiquary. Four dayes or a week before Mr Gandy tells me from Mr Davenant that I took away some writings out of Oriel College Treasury. . . . This report makes me a thief and a rogue ; the other a beast—I perused Oriel Coll writings 20 years before ; and never heard of this till now. All these things done by clergymen !

But his most serious trouble of all was when in 1693 Henry Earl of Clarendon prosecuted him in the Vice-Chancellor's court for a libel on his father contained in Wood's *Athenae Oxonienses* which had just been published. For this Wood was expelled from his University and the second volume of the book was ordered to be burnt. But neither on this or any other occasion does he enlarge at any length on his troubles nor does he ever return to them, so busy is he with the various public incidents which have to be recorded as they occur. In the long and elaborate recital of University affairs one is rather surprised to find so much of a private and personal nature. But Wood's diary method is peculiar. Self obtrudes, but only spasmodically and for no apparent reason. In the midst of pages devoted to burials, appointments, sermons, correspondence, researches, disputes, lists of names and heraldic and archæological notes, suddenly one day he writes as the only entry " my picture, by the eating of the rust of the naile it hung on fell downe on the face thereof."

He notes this probably as an unlucky omen. But we see that as a rule he is so much absorbed in his work that he only turns from it even in thought to register events which disturb and distract him or sometimes a very domestic memorandum such as "clean sheets and shirt."

Although by habit and disposition Wood was a confirmed bachelor we even catch just a glimpse, in a series of enigmatically brief entries, of a love affair. The lady is referred to as "E à D." She falls sick of the small-pox. Wood attempts to visit her, but the nurses prevent her from seeing him. The end of this episode he relates as follows:

> Dec. 16. Sunday E à D was unkind showed scorne and pride; now come into the city. From Oct 25 I discern'd a decay of love and she grew worse and worse. I waited for a return but found none, so at the conversion of Paul Jan 25 I left her.

From a perusal of his journal Wood does not strike one as being a ladies' man. The death of any member of his family is always noted as well as that of Oxford residents. When his mother dies he devotes a great deal of space to a description of her last illness and goes so far as to accuse the doctor of having killed her by "laying a thick prodigious plaister" straight on to her flesh. His concluding words are:

> And this was the doctor she loved and doted on soe much as so great, learned, and well-deserving phisitian! whereas noe unskilful quack or huswife would have ventured so much as he did.

Monthly accounts are also entered in the almanacs and they give a detailed list of all his expenses. A careful examination of these provides the small particulars with regard to food, drink, clothing, club subscriptions, journeys, books, etc., which help to make up the picture of Wood. For instance, we can dress him in "an English Tammy gowne which cost me with its appurtenances 21*s.* 4*d.*" "a rough Demy castor (hat) 18*s* 6*d*," "a pair of tan gloves 1*s*," "a black pair of round toed shoes 4*s* 6*d*," "haire powder 6*d*," "a pair of flannil loynings 2*s*," "a paire of wollen socks 6*d*," and "a paire of spectacles 1*s* 2*d*; they are green."

In the general memoranda concerning Oxford, which form the great bulk of Wood's diary, there is a mass of valuable information as well as a good deal that is of little importance.

A historian must weed, select and epitomize, as in their disjointed day to day form the notes are difficult to read consecutively. Wood occasionally gives little character-sketches and anecdotes of the people who die or receive appointments. For instance when Mr. William George of Christ Church dies, he writes:

> This person had been tutor to the children of John Wickham of that towne, gent; and when resident in the Universitie was accounted a noted Sophister and remarkable courser in the time of Lent in the publick scholes. He was poore and therefore ready to make the exercise of dul or lazy scholars. He could not for want of money take the degree of Master; yet the generality of scholars thought that if he had money, he would not because otherwise he should not be accounted the best scholar of a bach. of Arts in Oxon, as he was. He looked elderly and was cynical and hirsute in his behaviour.

And when Joseph Maynard is appointed Rector of Exeter:

> This man was good natured, generous and a good scholar but having been absent from the college neare 20 yeares had forgot the way of the college life and the decorum of a scholar. He was given much to bibbing; and would set in fellowes' chambers where there was a musick meeting, smoke and drink till he was drunk and led to his lodgings by bachelaurs.

Wood was by no means above gossip and scandal when making his comments:

> 5 Sept. Sunday at about 5 in the afternoon died William Lenthall of Burford at Burford only son of John Lenthall aged 27 or thereabouts. Left two children behind him (sons) by his wife. . . . Hamilton (of kin to Duke Hamilton) who left her husband's bed about halfe an yeare before his death and lived at Fulbroke. He was buried at Burford by his grandfather and grandmother. Thursday 16 Sept she was brought to bed a little before his death of a child, begotten by . . . Coss his servant (a Burford young man) ut fertur. The grandfather, a knave; the son, a beast; the grandson a fool, who married a court-whore.

Many entries refer to public events in London and elsewhere. But in Oxford he never fails to register the daily occurrences be they great or small. Here and there at the end of an entry he has written the word *False* at a later date. The variety of subjects he touches on may be illustrated by a few quotations:

1670. Jan 6. Th. Twelfe day in the morning at 4 or 5 of the clock a prodigious wind arose and did mischief. Some of the phanaticks stick not to say that the devill come to fetch away Monke.

1672. Jan 26. F. at night another fier in Toll's in the backside of the wheatsheaf, a malthouse or two, thatched, who had not obeyed the towne orders in slatting it before. Began at 9 and downe at 10 at night. Dr. John Fell very busy in quenching it.

1680. Mar. 15. Munday. Thomas Hovell that killed White a servitour of Ball: Coll. was hanged on a gallows against Ball. Coll. gate died very penitent and hang'd there till 2 or 3 in the afternoone.

1684 Dec 26 F. T. Hatton M.A. and one of the senior fellows of Bras. Coll. died suddenly of an apoplexy ; buried in the cloister neare to the grave of Ch. Sheringdon on the left hand. Apoplexeys now frequent in yong people.

1693. May 29 King's birthday and restauration Mr Sizer of Univ. Coll preached at St Marie's no musick or instruments from the organ loaft as formerly. Few or no bonfires in the great streets ; only some at Colleges.

There is frequent mention of Ralph Sheldon with whom Wood was on friendly terms. Sheldon promised him £100 towards printing his book, but Wood seems to have had some difficulty in getting the money from him.

Mr Ralph Sheldon of Burton and I being in an upper room at the Miter next to the street he told me that he would give me an 100 li: in the latter end of next summer towards the printing of my book. I writ twice to put him in mind of it. Candlemas day 1685 he told me 'he would pay me and that in good time'.

The accounts of royal visits are long and elaborate. Ceremonials appealed to him. After Charles II's visit in 1663, he notes :

It is to be observed that being a fashion among the courtiers to sing and especially whistle in a careless way as they went too and fro, the gentlemen commoners and other idle scholars followed it, after the courtiers were gone from Oxon, to the disgrace of the gown.

He also observes about this time :

A strange effeminate age when men strive to imitate women in their apparill viz long periwigs, patches in their faces, painting, short wide breeches like petticotes, muffs and their clothes highly sented, bedecked with ribbons of all colours.

Although he himself was absent when James II visited Oxford in 1687, he gives very full particulars, which he must have collected from friends on his return. Cosmo de'Medici's visit in 1669 he also relates in detail. His weather comments are frequent; sometimes lengthy and sometimes quite brief: "a flashing trite rain." Plays which are acted in the University are always set down and he is very fond of tracing genealogies. Wood's journal, however, is really a chronicle of Oxford more than a private diary. It is only incidentally that he talks about himself and except with regard to his health symptoms there is no attempt at self-analysis or introspection. At the beginning of his almanac for 1678 he writes laconically: "At 45 grave; avoid vanities." But the antiquary wasted no time in resolutions for self-correction.

Wood died at the age of 63, in 1695, on November 29. His last entry is dated November 12. On November 10, while discoursing on William III's visit, he makes a somewhat bitter reflection on his own treatment by the University:

> The University was at great charge in providing a banquet for the king; but the king would not eat anything but went out; and some rabble and townesmen that had got in by the connivance of the stairers (and some when the king went in and out) they seyzed up on the banquet in the face of the whole Universitie, and in spite of their teeth, all looking on and would not and could not help themselves; and after this the University caused this collation to be put into the Gazett.—This is partly my case. I have spent all my time in providing a banquet for the honour of the Universitie which being alone and applauded by the generalitie of the Universitie, come some barbarous people of the Universitie and spoyle the banquet, burne in the face of the Universitie and before and in the face of the Universitie and then make public proclamation of their most excellent dinner.

Nevertheless, there were times when Wood's work was greatly appreciated, as the following entry in 1673 shows:

> Mr Georg Verman, the senior proctor of Exeter Coll. laid down the fasces of his authority. In whose speech then spoken in the convocation he insisted neare a quarter of an hour in praise of me and my work then in the press. I was not then there and therefore cannot give the particulars, all that I heard was—that "there was nothing so antique, nothing so undervalued among the generality of people, but I made use of it for the honor of my mother the Universitie of Oxon." I desired by a friend to have a copie of as much as concerned me, but was denied.

Wood's autobiography, journal, accounts and notes have been most carefully examined, transcribed and published with copious notes and explanations by the Rev. Andrew Clark, M.A., in five volumes of the Oxford Historical Society under the title of *Wood's Life and Times.*

# SIR RICHARD NEWDIGATE

THE minutely kept record of daily life belonging to Sir Richard Newdigate was very nearly completely destroyed. Only a few sheets were torn out of the manuscript volumes and preserved because they contained matter of estate interest. Some curious entries have thus been retained owing to the fact that the folio sheets were closely covered with writing on both sides. Thus a note on a matter of mere local importance has safeguarded a more interesting entry of candid self-revelation, on the reverse side of the paper. These fragments show that Sir Richard kept a diary for his private and domestic life and referred little, if ever, to politics and public affairs. He wrote daily with the most punctilious exactitude and refers on one occasion to "transcribing my Diary," which shows that he kept rough notes.

Sir Richard Newdigate was born in 1644. He was the son of an eminent lawyer and judge, known as Serjeant Newdigate, who was made a baronet by Charles II. Sir Richard made an unsuccessful attempt to enter Parliament in 1661. He was elected in 1680 for the county of Warwick, but the Parliament was dissolved after a week. He therefore took no prominent part in politics, but he was in correspondence, and sympathy with Monmouth. He settled down as Squire of Arbury, and had eight sons and seven daughters by his first wife, and three children by his second. It was at his country seat in Warwickshire, that the Cavalier Squire seems to have spent most of his time.

The diary fragments are fortunately sufficient to give us a good impression of him. He was a man of hot temper and an autocrat, quarrelsome and in spite of his elaborate accounts, a hopeless man of business. Like so many diarists, he indulged in a good deal of self-disparagement and prayer in the secret pages of his diary.

Here are a couple of entries from 1680 which show that Sir Richard did not write at great length but noted everything:

June 13. Making ready to go to Church. Drove myself and failed exceedingly with my young horses; the ways are so very ill. At Church. Came home well, but by the Coach house failed for an hour and a half by Dodson's restiveness. Four o'clock dined. Five o'clock Prayers and homily. Six o'clock shaving and walked out. Eight o'clock, prayers; undressed.

June 16. To eight dressed. Forbore breakfast having much to do. Trifling. Went to the Lord Masserene's who had invited me to Dinner. Stayed there three hours before he came in. Had a perfect cold fit of the ague at three o'clock. His Lordship came in and I drank a good draught of Sack which with the help of Clothes that I had laid upon me, my Cold fit turned to a hot fit, but I could eat nothing. After some repose I went to Dr Lower. He ordered me a Pearl Julep and some powder to provoke to sweat; but I came home by five, got to bed and slept heartily and sweat before the things came.

Sometimes he records long conversations as if verbatim, notably on an occasion when there is an altercation in his Church with a newly-appointed Churchwarden. He never fails to note his ailments and his mood and attempts at self-correction are very frequent:

1682. Extremely troubled with the toothache which upon my prayers went away. Entered the birth and christening of Betty (his sixth daughter). Went with my Wife to Chapel to her Churching. Backed the five year old Grey Gelding which I call Ophthene and rode to the several grounds and woods upon him. Gave God thanks for preserving me tho' I think my method to be very safe. Prayed and slept soundly I thank God.

This day I fasted as a revenge upon myself for sin and prayed fervently tho' little. . . . Troubled with toothache, cured with sack.

He seems to have been very ready with his cures. Here is another:

While I thought this my old Distemper a Dizziness in my head, came upon me for which I did privately eat two bits of orange.

His house is searched by a detachment of soldiers for arms. Of this he gives a very full account. But we get a better view of the man himself in the routine account of his daily doings in which a note of melancholy and depression very often obtrudes itself:

if my own heart do not much deceive me I am very willing to die.

Was extremely out of Humor at the base reports that are raised of me.

was vext as yesterday.

Waked at five being disturbed by the Pewets flying in the Battery Chamber. Wrote to my sister and a resenting letter to the Lord Conway. Was extremely angry at some disturbance which I met with in the house. Retired to my prayers. Was better. Read the 8th of Deuteronomy. Ordered the coach to be got ready. Seriously wished myself in another world for life is very troublesome.

Was violently angry today on a small occasion.

His methods of disciplining himself are sometimes curious:

I have these three days abstained from eating one grain of Salt with my meat, which is very insipid, especially roast venison, without it. Merit I pretend to none; but O God sanctify the means I use to preserve myself from sin, that I may be made capable of the Atonement wrought by my blessed Saviour for whose sake I hope to become a member (though unworthy) of the Kingdom of Heaven.

In 1699 Sir Richard makes a tour in France, and there are several entries of this date in which he describes his preparations and the various places he visits. At Cherbourg he has some difficulty in ordering supper:

In the meantime I went to bespeak Supper, but could have no flesh: they durst not dress it. 'Twas Saturday a fish day and tho' to break the seventh Commandment is venial, eating Flesh is a mortal sin. Nor could we have fish; Mrs. Da Vall said 'twas all gone. But I spied Crabs of which she bought six for three pence and we got Thornback and made a pretty good supper.

One Sunday he notes as "miserably spent in this Popish Country." He makes remarks about agriculture and the price of food; but small worries occupy his attention very often. Dick is "extremely ill" and Betty has "spots which broke out on her neck and face." He himself occupies intervals in "studying the French Grammar." Another Sunday seems to have been a failure, as it was "Spent in too much altercation." He gives a summary of his impressions of France, of which we may give the concluding paragraph:

But their Superstition, Nastiness, Supineness, Swearing, Sabbath-breaking (even Acting Plays, Carting, Buying and Selling on Sundays); Exacting on Strangers; their hanging up the Dove which they call *le Saint Esprit* and an old Man which they call *le Providence* (God Almighty); their neglect of their highways but more of their Liberty and Property shews the Proverb to be true That the French King is Asinorum Rex.

He was delighted to return home:

I was overjoyed when we were drawing near England and was too lightsome and too brisk on board.

On May 2, 1704, Sir Richard, who was close on sixty, married a second wife. The entries in his diary a few days later, do not show that this had any great exhilarating effect on him either mentally or physically:

May 5. Was exceeding melancholy. At three o'clock this afternoon am three score years old. Went to Serjeant Selby.

May 6. Began to take my Pills today Took four.

May 9. Wrote to Sir Walter Bagot that I was married. Would give him account how it came about.

But the marriage with Henrietta Lady Newdigate does not seem to have been a great success. There are occasional references to "Henny," but when Sir Richard writes about "My dear Henny's Jointer," he subsequently draws his pen through the words "my dear." She renounced the executorship of his will and three months after his death she married again. She also found time and opportunity for a third husband before she died in 1739. From his will we gather that Sir Richard quarrelled with his children and died in 1710 without becoming reconciled to them. The last fragment of his diary, written in a trembling hand in 1706, shows him to be suffering from gout and "very ill." But there is evidence to show that he went on writing till 1709.

In addition to his diary Sir Richard kept an account book which is of a kind that makes it almost more illuminating than the diary itself. In it can be traced his domestic and monetary troubles, which were frequent. His comments are very entertaining. Of George Newton, one of his tenants who makes preposterous claims at a rent audit, he writes:

To avoid Wrangling and Clamour I submit but shall mark him for a Black Sheep.

In one of his attempts to balance his debt and credit accounts, he finds on paper a satisfactory balance in hand, but under this he writes:

'Tis false I have not so much by a great deal.

He makes his own ink, of which he writes down the ingredients and which, judging by the state of the manuscript, must have been very good. He is troubled by the large consumption of beer in the household and tries in vain, by the aid of a female butler, to reduce the quantity consumed.

To Mole Porter for four months 16s. To her at going off £1 which she ill deserves having been careless ; but according to the Proverb 'Set a knave to catch a knave' and having a great desire to know who my Secret Drinkers are that devour so vast a quantity of Ale I have given intimation (tho' I gave no positive Promise) that I would give forty shillings to anyone that would and could make a Full and Clear Discovery : which she has done of some, with some undeniable circumstances.

There are many other curious entries, of which a few examples may be given:

To my three Daughters because they came to Prayers, three shillings.

To Tom Cooper who worked hard after I had broke his head, 2s. 6d.

Nan Nuvton for breaking a Teapot in Phill's chamber 2s. 6d.

Ri. Knight for Pride and Slighting 2s. 6d.

Cook dead drunk 10s.

Wm. Wheeler Cook. Good if less given to drink.

Tho. Moseley. His faults are innumerable.

Perrugues.

| | |
|---|---|
| To wear abroad in winter | 2 |
| To wear in cold weather visiting. | 1 |
| For winter at home ith' house | 1 |
| For summer abroad. | 2 |
| For summer at home ith' house. | 1 |
| For London. | 3 |
| | 10 |

I find but nine which are more than enough at one time.

And there are many entries of payments, rents, allowances, etc., in some of which he speaks very plainly about members of his family. On his wife's death he started still more colossal account books, devoting a separate page to the expenses of each of his seven daughters. In his new account book in 1701 he writes on the title page: "This begins at Lady Day 1701 which contains the most uncomfortable part of my life."

Sir Richard Newdigate's father and his grandson the M.P. and antiquary may have been more eminent public men than he. But had his whole diary been rescued from destruction, his claim to fame might have been greater than theirs, for his record would have been handed down to us as a unique picture of the domestic life of a country gentleman in Stuart times; and the little outlines still preserved which tell us so much would have been filled in with a wealth of detail which would have brought not only the public and domestic life but the character of the author very close to us. There is an attractive portrait of him by Sir Peter Lely representing him in a flowing "perrugue," steel armour and lace cravat—a very distinguished figure.

Extracts from the diary, accounts and other papers are given in *Cavalier and Puritan in the Days of the Stuarts*, by Lady Newdigate-Newdegate (1901).

# EIGHTEENTH CENTURY

## JAMES CLEGG

BY combining the two professions of a Minister of Religion and a Doctor of Medicine the Rev. James Clegg led an unusually active life. His diary, kept from 1701 to 1755, gives a good picture of him. It contains rather more medical details than pious reflections. It is kept regularly and trivial matters as well as more important duties are carefully noted. He was the incarnation of energy, he works in his garden, he builds arbours, he turns on his lathe, he is busy with his haymakers, parcels of books are sent to him which he reads with delight, he scours the countryside (from Malcalf, near Chapel-en-le-Frith, where he was a Nonconformist minister) on his horse, having many an accident on his journeys, visits and attends the sick not only spiritually but physically and helps to compose differences among numbers of his flock and his friends, and after a week of incessant toil he preaches a sermon of three hours. Yet he is never satisfied that he is doing enough. "It fills me," he says, "with shame and grief to think how little I have done." He also sets down his resolutions:

This day I resolved especially to be more diligent in my work as a Minister and deal more freely and particularly with my hearers as to which I have been too negligent proud and cowardly.

(2) I resolved against unsuitable company.

(3) against unseasonable staying out of my house.

(4) against excess and intemperance as to which my conscience reproves me.

Lord humble mee, help mee, give mee zeal, blow the fire!

Being a doctor was not an unmixed advantage to him. He

has a chance of promotion, but he finds the people of Bolton unwilling to have a Minister " who practices physick " and he has misgiving that his practice as a doctor takes up too much of his time. Many entries are filled with medical particulars:

> Mr Richardson an Exciseman near Buxton, a serious young man, was seized with ye small pox. When I came to him I prescribed a vomit which succeeded well. Ye small pox appeared on ye 4th day of ye confluent kind and very malignant, with many purple spots intermixed. On the 12th day ye 2nd feaver was very high and on ye following day he was delirious. I prescribed opiates and alexipharmiks and 2 episparick plaisters. Through Gods assistance he recovered.

The following is his remedy for his own ague fit:

> I took powered sulphur and Balsam of sulphur mixed with conserve of roses drinking after it whey and small liquers but had a very bad day.

He also takes " apple tea " and " birch wine." With regard to his sermons he was very conscientious:

> I cannot satisfie myself in preaching old sermons unless in a case of extreme necessity and when I do so I find it neither so good for myself nor for others.

By the insertion of domestic trivialities an air of intimacy is imparted to the diary which is always valuable. The reverend doctor notes:

> This morning I began to use ye flesh brush and design to continue it.

Wife and children are of course constantly referred to:

> I had an unhappy difference with my wife and uttered some harsh and hasty expressions yt cost me trouble after.

This was his first wife. When she dies he writes:

> the widest breach that was ever made upon me—the greatest loss I ever sustained.

Time passes. One of his daughters lives with him and then she marries and he tells his diary:

> I am now left in a solitary state. . . . I am therefore advised by my children and friends to look out for a suitable companion.

And sure enough a few months later he refers to " my

wife." When he is an old man and still a diarist—as he kept up the practice to within a week of his death—his second wife dies and he writes out a long eulogy of her, saying:

> I am left at my advanced age in a solitary state. . . . I would submit but I cannot yet conquer griefe.

His son John causes trouble; in fact a sort of family conclave has to be held on John's misconduct, although it is not quite clear what particular form his failings took. At any rate his father is indignant:

> I said a great deal to him, but with too much passion.

Public events are commented on throughout the diary and there are many entries about the rebels in 1745 when "our town is full of refugees." Sometimes he makes reflections like the following:

> At home reading and writing. This is Black Bartholemew Day when so many of our pious and faithful predecessors were silenced.

He is much disturbed by the arrival in the district of a Methodist preacher whose doctrines he considers to be "Antinomian in the highest degree." He describes disputes with him and his own sermons which were directed against the preacher. But with serious theology and scientific medicine he never fails to mix the casual and domestic incidents of the day which, although they may be magnified in importance to a daily diarist, nevertheless give vitality to his record. When he nearly swallows a fishhook while eating trout we naturally get a full account of it.

The Diary, edited by Henry Kirke, was published in 1899.

## JAMES WOODFORDE

THE instinct or inclination to record public events or private affairs is often inherited. Diary writing may be found to run in a family. James Woodforde, than whom no more punctual diarist will be found in this collection, was a great-grandson of the Rev. Samuel Woodforde (1636–1701), Canon of Chichester and Winchester, who wrote a paraphrase upon the Psalms of David. Samuel and his wife both kept diaries, so also did his father, Robert Woodforde (1606–54), who was Steward of Northampton.

Of Robert's diary some extracts are given in the Historical Manuscripts Commission (Ninth Report, App. II). The entries are brief and of a more or less public character, but his strong Puritan leanings are very apparent. Passing through Oxford he notes: "this place is prodigiously profane I perceave for drunkenness, swearinge and other debauched courses, stage plays etc." He comments on sermons and preachers, but there are only a few entries in each month between 1637 and 1641.

Mr. J. Beresford, the editor of James Woodforde's diary, holds out some prospect of the diaries of Samuel and his wife appearing before long. In the meanwhile a great part of James's Diary has been published in two succeeding volumes and there is more to come.[1]

The Rev. James Woodforde was born at Ansford in Somerset in 1740, educated at Winchester and New College, Oxford, and after serving as curate in Somerset and residing as a Fellow at Oxford, he received the living of Weston in Norfolk, where he lived till his death in 1803. Woodforde was not a celebrity, nor did he consort with celebrities, yet we know much more about his life than we do of the lives of most of our eminent national figures. From the age of

[1] Quotations from *James Woodforde: The Diary of a Country Parson* are given with the kind consent of Mr. Humphrey Milford, Oxford University Press.

eighteen he kept a regular daily diary, which has survived in a more or less complete form. It covers a period of forty-three years. He is not morbid or introspective, he has no particular talents, he recites no sensational events, he himself is not an outstanding personality, and his life therefore provides nothing exciting or dramatic. It is a record of quiet days, redolent of the atmosphere of his time, intimate and peaceful, not profound or thought-provoking, yet drawing a reader into the inner passages of a human life more completely than the more elaborate and self-conscious productions of greater men. As a picture of village life 150 years ago it is unique. Quotation from such a diary spoils its chief merit, which is its detailed continuity. So much is this the case that Mr. Beresford, who has edited the volumes with great skill and tact in his thorough appreciation of his subject, was appealed to after the appearance of the first volume not to miss any days, not to disturb us as we live with the parson in his vicarage, but to give it all. In the second volume he did his best to comply with this request. There are indeed very few diaries in which the merit of continuity is so conspicuous. In so many diaries written with the never absent thought, if not the deliberate intention, of publication, the diarist in his fear of wearying a possible reader hesitates to repeat and tries to avoid what at the moment seems dull. Woodforde, entirely un-selfconscious, repeats time after time and makes notes whether they are dull or not because he wants to record all that has happened. Hundreds of entries begin "I breakfasted, dined, supped and slept again at home." He was never in a hurry when writing, because pressure and bustle did not enter into his life. He wrote out the entry neatly whether it was short or long and ruled a line across the page under it. He does not, like many others, discuss the principle of diary writing or tell us his purpose. He cultivates the habit to the highest possible degree without a thought of whom he is addressing or what the fate of his record will be. He does not tell us everything because his is not a revealing method but a recording method. He will tell us his mood without always explaining the cause of it. "Sister Jane and myself both very much in the dumps to-day"; "I was very stingy this morning alias in a bad humour," and sometimes he is "comical," which means dull. His disinclination for introspection makes him omit any analysis of the causes of depression or elation. We cannot help being very curious when he writes:

> Something very agreeable and with which I was greatly pleased happened this evening. It gave me much secret pleasure and satisfaction.

But we are given no clue. As we read we get vivid pictures of his brothers and sisters, nephews and nieces, of his neighbours in the village and of the Squire and his family, not from elaborate character sketches, but from repeated references to their visits and doings, with occasional brief comments. These comments on people and events which hardly amount to opinions, together with the punctual recital of his daily occupations, disclose little by little as the days and years pass the character of the Diarist himself. Amiel and Barbellion are nothing like as self-revealing. Moreover, a simple nature such as Woodforde's is far more difficult to dissect or even describe than a highly complex psychological disposition and can therefore only be grasped by the gradually unfolding vision of his habit of life over a long period.

Unlike the ecclesiastics of his century he never indulges in an orgy of self-disparagement nor an ecstasy of prayer. He is conscientious and punctual in his observances, but never sanctimonious. He loves company and hates being alone. One love episode and one alone enters the pages of his diary and this can only be detached from a few brief references. In 1774, when he was thirty-four, Mrs. White and her daughter Betsy are mentioned. Later she becomes "my dear Betsy." Then we read:

> I went home with Betsy White and had some talk with her concerning my making her mine when an opportunity offered and she was not averse to it at all.

Next year Betsy goes to Devonshire and he records quite simply in an entry that she is to be married to "a gentleman of Devonshire by name Webster." She returns with her husband to visit her mother at Ansford where Woodforde is staying. He refuses to go to Mrs. White's, but while walking with his brother he meets Mr. and Mrs. Webster by chance.

Mrs Webster spoke as usual to me, but I said little to her being shy, & she has proved herself to me a mere Jilt.

He remained a bachelor to the end of his days, Nancy, his niece, living with him. To her he is greatly devoted and is always dull if she is away. He teaches her, they ride together, visit together, play cards together, quarrel occasionally and then make friends.

Nancy by being with Mrs Davy had learnt some of her extravagant Notions and talked very high all day. I talked with her against such foolish Notions which made her almost angry with me, but when we went to bed we were very good Friends and she was convinced.

Nancy was low at Dinner owing to me—was sorry for it.

At cribbage this evening with Nancy won 0.2.0. She was very sulky and sullen on loosing it, tho' not paid. She did not scarce open her Mouth all the Even' after.

There is a great deal about other members of his family, specially in the earlier days, and it is evident that many of them were inclined to sponge on him. Brother John is a high trial not only to the parson but to the whole family. Try as he will to be tolerant James has to record backslidings every time he mentions his brother. John " is very indifferent by his being too busy with Girls " ; he is " very much disguised in beer " ; his way of life is " very disagreeable " ; " the house is in an uproar Jack abusing of them all in a terrible manner " ;

Brother John being very full of Liquor at two o'clock in the morning, made such an intolerable noise by swearing in so terrible a manner and so loud that it disturbed me out of sound sleep being gone to bed, and was so shocked at it that I was obliged to get up to desire him to go to bed, but all my arguments and persuasions were in vain and he kept me up till five in the morning and then I went to bed and he went on Horseback for Bath.

So it goes on. " He is the worst company I ever was in in my life when he is got merry." But the Diarist admits " he is very generous and too much company hurts him greatly." John's failings were crude, but repeated references to other members of the family with sometimes no more than a word of comment make us see very clearly Brother Hughes,

Brother William, Sister Pounsett, Sister White and Nephew William who causes him much anxiety. His servants too, with their virtues and shortcomings, come naturally into the daily story and also many of the villagers and the neighbouring parsons. But one of the best pictures we get is of Squire Custance, his wife and family. But again here there are few long quotable descriptions. The impression given, and very pleasant it is, comes from the repeated visits, dinners, and hours spent at Ringland and Weston House and the return visits of the Squire. Here is an early visit :

I took a ride to Ringland about 2 o'clock and there dined, spent the afternoon and supped and spent the evening at Mr. Custance's with him, his Wife and an old maiden lady by name Miss Rush. I spent a most agreeable day there and was very merry. Mrs Custance and self played Back Gammon together. Mr. and Mrs Custance are very agreeable people indeed and both behaved exceedingly polite and civil to me. I there saw an Instrument which Mrs Custance played on that I never saw or heard before. It is called Sticcardo pastorale. It is very soft music indeed. It is several long pieces of glass laid in order in a case, resting on each end of every piece of glass and is played in the middle parts of the glasses by two little sticks with Nobbs at the end of them stricking the glass. It is a very small Instrument and looks when covered like a working Box for ladies. I also saw the prettiest working Box with all sorts of things in it for the ladies to carry with them when they go abroad, about as big again as a Tea Chest, that ever I saw in my Life. It could not cost less than five guineas. We had for dinner, some common Fish, a leg of Mutton rosted and a baked Pudding the first course ; and a rost Duck, a Meat Pye, Eggs and Tarts the second. For supper we had a brace of Partridges rosted some cold Tongue, Potatoes in Shells and Tarts. I returned to Weston about ½ past ten o'clock. To servants at Ringland . 2 . gave 0.2.0. Mr. Custance also gave me to carry Home a brace of Partridges which my servant Will brought home. They keep 6 Men Servants and 4 Maids.

There are innumerable instances of Mrs. Custance's kindness to Nancy. Here is one of them :

Mr. Custance sent after Nancy this morning to spend the Day with Mrs Custance and to have her hair dressed by one Brown the best Ladies-Frisseur in Norwich. . . . Nancy returned home about ½ past 9 o'clock this Even' with her head finely dressed up but very becoming her. Mrs Custance would not let Nancy pay the Barber, but she paid for her and it cost no less than half a guinea. Mrs Custance gave the Barber for dressing her Hair and Nancy's the enormous sum of one guinea—He came on purpose from Norwich to dress them. Mrs Custance (God bless her) is the best Lady I ever knew.

He describes an informal visit from the Squire :

As I was out in my Garden this morning in my Ermine old Hat and Wigg, Beard long and dirty shirt on, who should walk by at the end of the garden but my Squire and Mr. Beauchamp with him, Mrs Custance's Brother. They walked into my garden and went over it, they liked it exceedingly.

Mr. Press Custance, the Squire's brother, causes a little trouble on account of his mistress, Miss Sharman, who makes use of the Parson's seat in the Chancel and " strutted by " Mr. and Mrs. Custance " in a very impudent manner coming out of Church." Woodforde acts with great tact, telling Miss Sharman she had better not use the seat any more. Indeed in a number of ways he shows himself lenient, good-natured, and kind. The only thing he could not tolerate was people being " rather high," whether it was his niece, his sister, visitors or his own maid. He is the very reverse of a snob and has no love of eminent personages. In fact, when he has been in high company at one of Mr. Custance's dinners at which Lady Jernegan (" a fine woman but high and mighty ") was present amongst others, he ends his daily note with " must confess that being with our equals is much more agreeable."

He enters a great many particulars about his servants. Some of them cause him a good deal of anxiety, but he takes much trouble about them. When he engages a new one he devotes a whole entry to the particulars :

Her name is Eliz: Caxton about 40 years of age but how she will do I know not as yet but her wages are £5:15:6 per annum but out of that she is to find herself in Tea and Sugar. She is not the most engaging I must confess by her first appearance that she makes. My other maid came to me also this evening. Her name is Anne Lillistone of Lenswade Bridge about 18 years of age but very plain, however I like her better than the other at the first sight, I am to give her 2.0.0 per annum and to make her an allowance to find herself in Tea and Sugar. Sukey this evening left us, but in Tears, most sad.

Woodforde tells us everything ; when he eats his first pine apple, when he performs an operation on the cat, when he goes out coursing, when he shoots his blunderbuss on the King's birthday, when his pigs are drunk, when there is a plague of toads, when his razor breaks while he is shaving on Sunday (which he takes as a warning), when he sees for the first time a peacock spread his tail, when he sees culprits whipped at the cart's tail, when smugglers arrive selling drink, when he wins or loses at cards, whether it be quadrille, loo, whist or cribbage, when he plays battledore and shuttlecock, when he witnesses a murderer being hanged, when he stays at the inn in Norwich, when he preaches in the Cathedral and every other possible event, including his purchases and expenditures. We get, therefore, a photographic picture of his daily occupations. He often gives some indication of his mood which is generally "merry." Even when things go wrong he has sense of humour enough to make the best of it. After a tiring day dining out and returning home at night in the wet and wind, he writes:

On the whole spent an odd disagreeable kind of a Day—as did also Nancy—we laughed much after we got home.

Health claims much of his attention, but it is more often the health of other than his own. Sometimes we have long descriptions of symptoms, the drawing of teeth and the nature of his pains: or sometimes just a sentence such as

My stomach rather sick this evening—Mince Pye rose oft.

Had the Cramp baddish in the Night in both legs, however had a tolerable good night on the whole and am greatly refreshed by it and am brave to-day.

Woodforde is good-natured even with a bad dentist:

My tooth pained me all night, got up a little after 5 this morning and sent for one Reeves a man who draws teeth in this parish, and about 7 he came and drew my tooth but shockingly bad indeed, he broke away a great piece of my gum and broke one of the fangs of the tooth, it gave me exquisite pain all the day after, and my face was swelled prodigiously in the evening and much pain. . . . Gave the old man that drew it however 0.2.6. He is too old, I think, to draw teeth, can't see very well.

Longer and more detailed accounts of Nancy's illnesses or those of his servants are carefully registered.

Of the common failing of the age—drink—Woodforde was not guilty. When at Oxford he tells us of a resolution he made after an orgy never to get drunk again. He kept this and although he has to record many lapses on the part of other people, there is never a word of self-righteousness about his own behaviour. At his annual "frolic," when he gave his tenants dinner, there was hilarity, not to say wild behaviour, but the parson, while keeping command of himself, was tolerant, perhaps a little over-tolerant of others.

In food he took a great interest. It would be quite a mistake to call him a glutton. He had a healthy appetite and was interested in his food, but he liked it plain and complains when it is "spoiled by being so frenchified in dressing." Dinner was at two or three in the afternoon and all the courses were laid out on the table. On most days he sets down what there was to eat whether he is at home or in other people's houses. "Plumb pudding" figures very often. Three examples may be given of dinners—with Mr. Custance, at home, and with the Bishop:

We had for dinner a Calf's Head, boiled Fowl and Tongue, a saddle of mutton rosted on the Side Table and a fine Swan rosted with currant Jelly sauce for the first course. The second course a couple of wild fowl called Dun Fowls, Larks, Blamange, Tarts etc etc and a good Desert of Fruit after amongst which was a Damson Cheese. I never eat a bit of a Swan before and I think it good eating with sweet sauce. The Swan was killed 3 weeks before it was eat and yet not the least bad taste in it.

I gave my company for dinner my great Pike which was rosted and a Pudding in his Belly, some boiled Trout, Perch, and Tench, Eel and Gudgeon fryed, a Neck of Mutton boiled and a plain Pudding for Mrs Howse. All my company were quite astonished at the sight of the great Pike on the table. Was obliged to lay him on two of the largest dishes and was laid on part of the Kitchen Window shutters, covered with a cloth. I never saw a nobler Fish at any table, it was very well cooked, and tho' so large was declared by all the Company to be prodigious fine eating being so moist.

There were 20 of us at the Table and a very elegant Dinner the Bishop gave us. We had 2 courses of 20 Dishes each course and a Desert after of 20 Dishes. Madeira, red and white wines. The first course amongst many other things were 2 Dishes of prodigious fine stewed Carp and Tench, and a fine Haunch of venison. Amongst the second Course a fine Turkey Poult, Partridges, Pigeons and sweetmeats.

Desert—amongst other things Mulberries, Melon, Currants, Peaches, Nectarines and Grapes. A most beautiful Artificial Garden in the Center of the Table remained at Dinner and afterwards, it was one of the prettiest things I ever saw, about a yard long, and about 18 Inches wide, in the middle of which was a high round Temple, supported on round Pillars, the Pillars were wreathed round with artificial Flowers—on one side was a Shepherdess on the other a Shepherd, several handsome Urns decorated with artificial flowers also etc etc. The Bishop behaved with great affability towards me as I remembered him at Christ Church in Oxford.

Parson Woodforde was an active man and socially in great request. He does not seem to spend much time in reading or study. But amongst other books he mentions *Roderick Random*, a life of Louis XIV and Evelina, which he describes as " cleaver and sensible." While kind and tolerant perhaps to a fault with his relations and friends, he is not without a critical faculty in human intercourse. When a clergyman, a former Oxford acquaintance, turns up to stay without having been invited, he writes:

He slept however in the Attic storey and I treated him as one that would be too free if treated too kindly.

We know the type.

In a short notice only a very superficial idea can be given of the excellence of James Woodforde's record. It is a window straight into the past through which we can follow in detail the life of an eighteenth-century village. No history book, no learned treatise on the customs and fashions of a hundred and fifty years ago can give the atmosphere and reality with which the consecutive reading of Woodforde's Diary furnishes our imagination.

The first volume was published by Mr. John Beresford in 1924, the second in 1926, bringing the diary down to 1787, and his readers are impatient for further volumes.

# THOMAS HOLLIS

UNFAILING punctuality in diary writing is rare. Never to miss a day means that many entries must often be made from methodical habit rather than from inclination. Nevertheless, by varying the length of the entries, daily writers have been able to write very fully. Thomas Hollis kept a diary from 1759 to 1770 without missing a day and that fact in itself tells us something of his character.

He was born in 1720, received a liberal education and travelled for considerable periods abroad. On the death of his father he inherited a fortune and settled in London as an antiquary and a collector. He was a great upholder of civil and religious liberty, a benefactor of several institutions and presented books to Harvard, Berne and Zurich. He was a fellow of the Royal Society of Antiquaries and other learned Societies and edited a book on Milton and Algernon Sidney's works. The eleven years of diary not only amplify the known facts of his life, to be found in biographical dictionaries ; but in spite of its dry precision, its brief businesslike notes, its entire absence of introspection, its rare expressions of opinion and still rarer reflections, the diary reveals his character and cast of mind in a way which no other document could. When a man sets out to write down his daily doings accurately and exactly, not only can a reader judge of his pursuits and interests, but sooner or later the even tenor of the coldest record is likely to be disturbed by something or other. And as we shall see, that was the case with Thomas Hollis. However, neither wife nor weather, perhaps the two chiefly disturbing elements to so many diarists, neither children nor illness are the subjects for joy or lament from the pen of this diarist, who was a bachelor and a townsman and appears to have enjoyed good health.

But before touching on the peculiarities of the diary let us get some picture of the routine of Thomas Hollis's life. Routine it certainly was with very little variety. Every day is spent sorting and arranging medals and coins or buying prints and books or collecting and conversing about objects of virtu, or preparing books to be sent away or attending learned Society meetings. He notes the coffee houses he frequents (though never the food he eats), the friends and strangers he see daily, the letters and articles he writes, the very occasional play or concert he goes to. He is always "busy" from morning to night and as often as not dines alone at home. No morbid reflections about loneliness ever occur and frequently the last thing at night he plays for an hour on the flute "to compose" himself. Occasionally he rides and fences. Hardly a mention of any woman of his own class is ever made and although he never writes of it we are left with the impression that the antiquarian bachelor was perfectly happy in the companionship he found in his collections and his flute.

A few sample entries may be given:

Perry with me for an hour, principally to weigh some of my gold coins for Dr Giffords account of the gold plates for the Society of Antiquaries. Buisy the remainder of the day in taking a catalogue of the books which I intend to send to Abbate Venuti as a present; and in copying of it fair twice once for the Abbate and once for myself. Dined at home alone. Played on my flute at night. Read.

Within the whole day buisied early and late about a great variety of odd matters. Dined at home alone.

Breakfasted at C. house in Maiden Lane. At Mr James's in the Tower to get a few copper medals from the dies in his possession. With Ned Burton on the custom house Keys, about sundry petty matters. At Mr. Whites got a curious gold coin there of the English Series for the Duke of Devonshire. At Snelling's about several matters relating to Virtu. At Pingo's. Dined at Townsend's with Mr Brand. Went with him afterwards to Vauxhall.

At home. Busied the whole day as yesterday. Snelling with me in the evening. Dined at home alone.

There are numberless instances of his generosity and

charity. He continually helps poor people in distress with a few guineas. But occasionally he is imposed upon and he notes it with a line or two such as " Mr Grimes, who has flagrantly and repeatedly ill treated me " ; and a young man who was " thrifty overmuch in petty matters " causes him to exclaim " What money, *thinking time*, has not this youngster cost me." He pays several visits to Speaker Onslow, where he is " entertained highly " and talks over medals and Milton. He also has talks with the Archbishop of Canterbury, corresponds with " the magnanimous Mr Pitt," has the brothers Adam to tea and meets Bartolozzi. Coins bring him into touch with the Duke of Devonshire, and he recounts how a fine collection being in the market he tells the Duke out of civility that he will not bid against him for it. He adds :

> Took the above resolution to thwart my Disposition which inclines at present too much to Virtu of this sort ; and to shew civility to the Duke, which, as expected, was not felt by him.

The Duke, however, presents him several times with a haunch of venison.

Hollis receives offers for a seat in Parliament. He refuses, saying :

> though I would give almost my right hand to be chosen into Parliament, yet that I could not give a single Crown for it by way of BRIBE.

Several years later another opportunity arises, but again he declines :

> I am advancing in age. The times seek corruption. " I can live contented without glory but cannot so for shame." I have passed the flower of my Life, as I have vowed in the Service of my Country. The remainder is at my own private disposal to pass in leisure with decorum.

His friends often come and " prate " to him about politics and he evidently follows public events pretty closely, although he only notes them briefly. When George II dies he breaks out into very pompous reflections, and when George III marries he expresses the wish that the new Queen may prove " the fruitful mother of a race of Heroes." " Fruitful " turned out to be correct, but Hollis did not live to see the

"Heroes." The following entry brings a political event of 1767 rather strikingly before us:

> Mr Wilkes having gained his Election for the County of Middlesex this day, and with great superiority, an universal illumination of the cities of London and Westminster ensued at night, but so late in Palmal that I and my family were in Bed and a Sleep, by which circumstances the Mob broke several of my windows.

Hollis has the reputation of being a republican, but there is very little to suggest it in the diary. He was, however, a keen advocate of the principles of the Revolution and the Reformation and his letters and compositions, his propaganda and projects for thwarting the advance of Popery are referred to in a number of entries. He often expresses himself strongly and makes notes of the letters and articles he sends to the Press. It is in connection with his activities in this direction that one very curious feature of the diary becomes apparent. He is persuaded that his neighbours are prying into his house in Pall Mall and considers whether he will not have "ground-glass" placed in the windows. Shortly after he notices that he is followed and spied on in different parts of the town by "Papists, from many circumstances it is possible." At brief intervals he returns to the subject. Six spies follow him, "one or two Spyes are constantly detached after me to watch me": "there are other spys effective, probably the whole body of the Papists who have received orders to follow watch me wherever they meet me and to report somewhere what they observe"; he is followed by "women and young Men especially." So it goes on from 1765 onwards till at last we find the two following entries:

> 1767. I have been followed, spyed on in some respects more closely than ever; and by very great numbers of Persons of both sexes, and seemingly of all Ranks. The Banks of the Thames too are now generally lined with spyes when I go out upon it; nor can I go into a Shop or C. House or Public place, in most parts of the Town, but I am followed thither by one or more of them.

> 1768. The generality of these Spyes, as from their office, affect obscurity, and are detected many of them by me only from my now great Experience relating to them and caution. No Quarter of the Town is free of them, no Public Place, nor even the Environs of London, as well on horse back as on foot. . . . The case of these

**Spyes is a clear one. The Papists, Jacobites, the Leaders of them, from long time and circumstances have found out that I am a hearty, ACTIVE friend to civil and religious Liberty and consequently a Detester of their Principles and Practices; and having Schemes of the highest nature in view, almost, it is probable, in execution; they are the Persons, who set these Spyes to watch, but for the scrub, base times, me a very ordinary Man.**

Although it goes on again after this it becomes clear to the reader of the diary that Thomas Hollis was labouring under a delusion. Whatever grounds there may have been for his original suspicions it is quite certain that the banks of the Thames were not lined with spies nor could he have been surrounded by a throng of spies wherever he went. The mania of persecution is the most common of all forms of insanity. While there is no reason whatever to suppose that Hollis was insane, he was evidently in this particular a prey to hallucinations. An obsession of this sort is not uncommon with people who in their ardour for some particular cause do not attract as much notice as they would like and consequently attempt to enhance their own importance by imagining they are the objects of special insult and attack. But the incidents have no culmination nor is there ever any proof or explanation. That is where the special fascination of a manuscript diary comes in. We just have the writer's impressions committed by him privately to paper, perhaps not communicated to anyone else, and we must make our own inferences without any editor's footnote to clear up and explain the mystery.

From this we pass to the other peculiarity in the long neatly written quarto sheets of what at first seems a dry and punctilious record. Neither his activities in the Protestant cause, nor his intercourse with the Speaker and Archbishop, nor his notable visitors, nor even his collections and antiquarian pursuits inspire Hollis to write at any great length. But there is one subject that does. It is what he himself calls "Domesticalities." Speaker Onslow, the Duke of Devonshire, Mr. Pitt and his brother antiquaries may receive a few lines, but Thomas, Jane, Betsy and Dy, his servants, receive pages. He notes when he washes "washed my feet and my bosom"; he notes trouble with pipes and the chimney ; he describes very fully an altercation with Mrs. Mott his landlady in one of his lodgings ; and he notes when he goes through his whole house to see that everything is in order, a practice he indulges in frequently. But when it comes to his difficulties with his servants he lets himself go even to the extent of recording *verbatim* dialogues. Of this feature in the diary some instances may be given, although it would be impossible to cover the whole ground:

> Gave my servant, Thomas Byrchmore, some old cloths and a suit of laced cloths now too little for me, but very good in order to induce him to continue to behave like a faithful and attentive servant.

But Thomas informs him one morning that he is married to Margaret, a former maid of his, and gives warning.

> Thomas has several good Qualities but has long since lost all true regard and reverence for his Master and become the most *sober impudent* Fellow that I ever knew.

Later on he records a talk with Thomas in which he asks him some " driving questions." Thomas goes, but turns up not long after, having " wheedled Harry to let him in." His maid at this time he says is " giddy pated at best " and he has to lecture her. Richard then appears on the scene, " good natured and honest " but " certainly very awkward " and " too small in person." Then comes an episode which reminds us of the spies and we refuse to believe that either Richard or the maid were to blame.

> The Door of my Bed chamber having been beated on from the outside for a year past, in an extraordinary manner and often with great violence in the Night time from 11 to 6 by a Person or Persons unknown with an intent as it should seem to destroy my Rest and vex me ; and other extraordinary noises having been heard by me . . . this evening thought proper to relate them to my servants with suitable observations upon them. Both the servants denyed repeatedly the having been concerned in them or the having heard them, Richard becomingly with humility and uneasiness the Maid with real Levity and Impudence.

Most of us would not stand violent blows on our bedroom door for even one night. When he says he had tolerated it for a year the maid's " Levity " appears to us pardonable. But some weeks later Hollis notes that Richard has become "sulky and improper" and he is convinced that both he and the maid are responsible for "the Beatings on the door of my Bed Chamber which still continue." But he concludes this entry "Yet I should wink on"; and a week or so later he refers to them both disparagingly and adds, "with such people it will still be convenient to wink hard at present." So it goes on—noises and suspicion—and he tells a friend who, he says, "appeared to be greatly surprized." At last the maid's Levity and Impudence reaches a pitch which Thomas Hollis, we fear, hardly appreciates:

This morning on my return home, the Maid desired to speak to me by Richard; and I saw her, being busy in my Bed Chamber, in the Landing place without it. She said in substance what follows in a very unexpected *bold* manner That she wished I would put a stop to the noises heard within the House in the Night time; that she felt herself *crawled* (or run) over by some kind of Creatures at times, as she lay in her Bed; that Long and I were the occasion of such proceedings; that Richard had talked something about a Court of Conscience, but said it would not do; and had added that I was a Heathin and a Devil. I replyed that I had been in her room but twice in the day time a long time ago, on account of Repairs; that a stop might probably be put to all noises in the House by bringing more servants into it; and that if she chose it, she might quit the House. She said, No, she would not be turned out of it, in so quick and sly a manner; or words to that effect. I replyed that she should mind her own right behaviour and not act *strangely* and so left her.

We can imagine the convulsions of laughter below stairs after this interview. But a day or two later Margaret takes her departure suddenly and Richard is dismissed in an interview in which he sheds tears. Jane, Margaret's successor, is at first satisfactory, but after a while he writes:

*Jane* becomes more and more careless of my instructions and her business; has lost much of her simplicity; is now reserved cunning and flaunty; and all this has happened to her probably through the machinations of those same base People who spoiled my former Servants!

He talks to her "roundly" a few days later. "At first she behaved rather stoughtly," but finally she is repentant and he forgives her. But a few months after there is trouble again; and he notes that she is "now actuated by the worst, a sober kind of presumption and impudence!"

This evening Jane appeared before me in a *laced* cap. I had reprehended her formerly on that account and for other indiscretions in her dress; adding "that neatness not finery should be the object of a Servant".

Jane explains that she had not a plain cap that was clean. Hollis adds that he suspects "She is engaged in some kind of intrigue that is neither suitable to my service nor becoming to Herself." Not long after Jane tells him she is going to marry a joiner which gives him an opportunity of "parting with her easily." She is succeeded by Elizabeth Dyet, known as "Dy," and he has much talk with the new maid "concerning domesticalities and some concerning the scrubnesses of Jane."

These extracts must suffice to illustrate the relations of the antiquary with his domestics. If prominence is given to this feature of the diary it is not only because entertainment is to be derived from these constantly recurring episodes, but also because a man's character can be judged better from his behaviour to his servants than by his behaviour to Dukes and Archbishops.

Each year, for Thomas Hollis began on his birthday, April 14, every section of the diary starts anew on that day and he makes a brief general reflection on the past year. A few of these may be quoted:

1759. Entered the fortieth year of my age. May the remainder of life pass steadily in active and extensive virtue, at least in innocence; and this I will endeavour.

1762. My birthday. Entered into the forty third year of my age. Reviewed the Diary of the preceding year. Many mistakes, many wrongnesses; yet, under some very discouraging circumstances have, in the general, acted like an honest man and an ingenuous one. O God in thy goodness aid me through the remainder of my life with thy choicest wisdom and grant me a perfect resignation to thy will!

1766. Another year of constant thinking, labor, expence has now been given in, by way of exceedings to the wonted Plan, and under many infirmities but much good will to the Public Service, it is hoped to some usefulness. May the future part of my life be passed, at least in Innocency and, if it shall please God, with greater Decorum and Wisdom to Myself and Benefit to others!

1770. I pray God, of his goodness, so to illuminate my mind long perplexed in uncertainty! that I may be enabled surely and speedily to fix on that Plan of Life, for the remainder of it, which shall be most conducive to his will and to my own private decorum and happiness.

In July of 1770 he retired to his estate in Dorsetshire and the last entries are concerned with his packing up and his departure. He died four years later.

Although the diary is objective we get a very clear picture of Thomas Hollis and we like him. He was a man of means who was not at all typical of the age he lived in, but devoted his time assiduously to learned and public work and never turned a deaf ear to the calls of charity. A full diary in which there is seldom any reference to weather, women, relations, deaths, food or gossip has a distinctive character of its own. Yet, full as it is, we know quite well he does not tell us everything.

The original manuscript diaries bound in six vellum-bound volumes are in the possession of the Antony family, by whose kind permission they have been examined and the above quotations made.

## NICHOLAS CRESSWELL

TRAVEL and adventure would seem to be very suitable subjects for diary writing, and there can be no question that they have impelled many people to keep diaries who otherwise might have had no inclination to do so. Yet those who have succeeded in making a diary of travel and adventure interesting and attractive are very few in number. Nicholas Cresswell, the son of a farmer, Thomas Cresswell, of Edale in Derbyshire, went out to America at the age of twenty-four in 1774. His journal gives perhaps the best model of this kind of diary.[1]

Nicholas Cresswell would have been surprised to learn that he had written anything remarkable. He started off against the wishes of his father and he completely failed to justify his adventurous journey. He wrote perfectly naturally for his own satisfaction without a thought of publication, and it is the very simplicity and unaffected candour of his record which makes it so greatly superior to a studied literary production carefully prepared for the Press. Nicholas was far from a saint and he tells us everything—not us, but his diary, because it is obvious that he was never conscious of a reader's eye. " Determined to keep a daily and impartial Journal from this day by which I hope to square my future conduct," he writes in his first entry in 1774, and in 1777, after he has returned a failure, poor and on strained terms with his family, he concludes his journal with the words, " Mem. Never to have anything to do with my Relations. I know their dispositions only too well, some of them begin to hint at my poverty already. I must be patient and if possible silent." Four years later he inserts a brief statement of his marriage to an heiress and under this he writes " My rambling is now at an end." A literary person would have found it

[1] Quotations from the Journal of Nicholas Cresswell are given with the kind consent of Messrs. Jonathan Cape, Ltd.

difficult to round off an episode with such art and dramatic restraint.

Nicholas Cresswell was never put off by obstacles. In the case of his father he had to get assistance in order to obtain his consent for the journey to America.

> This evening Mr. Carrington came and by his aid and assistance got the consent of my Father to go into America. I believe it is with very great reluctance he grants it. I am sorry he will not converse with me on the subject but am determined to persevere.

It is, of course, impossible to follow Cresswell in his wanderings in Virginia, Barbados, the Kentucky and the Ohio rivers, in his poverty and illness and narrow escapes. The outbreak of the War of Independence frustrates all his plans and places him in a very difficult position. He refuses to take up arms against his own country and is consequently always regarded as suspect. The excellence of the diary can only be appreciated by reading the consecutive entries and by being carried along with him in his ups and downs, his dangers, his hopes, his depressions and his illness. He never wastes words. Sometimes he only writes a sentence or turns off the character of those whom he encounters in a phrase. When he is interested in his work or in the experiences he is passing through he lets himself go. His style is surprisingly modern, his reflections discriminating and mature, and in spite of his lapses, caused generally by desperation, one can detect without any self-conscious assurances on his part an upright, unaffected and solid character.

From time to time he takes stock of his situation and faces his failure. He writes in an entry in which he is thrashing out the pros and cons of his adventure :

> All these summed together are not half so grating as the thought of returning to my native country in poverty and rags and then be obliged to beg like a criminal to get my debts paid which I am now contracting and in course must be obliged to contract before I get home. The bitter reflections, taunts and sarcasms of my friends will be submitted then upon my conduct. No matter whether it be right or wrong, I have been unfortunate, therefore, everyone think they have a right to find fault with my proceedings. I believe their reproofs will be tinctured with a good deal of acrimony, as I took this journey entirely against their consent. I must endeavour to brave all these rubs and

frowns of fortune with fortitude and patience, submit myself to them and follow their councils and advice.

He refers to his extreme diffidence and puts it down to the way he was brought up:

When I am in company with people of equal or superior abilities or those of an unconstrained behaviour, tinctured with a large share of assurance, my diffidence and temerity is so great that it renders me ridiculous, even when the discourse happens to turn upon a topic I understand as well as any of them (Mem. Never to enter into Political disputes again till I have more impudence or am in a free country).

He has no shyness, however, when he is with the Indians:

Saw an Indian Dance in which I bore a part. Painted by my Squaw in the most elegant manner. Divested of all my clothes except my calico short breech clout, leggings and Mockesons. A fire was made which we danced round with little order, whooping and hallooing in a most frightful manner.

His low spirits sometimes lead him into bad company:

Got up at 2 in the afternoon. Got drunk before 10 with the same company I was with yesterday and am now going to bed at 2 in the morning, most princely drunk indeed.

His poverty is a constant handicap. "To be poor and seem so is the devil." "O poverty poverty thou worst of curses tho' an old companion, I hate thee." "The thought of returning home a Beggar is worse than death." But a "cheerful glass" sometimes makes him forget it.

The war upsets all his calculations and of course he constantly refers to it and all the rumours true and false that he hears:

The people here are ripe for a revolt, nothing but curses and imprecations against England her Fleets, armies and friends. The King is publicly cursed and rebellion rears her horrid head.

He cannot always write fully of his projects because he carries his diary about with him and it might become "a capital witness" against him. Some of his adventures are very well described, but they cover several pages. On the other hand, he is very brief if he is off colour or has little to say. Here is a series of short entries:

1776. March 20. Have been confined to my room in violent pain A little better to-day and able to walk about my room. This is the first day I have been able to write since the 4th day of the month.

March 21. Much better but very weak. Taking a decoction of the woods. My spirits are good and I hope I shall get over this bout. News that the Great Sanhedrin, the Congress, had given the Colonies liberty to trade with all nations but Great Britain and its Islands and that they had begun to Bombard Boston.

March 22. Free from pain, wrapped myself up and went out to see the general musters of the Militia in town, about 700 men but few arms. Great confusion among them.

March 23. Am afraid I got cold yesterday violent pain in my back and head.

March 24. Confined to my room. The Doctor scolds me and brings more of his Damd nostrums.

March 29. Confined to my room these past five days and greatest part of the time in bed, unable to help myself. I am a little better to-day, able to walk about the room, but look like the picture of Famine.

He settles down on board ship on his way home to write very fully about the "cursed Rebellion":

I have seen thic a happy Country and I have seen it miserable in the short space of three years. The villainous arts of a few and the obstinacy of many on this side of the Water, added to the complicated blunders cowardice and knavery of some of our blind *guides* in England, have totally ruined the Country.

As for himself, he says:

A man suspected of loyalty is in more danger, by far, than an Old Woman and her Tabby Cat was formerly in England and Scotland if she was suspected of witchcraft.

Incidentally at the beginning and end of the Journal we get a sidelight on his stern father. We have Nicholas's reluctance to face him, the father's morose silence and on the very day of his return

My Father set out for Chesterfield Fair soon after I arrived, but remembered to order me to shear or bind Corn to-morrow. I think this is rather hard.

Nicholas Cresswell was not a diarist, he wrote for these three years because he wanted to record his adventures and had no one to write to. But when at home he finds " a sameness " in his life and thinks it is not worth while keeping a Journal. As it stands, however, there are few diaries which present a complete story with such natural art.

He died at the age of fifty-three in 1804, four years before his father.

## JOSEPH MYDELTON

A SMALL leather notebook on the title page of which is inscribed " The Memoirs, Life and Journal of Joseph Mydelton, son of Starkey Myddelton, Minister of the everlasting Gospel. 1774," contains, in addition to an autobiographical preface, a diary kept from 1774 to 1787. The entries are brief and irregular and deal chiefly with religious occupations, pious reflections and notes of the births and deaths of children. Struggles with poverty, failure in his pursuits, punctuated by constant deaths in the family, make Mydelton's diary a rather dismal record. Moreover, it is difficult to get close to the writer not only because of the scrappiness of his entries but because he shows no originality of expression but falls back on stock phrases favoured by Methodists of that date. " Had a good time " is varied by " Had a melting time," " had a glorious time," " a very dry time," " a dead time " or " a comfortable time," and when anyone is dying he says they " are ripening fast for glory." Sometimes his ecstasy seems almost excessive :

My poor vessel was so filled with the Love of God that I really thought it would burst and let my Soul out to wing its way home to Xt. A night never to be forgotten.

In the course of one day his mood may vary :

Had a comfortable time in riding to the Hay with Bro: Clayton when we parted I found sweet communion with God, preached in the Morn and had a good time but a dry one in the Even.

He very occasionally and very briefly mentions public events.

Saw the King go to the Parliament House and a solemn sight ; saw a poor man breath his Last, in Health one moment and dead the next, he was run over by the Kings State coach : Lord prepare me for all thy Will.

Went to see Mr Davis executed for Forgery who at the place of execution pray'd, sang and exhorted with great fervency both the spectators and the prisoners. I dont know that I ever saw a more solemn awful yet profitable opportunity in my Life and Blessed be God I trust there was some good done. 7 of the malefactors seem'd happy and Mr Davis died seemingly ripe for Glory.

He begins as a student at the Countess of Huntingdon's College and when he preaches before her he has "a pretty good time." However his marriage appears to be a barrier to his continuance at the College and although in one entry he writes :

Spoke to my Lady about my marriage and she behaved much kinder than I expected.

Later on the Countess sends for him and tells him that "her cause would be much injured" if he remained, so he goes to London and makes fruitless endeavours to get ordination. He accepts all his rebuffs with patience except on one occasion when he refers to the Bishop of London as a "haughty prelate."

But we need not follow Mydelton through his trials, his attempts to get pupils, his failure to be ordained or his voyage to China, during which his entries are still more meagre, although the King of Baba in Madagascar confers on him the "honour of knighthood." There is a good deal of "ripening for glory" on board ship, no less than twenty people dying, but the mortality in his own family is also severe.

On March 27, 1778, his wife dies giving birth to a girl, who dies also. He records the fact with all the suitable accompaniment of religious lament. But on May 9, about six weeks later, he writes :

Went to Warley Common to see the Camp with one who seems as tho' she would make a good companion for me. O Lord my God do thou guide and direct Me in all things.

In September he marries his companion of Warley Common and writes appropriate thanksgiving on "once more entering into the holy estate of Matrimony." In the same year he loses a son of two years old. The loss of a wife and two children and a remarriage might be supposed to make something of an impression on the baldest of diary writers, but Mydelton registers the events with no more comment than the usual pious tag with which he concludes nearly all his entries. We are, however, able to discover in a rather curious way by means of a mistake he makes that the year's events made a deeper impression on him than he allows us to see from the dated entries. He is accustomed at the end of each year to devote a page or half a page to "Observations on the year." In 1778 he very briefly but accurately records his three losses and his marriage. In 1779 he goes for his voyage and is in Canton at the end of the year. In his remarks for 1779 he repeats all over again precisely the same events of the previous year, although in slightly different language, adding the only event which correctly belonged to the year:

> Thro' many losses was obliged to leave Home got a place in an India Ship bound direct for China.

He was, in fact, deluded. The passage of time had failed to impress him and his memory went back to the year of sensational happenings which still seemed near and which he could not so readily forget.

He refers briefly but frequently to his own health and to his disorders without specifying them with any exactness, except to give on one occasion a description of a curious poultice he uses for the pain in his side:

> a top crust of a threepenny loaf toasted and spread with soft soap put between a flannel made hot and applied to the part affected.

He has an altercation with the taxation authorities and exclaims:

> Oh how vilely do these men in power abuse the trust reposed in them.

But Mydelton's piety as we see it in these neatly written little pages is concerned first and foremost with his "soul's advantage." He was self-centred but had no talent for interesting reflection nor sufficient sympathy to write about other people. The diary breaks off abruptly in March, 1787, the last entry being:

tho' tried in circumstances yet Blessed be God our Trust is He will safely bring us thro' all our Tryals.

Mydelton died in May of this year and was buried at West Ham.

The original manuscript is in the possession of W. M. Myddelton, Esq., of Woodhall Spa, by whose kind permission it has been examined and the above extracts made.

## WILLIAM JONES

NOT many people have heard of Broxbourne, and only some of those who have, will know that William Jones (a native of Abergavenny, born in 1754) was curate and vicar there for forty years from 1781 to 1821. If special prominence is given here to William Jones's diary, it is not because he was an eminent divine or a great writer, neither is it because he was acquainted with famous people nor because he collected important gossip and shed sidelights on public affairs which are of historical value, it is simply because a perusal of his record shows that William Jones was a great diarist. It is unnecessary to repeat the elements which constitute good diary writing [1] or to emphasize again that it is not the subject matter which counts but the attitude of mind and powers of perception and expression of the writer. There is nothing in William Jones's career that is noteworthy, nor were his daily pursuits, his domestic cares, or his intercourse with his neighbours of special interest, but he had individuality and character, original and peculiar powers of expression and an overwhelming desire to scribble down at all periods of his life and at all moments of the day and even night (for he kept a special slate by his bedside) the ideas and impressions which were continually bubbling up in his very shrewd and observant mind. His diary, which he began when he was at Jesus College, Oxford, covers 2,962 pages. He kept a Book of Domestic Lamentations as a safety-valve for his matrimonial woes and domestic grievances. There were two volumes of this unique record which, most unfortunately, he destroyed. He kept a Journal of Health dealing with his own and his parishioners' ailments and a Medical Common Place book recording the progress of local epidemics. There

[1] See Introduction to *English Diaries*.

were other Commonplace Books and rough notebooks ; the latter took the place of his journal from 1799 to 1814, and various detached manuscripts, one of which contained his "apology or defence" for keeping his coffin in his study. There can be few instances of a diarist in which the "itch to record" is so strongly developed and yet any desire for publication never seems to have entered his head. Of all his writings, except two volumes of Sermons published in 1823, his Diary alone has survived ; but luckily it amply suffices to give us a very remarkable and intimate picture of a human life.

William Jones returns time after time during the years he wrote to the benefits to be derived from journalizing. Originally his motive was purely disciplinary, but as time passed he certainly found pleasure in recording his thoughts, describing incidents and making character sketches :

1778. Am convinced every day more of the propriety of continuing my Journal ; for however tedius or foolish it may appear to any one else I know the pleasurable enjoyment of the mercies Deliverances etc here recorded and to my great Encouragement a retrospect has always yielded me redoubled capital pleasure.

1779. As my Journal swells so does the pleasure I feel in keeping one.

1786. (after a long interval) I really believe my neglecting to journalize, has very much contributed to my soul's decline in spiritual things.

1791. The good effects arising from my frequent use of my diary are hardly to be imagined. It leads to reflection and self converse which is not one of the least among its good effects.

1814. O ! that I could persuade all my fellow mortals to *journalize* ! if they were to begin in earnest they would be so delighted as to be unable to *discontinue*. It would insensibly lead their minds into a train of *thinking attentively* and I trust, I may add, that it would conduce to their *acting circumspectly*.

He realizes the difficulty, as other introspective writers have, of writing truthfully when he says :

Imagining that my Journal may fall into the hands of my friends or others I find within me, in spite of all I can do, a studious care employed tho' not to misrepresent the truth, yet to avoid setting it forth in glaring colours.

But towards the end he writes:

> This journal of mine! *Nostri farrago libelli!* how rambling and disjointed is its appearance! but I trust that every one of the 2898 pages already occupied, exhibits and maintains the *integrity* of *truth*.

The " bed slate " was used for catching passing thoughts at night or in the early morning:

> I frequently have a slate and pencil by my bed side and when I wake at perhaps far too early an hour to rise, I scribble down any thoughts or reflexions which present themselves to my mind.
>
> Often do I in the dark my means of *holes* in the frames of my slates and *moveable* pegs scribble my dawning morning thoughts.

The above quotations show that William Jones's equipment as a diarist was very exceptional.

Now as to the diary itself. By the opening entries when he is at Oxford a reader may at first think that it is going to be one of those numberless diaries so common in the eighteenth and early nineteenth centuries in which monotonous repetition of prayer and exaggerated self-condemnation become very wearisome reading. The practice is common with young divines. With age it becomes mitigated, but very often there is nothing much else to take its place. Although William Jones never left off his religious meditations, he began to observe the world outside as much as, if not more than, the recesses of his own soul. But even in the earlier entries his language is unconventional and his expressions so violent that one is forced to smile and read on and then to pity the mental suffering of an obviously sincere writer. In the very first line he refers to himself as " the Vilest of the Vile " and later as " the most daring Rebel against Heaven," " the vilest of Sinners, the most daring miscreant out of hell,' " a polluted Wretch," " a Monster of Iniquity all unholy and unclean." He speaks of his " Fillthiness Vileness and Wretchedness " and declares that his sins are more in number than the hairs of his head. But we need not dwell on this side of the diary because, although the language is picturesque, anyone who finds edification in perusing lamentations of self-reprobation will find enough and to spare in the diaries of this period.

Jones left Oxford in order to take up the post of tutor to the sons of Mr. Thomas Harrison, the Attorney-General of Jamaica. In Jamaica he remains two years, keeps his eyes open, observes the manners and customs more often with pain than with pleasure and notes it all down. At first he is amazed and shocked at the " herds of tawny sooty Beings," disgusted at their " sottishness and stupidity " and indignant at the " obscene and filthy language." But after a while he has talks with them, learns to appreciate them as " shrewd and sensible " and turns the vials of his wrath against the white population with their dissolute manner of living and their hideous cruelty to the natives ; and there are many entries which show him on the side of the negro and against the white man. However, he keeps his views to himself, for he writes :

Were I to say to these brutal Ruffians and Murderers of Negroes what I write of them I'm sure the least harsh term they would think I deserved would be " a hen-hearted simpleton " or " a *dammed* fool."

How disgraceful to Christianity are those professors of it who imagine poor oppressed negroes to be formed *by nature* for no other end than the exercise of their cruelty and the gratification of their brutish lusts.

And his " heart aches " when he hears " the loud smack of a barbarous villain's whip." Here is part of a conversation he has with a negro boy. He asks him whether

he ever had heard of God, Heaven or Hell ? He was a long time before he made any other answer than " No." He did not understand what I had asked him. At length he told me that " Dod " (as he called Him) " was live Top " (pointing with his finger upwards). Upon my enquiry " where he imagined all the negroes went after death ? " he said in his barbarous speech " dey fly up Top." This he supposed was the End of all Whites and Blacks except those " *Bokrahs* (white men) who fum (beat) Negers too bad." " Dey be boil in de Copper."

Of his patron, Mr. Harrison, Jones makes a very careful study, enlarging on his character on many occasions. He shows a certain generous broadmindedness which comes as a surprise from one who might be suspected of rather narrow and rigid piety. For Mr. Harrison was by no means religious in the restricted meaning of the word. But on both sides they were sensible men, each ready to appreciate the good in the other. Jones found himself in a difficult predicament. Here was a man who was obviously highminded and who soon gained his respect and his warm affection and yet Mr. Harrison's religious views fell far short of what the tutor considered essential. He jots down all his misgivings. After a description of his patron's position, income, family, etc., he writes:

> He is a person of a sprightly good-natur'd turn, the most respectable well-informed member of the Law in the Country without exception. I frequently see in him what attracts my love, tho' there appears more frequently what grieves and disgusts me. . . .
>
> But where oh! where shall his soul appear unless a prior change takes place, a spiritual renewal which he now scornfully derides and esteems Fanaticism? It must—shall I mention it?—cou'd he hear it without horror? scarce can I think of it without shuddering—it undoubtedly must yell forth in *Eternity* with his hellish Legions.
>
> The longer I live with him the more I *respect* and *love* him: and as my love increases so does my solicitude and concern in his behalf.
>
> I have never had such flattering marks of respect and attention from any; never been honoured with the intimacy of any, so affable and courteous as Mr. H. . . . In the midst of his jocularity at table he frequently looks towards me and enquires "Jones, don't you think me a heathen?" or "I am a noisy rattling fellow, am I not?"

He comes to the conclusion that Mr. Harrison does not "imbibe sin upon principle." And he rejoices when the Attorney-General leaves off swearing. On one occasion he goes so far as to express his disapproval of Chess on Sunday. Mr. Harrison remarks good-naturedly, "Jones does not like it, he looks very serious about it," and the game is abandoned. Many of the entries describing Mr. Harrison are of considerable length; pieced together they make a fine portrait of a charming gentleman and Jones confesses as he leaves Jamaica:

> My pain at the hour of parting with my dear friend Mr. Harrison was truly indescribable. He fell on my neck and embraced me in the most cordial manner, in a flood of tears. . . .

He writes about his pupils, of his drill as a private in the "Refermado Corps," of the threats of a French invasion and of many other adventures and experiences. Years after he refers to this period as the two happiest years of his life.

Throughout the diary we have to remember all the time that the repeated lamentations at his foulness and vileness are not only exaggerated but out of all proportion. He says himself:

> A Stranger who might chance to read some of these *dolorous* scrawls would imagine me to be one of the most *miserable* of all miserable unhappy beings—but is it so? No—no such thing.

Indeed we can detect from Jamaica days to the end that William Jones obviously had a social gift, was popular in company and enjoyed himself immensely, however much he may have bewailed his frivolity afterwards:

> O! sinful ill-judged complaisance to what Follies doest thou betray a weak Simpleton! This and a fear of displeasing some Ladies urged me to the public supper etc. etc. last night.

Revisiting Oxford on his return home "What an evening did I spend last night," he writes. "I have too many acquaintances in Oxford." At intervals he returns to the subject in later years:

> I have reason to lament daily a levity of disposition.

> Truly sorry am I that I staid so long at Mr. Cawthorn's particularly last night but my sorrow is unavailing. A clergyman's life should be chiefly spent among his books, and particularly in studying, upon his knees, that best and most useful of all books—the Bible. . . . his life cannot be too recluse. If he mixes with the rich, he will be very apt, if of my volatile naturally-gay temper to speak "unadvisedly" and "unguardedly with his lips."

> Alas! I too often feel that my natural *levity* and *folly* prevail over my better sense of things in my communications with the world. I, therefore, ought to mix as seldom as possible with what are called "joyous parties" for I am too apt to be off my guard.

All of which means that he was very good company and probably the life and soul of the "joyous parties." Moreover, he was not at all censorious, as the following shows:

> Thus have I seen some do wrong yet in such a manner (I am at a loss for an epithet to apply to it) that the edge of my disapprobation has been taken off and I have been unable to resist smiling while too

many others have I seen who have a most unpleasant way of doing right. I must and will do my dear wife the justice to say that she very often does right but I am sorry to be forced to class her with the above mentioned right doers.

This brings us to Mrs. Jones, of whom we get very entertaining glimpses throughout the diary. No doubt there was a good deal more about her in the Book of Domestic Lamentations. Of course we only get his side of the story, and in all fairness it must be admitted that a husband who was very seldom out of the house may have been a high trial to her. Not long after his return from Jamaica William Jones decides to marry and is " recommended " a young lady. He thinks her beautiful and charming, but the trouble is that " she seems to be an utter stranger to God." Nevertheless, " I cannot help finding my affections on the wing towards this object. Oh fickle, foolish heart ! " He thrashes the matter out in his diary very fully ; he describes her attractions and then breaks out, " But she knows not God, nay she despises religion. How then can I have thought of her ? " However, she marries some one else and five lines are erased from the diary in the entry where he records the receipt of the news. He eventually marries Theodosia Jessopp in 1781, but unfortunately the pages in which his courtship and marriage are described, and we feel sure very fully, are torn out of the Diary, and in 1782 we find him married, " happily married to one who is so good a woman." " The dear partner of my life—a better, one more calculated to make my life comfortable and happy I firmly believe Heaven could not have given me." After fifteen years and later he writes :

I with pleasure acknowledge that my wife tho' wanting in mildness and gentleness in her general behaviour to me, is in every other respect an excellent wife, frugal and attentive to her domestic concerns and a pattern of a mother.

My *dear* wife is a lawyers daughter and possesses such a wonderful volubility of speech such a miraculous power of twirling and twisting every argument to her own interest that I am no match for her High Mightiness. She right well knows how " to puzzle right and varnish wrong." No Old Bailey solicitor, no puzzle-cause throughout the kingdom better knows the *sublime* art. Whether she has by dint of application or in the management of me acquired this faculty I know not.

I do not expect to be consulted at all (about his son's affairs) my *sage* wife being well assured that she not only plays at *cards* and stirs a *fire* but does everything else better than her *dear* husband.

In money matters she *trusts nobody* ;—" for why ? " " because as how " she *suspects everybody.*

I can truly say that from my soul I wish everyone about me to be happy ; but my temper is alas ! too warm and hasty. And my *Dosy's* temper is too much like mine in this respect. Every misunderstanding we have I sincerely wish may be our last, but I too soon forget my good wishes and resolutions.

His poverty combined with a large family make his life both as curate and vicar very difficult. He denies himself everything in the way of clothes, so that when he is presented one Easter with a new " gown, cassock the whole paraphernalia of a parson " he is highly delighted. But he is very much afraid that it is vanity not gratitude that makes him look forward daily to this present. If it were vanity, he writes,

this would impeach my wifes insight into human characters, she having often told me that *she never knew any man so perfectly devoid of vanity as myself.* As she and I have been on a very *intimate* footing for more than 26 years and I cannot accuse her of flattering her humble servant of a husband ; I own that I feel not the least inclination to *weaken*, much less to *annul*, her verdict which in this instance is favourable to me.

On another occasion he gets what he considers a compliment from Mrs. Jones :

My *dear* wife calls such conduct *meanspiritedness* ; and in order to prove that I have not a spice only, but a large quantity of this scurvy quality in my composition she expressed herself some time ago in her very *strong* manner—that if a man were to *cut off one of my hands and offer to shake my other hand* under a mask of friendship she verily believed I would not withhold or refuse my hand.

A sidelight on their relations is cast by a very pathetic entry about the death of their daughter :

May *I* and may the *mother* of the dear angel never forget the *kind* admonitions which she gave us when she supposed herself departing not many days ago ! " Don't quarrel together ! You might be very happy."

His sons caused him a great deal of trouble and anxiety, but he constantly expresses his great devotion to his daughters ; and as to his wife in his old age there is an affectionate sound in his brief references to " my old mate," " My old rib."

Diarists do not describe their serious sins and vices, although we are always favoured with lamentations of remorse and repentance. Their minor peccadilloes are, however, often elaborated. William Jones conforms to this rule. He tries to cure himself of the " *filthy* and *beastly* practice " of taking snuff and incidentally he remarks " O that my deary would give up snuff and novels," which seems to show that Mrs. J. was a slave to the same habit.

I may write huzza ! huzza ! for I have hitherto succeeded beyond my most tiptop expectations. My poor grumbling nose has kept a complete fast since the last date ! ! In all this time my snuffbox has not been for many minutes together, forgotten. It may therefore be truly supposed that I have been in a sort of *snuffy* purgatory. And my *hands* have not been idle, for again and again have they involuntarily been rummaging all my pockets in search, I suppose, of my snuffbox ; for after every repeated disappointment they have generally rubbed my craving nose, as if wishing to solace it (see Snuff—Journal of Health).

But it only lasted three weeks and he begins again " to make a dust hole of my poor head with more eagerness than before." His hands were always " rummaging for a snuff-box to befriend my *craving discontented* nozzle." Seven years later he makes another attempt and with greater success :

I, now and then, the seldomer the better, indulge my " snub nose " with a sniff (at an empty box). . . . I trust I have done with snuff and I cannot sufficiently rejoice. I now carry a *decent* handkerchief, instead of a *portable* dunghill.

Spirituous liquors he likewise tries to abjure, but we do not gather with what success. But he reasons it all out and while praising abstemiousness he takes the other side fully into account. In a long entry on the subject he remarks :

I trust I shall not die either of *eating* or of *drinking* I never was a *great* eater and I rejoice that *I am not* for as I take very little exercise it would not suit me I have always abhorred *foul feeding* gluttons and cannot help thinking that excess in eating is infinitely more unnatural and more unpardonable than excess in drinking.

Even the subject of early rising, a favourite disciplinary theme with diarists, he treats in an entirely original way :

I went to bed about 10 o'clock last night and when awaked between 12 and 1 by my noisy family's going to bed I felt as if I had slept sufficiently. I however took another nap and unclosed my eyes about 5 o'clock when I seemed resolved to get up; but the morning was so dark and cold that ¼ of my reverend person which was enjoying the *warmth* of the bed *outpleaded* the ¾ which had quitted it and down I slunk again like an old hare into my *form* ; to my shame I did not get up till 8.

As he grows older thanksgiving rather than self-disparagement forms the theme of his religious reflections. Considering his upbringing and the beliefs of his day, his views are often enlightened. He writes at great length on the doctrine of Eternal Damnation, which he finds difficult to accept.

I have sometimes been sorry to remark a sort of *ill-nature* or spirit of *revenge* seeming to shew itself in some rigid professors of religion while they were contending for the *eternity* of Hell-torments. . . . Can any sins committed by poor wretched man during his existence here deserve to be punished eternally ? . . . Could I, for any possible offence, doom to a punishment of *years* or still less consign to *eternal* torments a child of mine—part of *myself* ! Nature even fallen nature shudders at the idea.

This entry covers several pages and ends " I hardly know how to break off. The subject is so rich and so delightful."

But a certain morbidity about death is noticeable in the later years. He raises himself up on his elbow in bed and looks at the yew tree in the churchyard under which he has decided to be buried and many gloomy meditations follow. Like Frederick the Great's father and Sarah Bernhardt he had his coffin made and kept by him. He calls it his " Elm case " and places it in his study.[1] Depression marks some of his days—poured out to his diary but probably concealed from his family and friends. He complains of a " despondency which oppresses and overwhelms his mind " and the trials of poverty are sometimes more than he can bear. " I seem to feel myself breaking up apace," he exclaims soon after he becomes Vicar of Broxbourne and he reaches a very low point when he writes :

The sun shines. I hear the birds singing and all nature looks *gay*

---

[1] This actual coffin was never used, for when he died he had grown too large for it.

but not to *me*, my cup of life is *embittered* my mind is *unsettled* and *beclouded* : and instead of actually *enjoying* anything round me, I seem like a *sentinel* longing impatiently and looking out for relief. Heaven forbid that I should ever be tempted—or rather I ought to say—prevailed upon to *quit* or *desert* my *post* till my *all-merciful* and *all-powerful* Commander shall be pleased to release me.

But in the very next entry he is alert again, watching from his window the young men and women "pairing off like birds." Here is a sad birthday:

My birthday. Alas! it has never to the best of my recollection been *kindly* distinguished! neither a *kid* has been *killed* nor even a *plum-pudding* made, more than usually *large* and *richer of fruit* which might induce my children to welcome the day—nor a glass of *wine* poured out to drink me "*many and happy* returns of the day"—But this day! alas! so far from noting it with *white—ochre* will not suit it: *black* chalk alone must mark it.

After this we cannot help thinking rather bitterly about Mrs. Jones; for in the same entry he speaks of his "usually merry heart which maketh a cheerful countenance." But fortunately we have pictures of the Vicar in a different mood and we like to think of him as he describes himself in the following:

How happy, how very happy do I feel myself in my dear little room which some *delicate* folks would, perhaps, rudely call a *hog-stye*! I am undisturbed I have my cheerful little fire, my books and in short every comfort which I can reasonably desire. I read, I reflect, I write and I endeavour to enjoy, as far as I can, that blessed leisure and absence of care with which the good Providence of my Heavenly Father has indulged me.

There is a Pepysian touch in his delight at curing a smoking chimney:

I may cry out with *Archimedes*, the famous *geometrician* of *Syracuse* "*I have found*! *I have found*!" He did it in Greek—I will do it in plain English. I have *found* that the little chimney in my *dirty* study has a communication with the chimney of what we call our *best parlour* and that by *stopping* the draft of the register-stove, I am delivered from *one* of the two *curses* which harass many poor devils of *husbands*. May not this furnish a hint to *chimney*-doctors in other *parallel* cases? How rejoiced I am at this grand discovery!

He loved his study—"I am nowhere so *safe* as in my own *dirty* study—alias doghole!"

The Diary is so rich on the intimate and domestic side that we have left little space for instances of his record of objective matters. There is a graphic description covering some weeks in which he describes the "flashing and dashing" Colonel Rawlins for whom he rashly became surety at an election and by whom he was repaid only after a very long interval. Jones is unsparing in his criticism and there is a scoundrel called Rogers who is his implacable enemy and whom he denounces with great violence. He takes in foreigners as pupils and writes about them and the flirtations of a German pupil in another book. But their presence was a burden to him:

Though my wife often reminds me that I could not have *this* and *that* without *foreigners* and now and then threatens to put me on course fare and short allowance, when we have none of *these* inmates; yet I cannot help thinking that I shall never truly enjoy my *dear* cottage till it is clear of *all* but my *own* dear family except a visitor or two *now* and *then* to vary the scene.

London had no attractions for him. After one of his very few visits, he writes:

'Twas misery to hear the *wretched* Londoners *wheezing* and *coughing* and *gasping* for breath as they walked the streets; and I myself was a *fellow-sufferer* for fogs and damps and night air by no means suit my lungs: medical *jockeys* would pronounce me *thick*-winded if not *touched*—or *broken-winded.* I sometimes think I shall never again spend another week in Town unless I can contrive to carry my little *study*—my *hutch* with me as the *snails* do their shells on their backs.

His hatred of shams and pretension of any kind and of people who were "in the front rank of the insolent squad" is shown in many of his notes. We may give a few examples:

As some *pure prime faded* females with all the airs of *antiquated virginity* have been heard to say "*I might have been married* if it had not been etc etc" so on the death of this or that Bishop some parsons ashamed of being *unwedded* to a *benefice* have pretended to have been *on* and very near the *top* of the Bishop's list of preferment.

*Gemmen!* Ought I to wish that it were in my power to furnish my sons with 5 or 600£ a year each? I "*trow*" *not*; for it would probably transform them into "*Gemmen*" alias—*idle useless* and *worthless* beings.

*Learned ladies* are said to be negligent of the drawers that contain the *family-linen* etc and to cease studying the *pantry* and the comforts of those who are *alive* around them when they conceive a *passion* for the *dead* languages.

Jones was a student and a scholar, as we can gather from his many quotations. Occasionally he discourses about books and of his reading he says:

I am, indeed, a *desultory* reader at present ? four books at a time! I could not forbear smiling when I just now observed them all open, at once, in different parts of my study. *Skimming* rather than reading!

Of public events he writes rarely. In 1803 he takes a survey of the world in which he says:

Those *little great* men—ycleped *Kings, consuls, emperors* etc seem to be bargaining and parceling out this earth, as if it were their own *inalienable* inheritance and they were to live here for ever. They in general *abide* by their agreements no longer than they think *convenient* to themselves; hence fresh quarrels and wars make fresh *arrangements* soon necessary.

In 1816 he writes:

Covered with glory! for how many *long* years did we read this *hackneyed* and *absurd* phrase in bulletins alias bills of *bloodshed.*

Although there are several "chasms," as he calls them, in the diary, he keeps up writing very fully till within four months of his death. Of his health, his gout, his swollen legs, his inability to walk he writes from time to time, but the Journal of Health must have contained more elaborate accounts of his symptoms. In spite of physical troubles he remains cheerful:

While I am *shaving* myself I sometimes look into my almost *untoothed* mouth; and at the same time consider my various other infirmities which render me not unlike to a "broken vessel." I thank Heaven that I am not dispirited; my spirit bears me up under all my "*infirmities*"; it is not "*wounded*" by them.

He was in the habit of reading over his past "scribblements" and reflecting again over the bygone days. We cannot help regarding as a calamity the destruction of the book of Domestic Lamentations. It took place after he had become Vicar. He argues out the pros and cons. He acknowledges that "midwifing" his complaints upon paper has eased and relieved his mind, but comes to the conclusion that

> passing my eye over them may keep my mind in a state of *irritation* which is not, I believe, any one of the *attributes* of *mercy* and *forgiveness*.

We must part from William Jones, although we might find many more intensely human extracts showing him in his beloved study with " unbuttoned knees," or at the funeral feast at the " Bull " with " a set of merry mourners " or walking in the churchyard with his little grandchild who cries, " let us read the dead," or addressing his " simple folk, familiarly and affectionately " from his reading desk in the dusk of a winter afternoon " on the duty of loving and fearing and worshipping the good and gracious God in spite of wind and weather." The old scholar, hasty perhaps, and easily offended, but keenly observant, humorous, generous to a fault and always the friend of the under-dog, has left us the full story of his life.

The complete manuscript is in the possession of Mr. O. F. Christie of Much Hadham, Herts (the Diarist's great-grandson) who has been good enough to allow a careful transcript he has made of the diary to be examined. He has also kindly given permission for the above extracts to be quoted here.

This diary is one of the manuscripts which certainly ought to receive greater publicity in a printed volume.

## HENRY WHITE

THE rector of Fyfield in Hampshire, Henry White, was a brother of the famous naturalist, Gilbert White of Selborne. Like his brother, he was a constant and regular observer of all that was within his reach in matters of natural science and he was also a methodical diarist. The available volumes of his diary are for the years 1780 to 1784. They are large folio size ; each page is divided into three columns ; as one column serves for each day, when the book is open the record of a week's doings is before the reader, Sunday's doings being entered under the heading of "Yesterday" in the Monday column. A horizontal line across the middle divides each day into two parts. The upper half is used for domestic notes, the lower half for recording how his team of horses were employed and what the men in his service were working at. At the bottom there are readings of the thermometer and barometer and the direction of the wind. When a diarist deliberately restricts himself to a confined space for each day the chances are that his necessarily brief notes will be matter of fact and colourless. But this is not the case with Henry White. He manages to imbue his few lines with the colour of his personality and besides showing the strenuous activities of his life as a parson and an agriculturist and giving his observations as a naturalist, he makes many notes which are interesting from the point of view of local history. He does not indulge in the expression of any opinions, make any reflections, or break out into prayer. His busy mind was turned outwards not inwards. An account of a typical Sunday shows that he "served" other churches besides his own.

**1783. May. Monday 26.** Yesterday Very bright night and morn. White Frost and Ice enough to scorch ye young French beans and Potatoes at Tidworth, incessant parching wind continues night and day. A most dreadful severe season to all countries especially this. Even ye wheat seems to languish. Served Kingston and Fyfield A.m. Ludgershall and N. Tidwth. p.m. called on Messrs Humpris and Goddard, vast multitudes of hares by Ashen Copse. Beautiful even tho cold. Great Coat necessary all day in ye full Sun. Mrs. Pn and Mrs. Wildg at Church mat.

There are many details about the making of wine from raisins, as well as cyder, perry and various other home-brews :

Sheppard ye Cooper unheaded the taper barrel and put in 1 cwt of Malaga Raisins. Bottled off ye Shrub from Saunders 8 bottles and about 1 pint. Bottled off Siberian Beer 7 doz and 5 bottles, more left and worth preserving having no seed of ye Hordeum Nuda to sow.

Very few public matters are mentioned. There are a few lines about the sinking of the *Royal George* and a brief note of " Rodney's conquest " and the " Thanksgiving Day for Lord Nelson's Victory over the French." There are some archæological memoranda and the weather is given a great deal of notice.

During the severe frost of December, 1784, he takes note daily of the low temperature and its effects. There is a picturesque touch in his Christmas Day entry :

Christmas Day. very bright morn. Trees beautifully powdered with Rime, more severity of Freezing than any since the first beginning, very little wind but ye Air amazingly keen. Sound of Bells heard from all ye Villages on every side. Sac$^{rt}$ at Fyfield. Riding not unpleasant over ye open Fields and Downs. Trees powdered most amazingly by ye Rime make a very picturesque appearance at Tidworth. Pump frozen in ye Wash House ! so that ye Frost tho not quite so cold as ye 2 first days yet operates more strongly within doors. Winter reigns in all its rigour and yet ye Sun shines unusually warm p.m. every day which seems to destroy every sort of broad leaved evergreen. Holly and Ivy leaves brt to decorate the churches and houses seem scorched and blasted.

Notes on gardening, agriculture and animals, including vipers and a tortoise, abound, and birds more especially come in for many comments :

A bird with a soft, gentle, delicate laughing note appeared with ye blackcap supposed to be of ye Titmouse tribe.

The rector has several visits from his distinguished brother and from time to time has news of him:

> The new Path up Selborne Hanger cut obliquely fr ye foot of ye Zigzag to ye corner of Waddon Close, opens the most picturesque View of the inside Wood in ye style of Reubens; and the most amazing View ever seen.

He also stays at Selborne. "Set out for Selborne ab' 10 a.m. dined at Lunways arrived ab$^{t}$ 7 vesp. at G.W's" and "H W and G.W. saw the new altar Piece at Winchester Cathedral; ye raising of Lazarus by Mr. West—very fine, ye Frame gone to be changed."

So methodical a writer naturally enters full particulars with regard to stores laid in and the prices of the various commodities and of farm produce. Not only Nature but human nature occupies his attention in the shape of his servants. A few examples may be given:

> Hannah French dismissed from her service; Robt gave much sage advise thereon. Servts now past all reprehension.

> Robt delirious and absurdly saucy and obliged to be desired to take his leave.
>
> Robt discharged and paid off.

> Goat at ye Farm, ye Male killed by a kick from ye Poney in ye straw yd, ye carcass by way of Perfume put just under ye Fir Trees facing ye house.

> After 26 Hours obstinacy and confinement Betty Oak confesses to have hid ye broken handle of ye Dessert Spoon in a chink of ye Laundry Floor where it was found and she was dismissed after a very severe reprimand.
>
> More discoveries of Betty Oke's thieving—Linnen given to ye neighbours.

Various other incidents which illustrate the reverend gentleman's pursuits may be quoted:

> Ruff's finest Dog puppy run over by Fr Berrett's Cart of Green Vetches and killed on ye Spot to ye great delight of ye savage Race of Swinish carters!!!

> Curtis's Flora Londinensis ye 3 vols returned from Chute Lodge in ye Butcher's Hampers with abundance of Suet etc etc etc yet escaped unhurt!!!!

Penton, Clanville and Blismore Hall families to dinner. Cards, cards cards et praeterea nihil.

Dined at Redenham with Mr. & Mrs. Butcher ; Chute Lodge family came to tea. Whist instead of Music, dreadful alternative. Alas ! alas ! ! alas ! ! !

Harpsicord unpacked and b[rt] very safe. Its touch is not inferior to that of any new instrument and the tone very soft and equal to any new or old and it is very complete indeed well worth the expense.

Began tuning ye Harpsicord and quilling it. Took out ye Piano top and discovered ye reason of ye keys sticking so sadly, it was ye want of more play in ye pinholes and also casting of two of ye long keys Mr Pether's wood not being well seasoned ; soon rectified by ye assistance of ye carp[r].

Harpsicord carried upstairs for ye summer.

Henry White could not only tune and requill the harpsicord, but he could play on it, and there were also in the Rectory a pianoforte, Spinet, Fiddle and Violoncello, played on by members of his family.

There are several memoranda of concerts he attends. Cricket matches, dancing, and appetizing dinners are also noticed. Except for services taken on Sunday and burials there is nothing distinctively ecclesiastical in the diary. Here is a visitation by the Chanceller of the Diocese :

Chanc[r] Sturges sine Perriwiggs. Visitation day at Andover 20 dined at ye Star 6[s] for a very middling ordinary and wretched new nauseous black strap. Winter peaches and sour grapes. Fish rather antient.

Keen, active, practical, epicurean and an ardent lover of nature, Henry White was not troubled by spiritual heart-searchings ; nor did he ever allow his pen to indulge in personalities either about his family or his friends. As much by what he omits as by what he records in his very brief entries does the Rector of Fyfield give us his portrait ; and we find ourselves constantly reminded of the Vicar of Wakefield.

The original manuscript is in the possession of the Misses Martelli of Bexhill, great-granddaughters of the Diarist, who kindly allowed it to be viewed. Extracts from it were published by the Rev. R. H. Clutterbuck in *Notes on the Parishes of Fyfield, Kingston, Penton Mewsey, etc.*, 1898.

# SAMUEL TEEDON

HAD it not been for the references to William Cowper, the poet, which are contained in Teedon's Diary, it is doubtful whether the little memorandum book, covering October 17, 1791, to February 2, 1794, would have been preserved and certainly it would never have been printed. There is indeed nothing in the brief daily notes which calls for special comment. Teedon, however, is rather a picturesque figure. His correspondence with Cowper and Mrs. Unwin has also been preserved. He was a schoolmaster at Olney. Cowper lived there and subsequently at Weston near by. There is a manuscript biography of Teedon written by a contemporary, a Mr. Soul, a designer of lace patterns who lived at Olney, from which we gather that the schoolmaster was originally educated for the Church. Of Teedon and his assistant master, Mr. Soul says: " they deserved a popular and flourishing establishment. Their work however was not appreciated and in consequence they never rose above the condition of poverty." The assistant master, Eusebius Killingworth, who lived with Teedon, is referred to in the Diary as " Worthy " and seems to have been constantly ill:

Worthy so ill I was forced to dress him.

Worthy took a dose of sennae which removed his complaints in a wonderful manner.

Worthy ill with a swelling in his neck.

Worthy and Mammy both very ill.

" Mammy " is Killingworth's mother. She was part of Teedon's household; so also was " Polly," who, Mr. Soul tells us, " called Teedon her cousin; the common sense or natural intelligence of the place called her his daughter." She suffers from fits:

Went to bed as usual but called up in the night before I got to sleep by Polly being taken in fits which continued very violent all the night.

Polly took in a fit and Mammy both very ill and so was I from a brisk purge.

Ailments, in fact, figure very often in the diary, both those of his household and his own.

Every letter Teedon writes and every visit he pays to Cowper and Mrs. Unwin, who are referred to as "the Esquire" and "Madm.," are carefully noted. Cowper must have regarded the schoolmaster as rather a bore, although he was very generous to him. In one of his letters Cowper refers to Teedon's indigence and says "with all his foibles he is a deserving man so far as the strictest honesty and the most laborious attention to his school can entitle him to that character." He also refers with amusement to "the many providential interpositions that had taken place" in Teedon's favour.[1] The relationship between them was curious. Cowper, as is well known, had bad dreams, heard voices and came to regard himself as a man whom God abhorred. Teedon, on the other hand, felt himself to be in close touch with the Almighty and believed himself to be Heaven's special favourite. The poet therefore was inclined to listen to the pompous schoolmaster and accept his advice, which unfortunately seems to have done far more harm than good. All this is made more clear in the correspondence. In the diary we get brief references which without further knowledge might be rather puzzling. A few of these may be given:

1792. (February) I received this day a mournful letter from the Esqr. declaring his firm belief God was his enemy not Satan. I was overwhelmed with grief and sorrow.

(November) Met the Esqr. who gave a most dreadful acct of the state of his mind.

Writ to the Esqr. advised 7 days prayer morn and eve from the example of Elijah's servant.

---

[1] *Selected Letters of William Cowper*, pp. 195–6.

**1793 (August) I writ to the Esqr. but before the the letter was sent I recd from him a most sorrowful note that he believed himself on the verge of madness.**

**(December) I went over with my letter to the Esqr who in pursuance of my advice has been visited with a glimpse of the Divine presence.**

**1794. I went to the Esqr and found him deplorably bad and told me he never was so bad and desired me to pray for his immediate help.**

Judging by the regularity of the entries it looks rather as if the little diary book of 122 pages was one of a series, the rest having been lost. It was not discovered till 1890 and is now in the Cowper Museum at Olney.

Samuel Teedon died in 1798 and there are records to show that after Mammy's death Worthy married Polly.

The Diary, edited by Thomas Wright of Olney (Cowper's biographer), was published in 1902.

## JOHN MARSDEN

IF some space is devoted to John Marsden's diary it is not because it is a particularly good one nor because the diarist was in any way celebrated. It is because this is one of the instances in which it has been possible to examine all of the manuscript that exists through the courtesy of his granddaughter in whose possession it now is. The handling of a series of manuscript books covering a number of years brings one into very close contact with the writer. Whatever the style, method or calling of a diarist may be, as one peruses the pages of the old notebooks the character and habits of the writer are disclosed with a degree of intimacy which it is not possible to reach even in intercourse with friends and contemporaries.

The diary is contained in some ten volumes, mostly folio size. The writing is very legible, although here and there the ink has faded. Between 1795 and 1816, with a few breaks and perhaps one missing book, the diary is complete and kept regularly. There are also small travel diaries of 1819–1822–1826 and a later one of 1831.

Marsden was a member of an old family of yeoman farmers whose history has been traced back to the end of the twelfth century. He was born in 1768 and by profession he was a Manchester corn merchant. The appearance of the first volume (a quarto notebook) and the first entries certainly suggest that he began diary writing before 1795, but if so the earlier volumes are missing. The last volume, a large folio book filled to the last page, also suggests that he continued after 1816. In 1806 he seems to have begun the practice of writing extra travel descriptions and the existence of one of these in 1831 does not necessarily mean that he was not still keeping a regular diary at that time as well.

Except for a very occasional reference to "the warehouse," John Marsden makes no mention whatever of his professional work. His father, William Marsden, was "a friend" and a disciple of John Wesley and there can be no question that diary writing was undertaken by Marsden solely for religious disciplinary purposes. A reader not noticing the few references to the warehouse would certainly suppose that the diarist was an exceptionally devout and active minister of religion. The great majority of entries are occupied with self-examination and more especially self-disparagement, ending in prayer. He complains without cessation of his deadness, depravity, ignorance, sluggishness and unfaithfulness, weakness, pride, folly, unfitness, unworthiness, stubborn-will, straying thoughts, insufficiency, vanity, and vileness. All this exaggerated self-abasement was common form, and one must not allow one's exasperation in reading it to make one condemn the writer as insincere. In 1804 Marsden was offered a partnership in a "liquor business," but for conscientious motives which he explains in his diary he refuses.

Marsden's religious activities were the central interest of his life and were indeed colossal. It is difficult to believe that anyone could listen to as many sermons as he did and survive ; eight or nine during the week was usual. Three in one day was quite common and the text and the name of the preacher is duly noted. But this was by no means all. He conducted a "class" which at one time numbered over fifty, he attended "Leaders meetings," "prayer meetings," "Band meetings," "Breakfast meetings," "Quarterly meetings," "Sunday school" and "Love Feasts." Here are some typical entries :

> Mr. Atmore preached from ye same text as last evening. In ye afternoon big Church Sunday I had the opportunity of hearing Mr Jack in Lloyds from Matt. 13—the parable of the sower. In the afternoon I heard Mr. Smyth from 2 Peter 1 Ch. V and in the evening Mr Lomax from Amos 4. C. 12. I attended prayer meeting at Whittles Croft.

> The Society breakfasted at our house the subject was Is the imputation of Christ's active obedience a scripture doctrine ? In the Evening I met both Band and Class not without deriving good from each.

> Mr Jenkins preached from 1 Peter 2. C. 9v. afterwards a Love Feast

was held for the Bands and the conductors of the Sunday evening p^r meetings.

Mr Rutherford preached at 7 in ye morning to a very full Chapel from 1 Cor. 16. Mr Benson preached in the forenoon from Heb. 9 many more came than the Chapel could hold, and Mr Bradford preached in Dale Street—Dr Coke preached in the Chapel at ½ past 5 to as many as could come in and Mr Pipe upon our steps to the rest.

Yet he complains at one time that what he wants is "more religion." But in one passage he admits

it is a melancholy consideration that religion which is certainly the most profitable subject is not the most pleasing one.

His perpetual self-examination as to his relations to the Almighty, as is the case in so many other diaries, is repeated time after time in the same conventional phrases which were in use in his sect and has a perfunctory tone which is not relieved by spiritual exaggerations. As time passes he seldom admits of any improvement, which seems to imply that the method of constantly recording his supposed shortcomings in writing was of little avail.

Apart from self-depreciation he is at first rather at a loss how to make use of his diary:

I am so much at a loss what to write that I frequently think of giving up my attempt to keep a diary.

I go from week to week in the same dull way.

And later, when he has allowed himself to record more mundane matters, he pulls himself up:

I sometimes think what does my journal consist of besides an account of where my time is spent—where the principal design ought to be—how does my soul prosper? What are the dealings of God with me?

We are glad that Marsden strayed away from the "principal design," otherwise the effort of reading the ten notebooks would have been beyond the power of the most enthusiastic reader of diaries.

John Marsden was a human being and in keeping a regular diary was bound to enlarge sooner or later on the human affairs which were occupying his thoughts. It is with great relief, therefore, that we come on the entry in which he confesses that in listening to sermons his mind wanders: "I cannot keep from thinking of women." Then, sure enough, for five or six years he confides to his diary his love affairs. It is true that even love has to be regarded from the point of view of salvation. Powder has to be mixed with the jam; but this is inevitable. A diarist's love affairs are always difficult to follow not only because of the blanks and stars but because of the omissions and the difficulty of detecting when the last love has been superseded.

Marsden was certainly attracted by beauty. Surely this was no sin; but it sometimes produced some spiritual conflict within him:

> Our company was again gay particularly two young women whose conduct evinced a very dissipated education. I was sorry for them and rather more attached to them on account of their being pretty than I otherwise should have been.

His three favourites were Miss L., Miss F. and Miss B. Miss L. he respects, his friends "strongly recommend" her, but he is doubtful:

> she is young and has not the most aimiable character being reported not of good temper, in her favour there is a similarity of situation and an attachment to her.

Owing to the superior charms of the others he decided against her. Although Miss F.'s "disposition and situation are such as would be very agreeable," he finds himself at a loss. Her conversation is "pleasing and artless" and he goes so far as to confess that he really loves her, "though she is not handsome, looks very ill, and has no certain property." But eventually she, too, drops out and Miss B., who has "engaged his attention" from the beginning, becomes first in the field. She holds him "in bondage," diverts his thoughts "from the chief concern," makes him "uneasy." He proposes and leaves Miss B. to consider it. Although "not willing to give her up," while she hesitates he himself has doubts:

> respecting Miss B. there are in my opinion several reasons why a union would not be likely to be attended with that similarity of manners and thinking which ought to be attended unto.

He finds her "too easy and civil," but nevertheless she

absorbs his thoughts. In a discussion on marriage with friends who were agreed that it was high time for him to take the step, he writes:

> I told them I considered three things as requisite in a wife, piety, good sense and an aimiable disposition in addition an agreeable person wd be desirable; but what is before me is at present so hid from my view that I cannot form the most distant conjecture.

A missing volume prevents us from following the further stages of his suit. But on the first page of the next volume of 1801 we find a passage which a subsequent entry shows us refers to Miss B. He receives a letter of definite rejection:

> I did not expect she would have acted in the manner she has; had she designed me all the ill in her power she could scarcely have placed me in a more unpleasant situation.

However, he recovers and the next year he goes to Hull to see Miss Jane Key. So little did he know of her that at first he calls her Miss Hay. She had been spoken of highly "as a suitable person for a wife." The poor young lady "having learned the purpose of our journey was so much affected as to cause us almost to fear whether we could see her."

However she appears:

> Miss H. & I were left alone and I introduced the business as well as I cld. She replied by saying how much she had felt on the occasion, freedom in conversation soon took place and I very soon entertained the highest opinion of her piety and good sense.

Correspondence followed and in June he marries her.

In detaching the love and courtship *motif* from the diary we reach the human side, and so far from there being anything discreditable in the various episodes, it would seem that Marsden exercised some discrimination, for his eventual choice was completely successful, as is shown by numberless entries in the subsequent volumes in which love and gratitude to his "dear partner" are frequently expressed, anxious solicitude for her health and satisfaction at her constant companionship. They rode together or travelled about in the whiskey, gig, chaise, sociable or coach in all weather with occasional accidents. Many visits were paid to the ancient home of the Marsden and Buxton families in Derbyshire. But his punctual recital of his religious duties and visits he pays and tea parties he attends is not very interesting. Almost everything that happens, deaths, births, marriages, accidents and journeys, serve as an excuse for breaking into ejaculatory imprecations and resolutions of repentance which become very tedious. Public events are occasionally mentioned. Here is Marsden on the death of Nelson:

> in the hour of victory a musket Ball entered his left Breast and he fell. The country knows not whether to rejoice or mourn, the victory is great, but so is his loss, perhaps never was a greater loss, sustained by the death of one man; he was justly dear to every true Briton; such are the dreadful effects of war, horrid war, offspring of sin and source of misery—with the gallant, the undaunted, the much to be lamented Nelson numbers of the brave defenders of their country have fallen and where are they if they died in their sins, they cannot be with God, awful consideration; they have bravely fought and gloriously fallen but many of them it is much to be feared have fallen never, never, never more to rise; I respect their memories, I honour their courage, but I feel for their souls.

He gives an account of the Weavers' riot in Manchester in 1808 and the entry of the allies into Paris in 1814, but there is no mention of Waterloo. The end of the year as well as his birthday and later the anniversary of his marriage give him an opportunity for pious reflections. He led a very strict life of religious duty and was upset if he ever was obliged to journey on the Sabbath. Fears of hell and hopes of heaven run through every page of the diary. No joy, no merriment, no humour is allowed to creep in. There is a grim severity which is very depressing, however admirable the self-discipline may have been. The most dissipated entertainment would appear to have been on the anniversary of his marriage when "my dear Jane prepared a large posset," to which several were invited. His health notes are very full and are always linked to a few lines of prayer. It is difficult to see how a regularly kept diary could be more rigidly disciplinary in its character. But Marsden was not satisfied. In 1802 he writes:

> Reflecting upon the manner in which I keep my journal (if it may be so called) I am convinced as indeed I have frequently been that I do not conduct it as would be most conducive to my real good, it is of little importance where my time is spent, the consideration ought to be have

I continually an eye to the glory of God and is my soul growing with a greater conformity to the image of Jesus. I have been led into my unprofitable method by not allowing myself sufficient time for the important design and daily experience convinces me that resolution accompanied by constant care to solicit divine aid is absolutely necessary to real improvement. I think my soul does grow in grace but pride and unwatchfulness appear to be my greatest enemies and I resist these too feebly. O may my God give me more of the spirit of true Humility and enable me to guard against that carelessness and inattention which (may) prove to be so prejudicial to my best interests.

This gives us a good idea of the motive and "design" of diaries of this character.

The later travel diaries may or may not have been written in addition to his regular journal. He is "appointed by the Conference" to visit Ireland and Scotland and the last one in 1831 records a visit to London, Rochester, Cambridge and Nottingham with his wife and children. He writes daily, preaches, has a good deal to say about the Roman Catholics in Ireland, and in London attends anti-slavery meetings and is impressed by the occasional sights he catches of royal carriages and minor royalties. But his descriptions of places are bald and of little interest.

John Marsden died in 1840. His granddaughter, Miss Georgiana Gibson, inherited his diaries and letters and has kindly allowed them to be fully examined.

# NINETEENTH CENTURY

## DOROTHY WORDSWORTH

THE omission of Dorothy Wordsworth's Journal from the first volume of *English Diaries* enables the present volume to contain the notice of one of the best diaries written by an Englishwoman.

The comparison of diaries is always a difficult matter because the style and method may vary so widely that a different standard of valuation must be used. Fanny Burney's intimate gossip and brilliant dialogue are hardly comparable to Caroline Fox's philosophic reflections and shrewd characterization. Both wrote excellent diaries but they attract different classes of readers. Dorothy Wordsworth has none of Fanny Burney's ebullience nor has she Caroline Fox's power of analysis. But she is able to describe the sights and sounds of nature as they reach the eyes and ears in a way which neither of the other two women could ever equal; and consequently she is able to impart to a record of seemingly uneventful days an atmosphere and a fragrance which are beyond the reach of anyone but a poet. Dorothy Wordsworth's sunshine and storm, her stars and flowers, the waters of the lake and the coursing clouds, do not make one just imagine, they make one feel, see, hear and smell. Yet there is no word of elaboration, it is all simplicity itself. Her notes are the product not so much of an observant and imaginative mind as of a loving spirit to whom the moods of nature, its brilliance or its gloom and more especially its little mysteries were subjects of unceasing and unstinted admiration. There is no rapture or gush and no exaggerated colour, nor is there polish and prettiness. It is all her natural way of expressing herself and the less obvious and the more elusive the scenes she writes of, the more strikingly beautiful are her descriptions. So much writing is called romantic which fails to be romantic because it is intended to be romantic. Dorothy Wordsworth has no intention to be romantic. Indeed she probably never used the word or thought about what it implies. But this product of her personality in its particular setting and surroundings is as purely and genuinely romantic as any pages ever penned by man or woman. This applies only to her Grasmere Journal which stands apart, almost in a different category from her other travel journals.

Diarists, as we have often had cause to remark, are particularly fond of scenic descriptions. When it is a case of a cathedral or a town, a mountain range seen for the first time, a waterfall, a statue or a picture, there it is before their eyes and they select the qualities and attributes which strike them. When it is the familiar everyday scene varying only through the seasons or in sunshine and rain, they either do not see it at all or they make some brief meteorological remarks. Diarists rather fancy themselves in these descriptions ; but whether it be from lack of imagination, defective powers of observation or want of literary skill, they very rarely succeed in making their observations on art or nature interesting. They either just scamp them or else they give one the idea that they are settling down to " a fine bit of writing." Many of them feel no doubt that they must write it down and however bald their remarks may seem to us, the little notes help to bring the scene back to them when in the evening of life they are perusing the old volume by the fireside. When, therefore, as a wonderful exception we find a diarist who can give us, the readers, real pleasure in what she saw, and make us feel the drops of rain and smell the rose, we ought to be, and indeed we are exceedingly grateful.

Dorothy Wordsworth kept various journals from 1798 to 1828. From the days she lived with her brother William at Alfoxden, through the Grasmere period, 1800 to 1803, when she was his constant companion, and on several occasions of tours in Scotland and abroad. The Grasmere journal reveals Dorothy Wordsworth more than the others because it is written in repose, and there is an absence of the incidents and the stress which invariably characterize travel journals. Her brother's movements, his moods and his work, are all faithfully recorded. She remained his companion even after his marriage. That event must have made a deeper impression on her than she cares to admit in the journal.

She did not write for publication but from a desire to record and so preserve, because of their beauty, the moods of nature day by day. The prevailing note is reverie rather than melancholy, although, except when nature's radiance prompts, there is an absence of joy in many of her reflections. It is difficult to indicate by quotation what makes simple descriptions of fugitive beauties arresting. Only by the perusal of consecutive entries can the delicate sensitive spirit of the diarist be discovered. The eye never wanders or wants to skip a line, but often it wants to read again a happy phrase such as "the crooked arm of the old oak points upwards to the moon," or "one only leaf upon the top of a tree—the sole remaining leaf—danced round and round like a rag blown by the wind," or "glow-worms—well for them children are in bed when they shine," or "I want not society by a moonlit lake." There are indeed few entries in which she does not make some note of the sky, the trees or the flowers and sometimes the scene absorbs her completely:

. . . our favourite birch tree. It was yielding to the gusty wind with all its tender twigs. The sun shone upon it and it glanced in the wind like a flying sunshiny shower. It was a tree in shape with stem and branches, but it was like a spirit of water. The sun went in, and it resumed its purplish appearance, the twigs still yielding to the wind, but not so visibly to us. The other birch trees that were near it looked bright and cheerful, but it was a creature by its own self among them.

As we ascended the hills it grew very cold and slippery. Luckily the wind was at our backs and helped us on. A sharp hail shower gathered at the head of Martindale and the view upwards was very grand—wild cottages seen through the hurrying hail showers. The wind drove and eddied about and about and the hills looked large and swelling through the storm. We thought of Coleridge. O! the bonny nooks and windings and curlings of the beck down at the bottom of the steep green mossy banks. We dined at the public house on porridge with a second course of Christmas pies.

We heard a strange sound in the Bainriggs wood, as we were floating on the water; it seemed in the wood, but it must have been above it, for presently we saw a raven very high above us. It called out and the dome of the sky seemed to echo the sound. It called again and again as it flew onwards and the mountains gave back the sound, seeming as if from their centre; a musical bell-like answering to the bird's hoarse voice. We heard both the call of the bird and the echo after we could see him no longer.

The Lake was still, there was a boat out. Silver How reflected with purple and yellowish hues, as I have seen spar; lambs on the island, and running races together by the half-dozen in the round field near us. The copses greenish, hawthorns green . . . cottages smoking. As I lay down on the grass I observed the glittering silver line on the ridge of the backs of the sheep, owing to their situation respecting the sun, which made them look beautiful, but with something of strangeness, like animals of another kind, as if belonging to a more splendid world. . . . I got mullins and pansies.

Day by day the diary relates her brother's pursuits, his varying moods, his coming and going, her anxiety when he was away and her joy at his return; as well as Coleridge's visits and letters; and her devotion to both of them is the keynote throughout. Passing references to her own household duties and gardening give a natural touch of homeliness:

I brought home lemon thyme and several other plants and planted them by moonlight. I lingered out of doors in the hopes of hearing my brother's tread.

sitting at work till after 11 o'clock I heard a foot at the front of the house, turn round and open the gate. It was William! After our first joy was over we got some tea. We did not go to bed till 4 in the morning so he had an opportunity of seeing our improvements.

All the morning I was busy copying poems. Gathered peas and in the afternoon Coleridge came. He brought the 2$^{nd}$ volume of Anthology. The men went to bathe and we afterwards sailed down to Loughrigg. Read poems on the water and let the boat take its own course. We walked a long time on Loughrigg. I returned in the grey twilight. The moon was just setting as we reached home.

Sometimes William is "highly poetical," sometimes "tired with composition," or "tires himself by hammering at a passage," or even "Makes himself ill" in his endeavour to alter poems. Many entries show his extreme sensitiveness.

William went into the orchard after breakfast to chop wood. We walked into Easedale . . . walked backwards and forwards between

Goody Bridge and Butterlip How. William wished to break off composition but was unable and so did himself harm. The sun shone but it was cold. William worked at *The Pedlar*. After tea I read aloud the eleventh book of *Paradise Lost*. We were much impressed and also melted in tears. The papers came in soon after I had laid aside the book—a good thing for my Wm.

Two very affecting letters from Coleridge ; resolved to try another climate. I was stopped in my writing and made ill by the letters.

Before sunset I put on my shawl and walked out. The snow-covered mountains were spotted with rich sunlight, a palish buffish colour. . . . I stood at the wishing gate and when I came in view of Rydale, I cast a long look on the mountains beyond. They were very white, but I concluded Wm would have a very safe passage over Kirkstone and I was quite easy about him.

There are days when her spirits rise as when " the thrush that lives in our orchard has shouted and sung its merriest all day long." She confesses, too, to being " cheerful and happy " ; and in one entry she writes : " Sara and I had a grand bread and cake baking. We were very merry in the evening." But more often she is just contemplative and the moments of anxious melancholy are frequent. Here is a very full description of a day when William goes away :

Before we had quite finished breakfast Calvert's man brought the horses for Wm. We had a deal to do, pens to make, poems to put in order for writing, to settle for the press, pack up ; and the man came before the pens were made and he was obliged to leave me with only two. Since he left me at half past eleven, I have been putting the drawers into order, laid by his clothes which he had thrown here and there and everywhere, filed two months newspapers and got my dinner, 2 boiled eggs and 2 apple tarts. I have set Molly on to clean the garden a little and I myself have walked. I transplanted some snowdrops—the Bees are busy. Wm has a nice bright day. It was hard frost in the night. The Robins are singing sweetly. Now for my walk. I *will* be busy. I *will* look well and be well when he comes back to me. O the Darling ! Here is one of his bitter apples. I can hardly find it in my heart to throw it into the fire. . . . I walked round the two lakes crossed the stepping stones at Rydale foot. Sate down where we always sit. I was full of thought about my darling. Blessings on him. I came home at the foot of our own hill under Loughrigg. They are making sad ravages in the woods. Benson's wood is going and the woods above the river. The wind has blown down a small fir tree on the Rock, that terminates John's path. I suppose the wind of Wednesday night. I read German after tea. I worked and read the L.B., enchanted with the *Idiot Boy*. Wrote to Wm and then went to bed. It snowed when I went to bed.

Poems were sometimes written in peculiar circumstances, as the following shows:

Just when William came to a well or trough which there is in Lord Darlington's park, he began to write that poem *The Glow-worm*; . . . interrupted in going through the town of Staindrop, finished it about 2 miles and a half beyond Staindrop. He did not feel the jogging of the horse while he was writing; but when he had done, he felt the effect of it, and his fingers were cold with his gloves. His horse fell with him on the other side of St. Helens, Auckland. So much for the *Glow-worm*.

On a wintry day in early May she writes:

The oak trees are just putting forth yellow knots of leaves. The ashes with their flowers passing away and leaves coming out; the blue hyacinth is not quite full blown; gowans are coming out; marsh marigolds in full glory; the little star plant a star without a flower. We took home a great load of gowans and planted them about the orchard. After dinner I worked bread, then came and mended stockings beside William; he fell asleep. After tea I walked to Rydale for letters. It was a strange night. The hills were covered over with a slight covering of hail or snow, just so as to give them a hoary winter look with the black rocks. The woods looked miserable, the coppices green as grass which looked quite unnatural, and they seemed half shrivelled up, as if they shrank from the air. O, thought I, what a beautiful thing God has made winter to be by stripping the trees and letting us see their shapes and forms. What a freedom does it seem to give to the storms!

One can gather from a sentence in the following entry in April, 1802—a sentence of beautiful but almost tragic eloquence—something of her deep unexpressed feelings when the poet contemplated marriage:

Walked to T. Wilkenson's and sent for letters. The woman brought me one from William and Mary. It was a sharp windy night. Thomas Wilkenson came with me to Barton and questioned me like a catechiser all the way. Every question was like the snapping of a little thread about my heart. I was so full of thought of my half-read letter and other things. I was glad when he left me. Then I had time to look at the moon while I was thinking my own thoughts.

Wordsworth married Mary Hutchinson on October 4, 1802.

Dorothy did not, probably could not, attend the actual ceremony :

At a little after eight o'clock I saw them go down the avenue towards the church. William had parted from me upstairs. When they were absent my dear little Sara prepared the breakfast. I kept myself as quiet as I could, but when I saw the two men running up the walk, coming to tell us it was over, I could stand it no longer and threw myself on the bed where I lay in stillness, neither hearing nor seeing anything till Sara came upstairs to me and said : " They are coming." This forced me from the bed where I lay and I moved, I knew not how, straight forward, faster than my strength could carry me, till I met my beloved William and fell upon his bosom.

The Grasmere journal continues for a few months till January, 1803. Mary is referred to with affection. William is still her all-in-all, but Mary is there. She concludes her last entry :

Since tea Mary has been down stairs copying out Italian poems for Stuart. William has been working beside me and here ends this imperfect summary.

One almost feels an emphasis on the " me."

The value and importance of Dorothy Wordsworth's Journal does not rest on the careful accuracy with which she relates the poet's doings. In one entry she confesses that she herself feels " more than half a poet " and in Wordsworth's own writings we can gather how largely he was indebted to the inspiration which Dorothy's alert and poetic observation afforded him. Years later, in 1832, he wrote " S.T.C. (Coleridge) and my beloved sister are the two beings to whom my intellect is most indebted " ; and there are several passages in his poems in which he pays a tribute to the sympathetic originality of her perceptions ;

She gave me eyes, she gave me ears ;
And humble cares, and delicate fears ;
A heart the fountain of sweet tears ;
And love and thought and joy.

Mr. Maurice Hewlett says, referring to her relations with Wordsworth and Coleridge, " She was the Muse of those two and had perhaps more of the soul or substance of poetry in her than either." [1] Indeed there is abundant proof of

[1] Maurice Hewlett, *Last Essays*, p. 229.

thoughts, incidents and even actual phrases noted by Dorothy becoming the theme for Wordsworth's poems. The detailed story she tells of the wandering tramp and the children Wordsworth took for his poem *The Beggars*. Her telling him that when a child " she would not have pulled a strawberry blossom " produces *Foresight*:

> Strawberry blossoms one and all
> We must spare them—here are many;
> Look at it—the flower is small,
> Small and low, though fair as any.
> Do not touch it! Summers two
> I am older, Anne, than you.

Dorothy's influence is very apparent when we find this jotting in her diary as they pass over Westminster Bridge in the Dover coach:

> The city, St. Paul's with the river and a multitude of little boats made a most beautiful sight as we crossed Westminster Bridge. The houses were not overhung by their cloud of smoke, and they were spread out endlessly, yet the sun shone so brightly, with such a fierce light that there was even something like the purity of one of nature's own grand spectacles.

When she tells of William resting on the bridge at the foot of Brothers Water and "writing a poem descriptive of the sights and sounds we saw and heard," we see by the description she writes herself when compared with the poem that there was collaboration to the extent that Wordsworth was using his sister's eyes and ears. The two may be given together:

> There was the gentle flowing of the stream, the glittering, lively lake, green fields without a living creature to be seen on them; behind us a flat pasture with forty two cattle feeding; to our left the road leading to the hamlet. No smoke there, the sun shone on the bare roofs. The people were at work ploughing, harrowing and sowing . . . a dog barking now and then, cocks crowing, birds twittering, the snow in patches at the top of the highest hills, yellow palms, purple and green twigs on the birches, ashes with their glittering stems quite bare.

> The cock is crowing,
> The stream is flowing,
> The small birds twitter,
> The Lake doth glitter,
> The green fields sleep in the sun;

The oldest and youngest
Are at work with the strongest;
The cattle are grazing,
Their heads never raising;
There are forty feeding like one.

But of the many that might be given, by far the most striking instance of "She gave me eyes" can be shown by putting side by side Dorothy's description of daffodils in a wood and Wordsworth's well-known lines. While the one is only a roughly scribbled impression of the moment, and the other a finished poem, the beauty of thought and imagery is in the diary note, although the charm and perfection of language may be in the verses. Sketches often have a merit of their own which may not appear in the great pictures composed from them.

Dorothy writes:

When we were in the woods beyond Gowbarrow Park, we saw a few daffodils close to the waterside. We fancied that the sea had floated the seeds ashore and that the little colony had so sprung up. But as we went along there were more and yet more; and at last under the boughs of the trees we saw that there was a long belt of them along the shore about the breadth of a country turnpike road. I never saw daffodils so beautiful. They grew among the mossy stones about and above them, some rested their heads upon these stones, as on a pillow, for weariness; and the rest tossed and reeled and danced, and seemed as if they verily laughed with the wind that blew upon them over the lake; they looked so gay, ever glancing, ever changing. The wind blew directly over the Lake to them. There was here and there a little knot and a few stragglers higher up; but they were so few as not to disturb the simplicity, unity, and life of that one busy highway.

And then the two first stanzas of the poem:

I wander'd lonely as a cloud
  That floats on high o'er vales and hills,
When all at once I saw a crowd,
  A host of golden daffodils;
Beside the lake, beneath the trees,
Fluttering and dancing in the breeze.

Continuous as the stars that shine
  And twinkle on the Milky Way,
They stretch'd in never-ending line
  Along the margin of the bay:
Ten thousand saw I at a glance,
Tossing their heads in sprightly dance.

There were no lines of poetry to be found to improve on "some rested their heads upon these stones, as on a pillow, for weariness." No wonder Wordsworth wanted his sister to be with him. In a poem dedicated to her he says:

Then come, my Sister! come I pray
  With speed put on your woodland dress;
And bring no book: for this one day
  We'll give to idleness.

A week of consecutive daily entries may be given as illustrating the life and close companionship of brother and sister in 1802:

*Monday morning.* A soft rain and mist. We walked to Rydale for letters. The Vale looked very beautiful in excessive simplicity, yet, at the same time in uncommon obscurity. The Church stood alone—mountains behind. The meadows looked calm and rich bordering on the still lake. Nothing else to be seen but lake and island. . . . On Friday evening the moon hung over the northern side of the highest point of Silver How, like a gold ring snapped in two and shaven off at the ends. Within this ring lay the circle of the round moon as distinctly to be seen as ever the enlightened moon is. William had observed the same appearance at Keswick, perhaps at the very same moment hanging over the Newland Fells. Sent off a letter to Mary H., also to Coleridge, and Sara, and rewrote in the evening the alterations of *Ruth* which we sent off at the same time.

*Tuesday morning.* William was reading in Ben Jonson. He read me a beautiful poem on Love. . . . We sat by the fire in the evening and read *The Pedlar* over. William worked a little and altered it in a few places.

*Wednesday.* Wm read in Ben Jonson in the morning. I read a little German. We then walked to Rydale. No letters. They are slashing away in Benson's wood. William has since tea been talking about publishing the Yorkshire Wolds Poems with *The Pedlar*.

*Thursday.* A fine morning. William worked at the poem of *The Singing Bird.* Just as we were sitting down to dinner we heard Mr. Clarkson's voice. I ran down, William followed. He was so finely mounted that William was more intent upon the horse than the rider, an offence easily forgiven, for Mr. Clarkson was as proud of it himself as he well could be.

*Friday.* A very fine morning. We went to see Mr. Clarkson off. The sun shone while it rained and the stones on the walls and the pebbles on the road glittered like silver. . . . William finished his poem of *The Singing Bird.* In the meantime I read the remainder of Lessing. In the evening after tea William wrote *Alice Fell.* He went to bed tired with a wakeful mind and a weary body.

*Saturday morning.* It was as cold as ever it has been all winter, very hard frost. . . . William finished *Alice Fell* and then wrote the poem *The Beggar Woman*, taken from a woman I had seen in May (now nearly two years ago) when John and he were at Gallow Hill. I sate with him at intervals all the morning, took down his stanzas, etc. . . . After tea I read William that account of the little boy belonging to the tall woman, and an unlucky thing it was, for he could not escape from those very words, and so he could not write the poem. He left it unfinished and went tired to bed. In our walk from Rydale he had got warmed with the subject and had half cast the poem.

*Sunday morning.* William got up at nine o'clock but before he rose he had finished *The Beggar Boy* and while we were at breakfast . . . he wrote the poem *To a Butterfly.* He ate not a morsel, but sate with his shirt neck unbuttoned and his waistcoat open while he did it. The thought first came to him as we were talking about the pleasure we both always felt at the sight of a butterfly. I told him that I used to chase them a little, but that I was afraid of brushing the dust off their wings and did not catch them. He told me how he used to kill all the white ones when he went to school because they were Frenchmen. . . . I wrote it down and other poems and I read them all over to him. . . . William began to try to alter *The Butterfly* and tired himself.

Many good extracts might be taken from Dorothy Wordsworth's other journals. Nevertheless these are different. They are heavier and more elaborate. There is even a feeling of conscientious effort about them and their only real interest is to tell us where Wordsworth was and what he was doing. The motive and intention seem not to be quite the same and after the vivid inspiration of the Grasmere diary they come as an anti-climax and should be kept apart.

Dorothy fell ill in 1829 and a few years later she began to suffer from a serious mental derangement from which she never recovered. She survived her brother five years, dying at Grasmere in 1855.

Her journals were collected and edited by Professor William Knight in 1897.

## THOMAS ASLINE WARD

LIKE Crabb Robinson and Pease, Thomas Asline Ward kept up diary writing from an early age until he was 90. He was a local celebrity, but he never reached any position of particular distinction except that of Master Cutler of Sheffield in 1816. He stood for Parliament but failed to be elected; and his long life was devoted to good works and public service in his native town of Sheffield. He really kept two diaries—one for brief jottings—the other a more elaborate local chronicle and personal diary. The latter was only kept for a few years with any regularity, but the entries are exceedingly long and exceedingly dull even for the student of local history. They are illustrations of the snare of the flowing pen.

He starts at the age of nineteen in 1800 and he writes his entries very often in French, Italian or Latin. He is evidently learning the languages:

> Sarah retourna de Chesterfield ce soir pour être confirmée.

> La famille de Morton prirent thé et du souper chez noos.

There are nice little nature notes such as "daffodils flower," "cuckoo sings."

But when he begins really to let himself go in his larger notebooks we get interminable and almost unreadably dull descriptions of local events such as the volunteer movement in Sheffield and wordy comments on public events. In fact, he cultivates a style as a chronicler and makes use of heavy and pompous language and from time to time breaks into apostrophe; as when leaving London he writes an immense passage filled with expressions such as "Thou art the centre of Good and Evil, of Virtue and Vice," "Thou Queen of

Cities," "the shrine of fickle fashion." He was twenty-three at the time and ought to have known better. But he probably felt a desire to get this sort of thing off his chest and instead of disgorging it in a speech or a letter he let it out in his diary and therefore no one was any the worse. In this sententious record he becomes quite unable to express himself simply. When parting from a friend instead of saying naturally that he cried, he writes:

> My eyes refused the friendly tribute of tears so long as he remained in sight: but when he was gone my cheeks became the channel to a flood of them.

Here is an account of a proposal and a rebuff:

> Long had I felt a tender passion for her; sometimes I thought she returned it. Anxious to be assured of the state of the heart, determined to put an end to the disquiet and suspence which agitated me I asked her if she loved me. How cold her answer, how freezing to my fondest hopes, how destructive to my aspiring views. "As a cousin" she replyed.

If Ward's conversation and love-making were anything like his writing at that time our sympathies are with the young lady.

He sometimes begins his year with a moral reflection such as,

> Another grand division of time has elapsed and yet—through the goodness of God—I exist.

In this section of the diary even the Editor has to omit many long passages which he says are too much like a guide-book. Sermons are reported at great length; yet after a very long account of a sermon, he writes:

> I regret much that my memory is too treacherous to allow me to give a more perfect sketch of this affecting discourse.

He has close associations with Chantry and a voluminous correspondence with the Rev. Joseph Hunter. He notes the daily tea drinking with friends. On one occasion he drinks "tea and madiera" with Macready's father. We feel inclined to exclaim like Dr. Rutty, "tremble at the mixture." He puts down his gains and losses at swisk ho, commerce, loo, vingt-et-un, quadrille and whist, and dances and public dinners are fully described. In politics he was an advanced supporter of Sir Francis Burdett and the Reform movement and he goes up to London to do a little lobbying in the House of Commons. In 1809 he begins writing in the smaller diary in a sort of shorthand which consists in leaving out all vowels, a method which must have been more difficult to write than it is to read.

But his voluminous writing suddenly ceases and when we should have expected pages on his engagement and marriage all we find is

1814. Nov. 17. I married Ann Lewin.

It is clear that Ward now found a confidante other than his diary and consequently his diary was neglected. Except for a description of the riots in Sheffield in 1816 his entries are quite brief and the single word " Alone " often occurs. On the anniversaries of his wedding there are no rapturous outbursts but just a simple sentence such as:

1818. The anniversary of our wedding day. Four years have elapsed happily.

In 1826 his wife dies. He gets out his large notebook, which he had discarded since 1806, and soothes himself in " the sad mechanic exercise of verse." " Written at midnight on December 31, 1826, on viewing my wife's corpse." The Editor says that as poetry the lines are poor stuff, but he rightly thinks it would be too great a violation of the privacy of the soul to publish them. There are long passages also in prose. A few of the least intimate passages are given. Although stilted they are pathetically sincere and end with the simple phrase " I have now known her for 18 years and I cannot say she had a fault."

Not till 1869 does he take out the large notebook again, while intermittently the pocket-books continue to have brief notes. The musings of the old man of 88 who has dropped the manner of the chronicler of events are charmingly natural. A few may be given:

I read the papers etc but am soon wearied, the small print is difficult to read and I soon tired by sitting up.

. . . my deafness makes conversation irksome and my time is chiefly spent in solitary musings in bed.

. . . I have one curious and uncommon amusement. A tall honeysuckle is nailed against the house and mounts higher than the windows. I admire its branches waving in the wind. Birds dart up and down searching for food, conveying it into their nest. If this honeysuckle were taken from me I should lament its loss as Jonah his gourd but not I hope like him, be angry.

. . . many solitary hours with little but my own thoughts to divert me. These become stale and I resort to murmuring a tune and singing a song or psalm, not loudly articulately or whispering but silently in my own mind which is sufficient for my purpose.

Such sentences as these are the gems in the diary. They give us a real picture of the old man lying back on his pillow, the newspaper having fallen from his hands, staring out at the honeysuckle and smiling as some old tune in his head helps to chase away the stale revolving thoughts. He adds some reflections about his grandchildren and two prayers which he says are his "daily devotions." The pocket diaries are kept up till within two months of his death in 1871.

Although in no way a remarkable diary the notebooks of Thomas Asline Ward disclose by their manner and method rather than by their contents the changing moods in a long life. Copious extracts from them, together with many of his letters, were published in *Peeps into the Past,* edited by Alexander B. Bell.

## COLONEL PETER HAWKER

IN *English Diaries* comment was made on sporting diaries and a few instances were noted. Sport, like religion, war, and visions of great people, is one of the subjects which encourages diary writing. But no sporting diary previously mentioned is so good an instance of the sportsman's desire to record his exploits as the diary of Colonel Peter Hawker, the greater part of which was published in two volumes in 1893.

Hawker was the author of *Instructions to Young Sportsmen*, a very popular book which went into several editions. He was born in 1786, saw active service in the Peninsular War and was obliged to retire owing to a severe wound he received at the battle of Talavera. He was a crack shot and his diary gives a fairly complete record of the birds which fell to his gun and of his various guns and punts and devices which he invented for shooting. Fishing he also indulged in but only as a side issue when something prevented his shooting; he confesses he never much cared about it "except to supply his friends." He killed, however, above twelve thousand trout in the river Test at Longparish, which was his home. The number of birds he shot could only be computed by some one who was accustomed to astronomical figures.

The Colonel's conceit is quite boundless. He is aware that he shoots better than anyone else and is never tired of saying so, "I have never yet been beat by anyone in any country that I have ever yet seen," and it is exceptional if he does not kill everything he fires at. He cannot bear anyone shooting with him, they disturb him, and people who happened to be shooting in the neighbourhood he refers to as "snobs." Nothing daunts him, wind, weather, frost, hurricane or seas of mud. He is up at daybreak and often out all night and in entry after entry his full bag is given in whatever part of the country he happens to be in ; and he visited practically every county in England. He crawls for miles, rows out in one of his strange craft or buries himself " in an old sugar cask in the mud " and if he is ill he shoots from his chaise or his buggy. There are a good many fairly monotonous entries in the diary merely describing the birds he saw and registering exactly his bag of snipe, duck, water rail, mallard, dabcock, widgeon, coot, curlew, plover, godwit or whatever it might be his quarry at the moment. If this were all, the diary might be dismissed with only a passing reference. But Colonel Peter Hawker was a good diarist with a style of his own. His weather remarks are full of colour and atmosphere. His travel descriptions, especially when he goes abroad on shooting expeditions, are unusually vivid. His sanguine, buoyant, breezy self-confidence gives an individual stamp of life and freshness to all he writes. First of all we will give a few examples of his sporting entries :

At Longparish 8 trout and shot 1 heron 1 snipe and 1 green sandpiper. Received my new double gun No. 4699 from Manton.

Mr. Cudmore never having seen a bird killed flying I took him out to see me fire 10 shots at swifts and swallows, 2 at moorhens, 2 at sparrows and 1 at a halfpenny thrown up. I killed every bird and handsomely marked the halfpenny.

Till this day I have been laid up with an inflamed sore throat and finding I could get but little better I went out on my old mare armed with gargle and hartshorn, to try for a few birds as the coveys were so wild that almost all the shooters had given up doing anything. I bagged 10 partridges, lost 2 more and missed but twice, one shot a long way off and another in the sun.

In Holland he is tantalized by seeing birds when he has no gun :

Here the wall on which we drove was made delightful by a refreshing breeze from the Het on the left and on our right was an object not a little interesting to Peter Hawker the *chasseur Anglais*—a marsh swarming with birds of every description : ducks, teal, curre, shovellers, spoonbills, snipes, storks, great snipes, plovers, etc., within shot of the road and bidding defiance to me as I waved my hat at them. How my fingers itched for my Joe Manton much more for my duck gun.

Colonel Hawker, however, was a man of many interests and many talents. Although as a shot he was pre-eminent, he was by no means narrowly confined to absorption in sport alone. Curiously enough his other great passion was music. If he were confronted with the choice of a day's shooting or a concert he would certainly have preferred the former—a brent-goose would have drawn him away from Bach. Nevertheless he managed to find time and opportunity for both, as the following extracts will show :

(Manchester) I went on a musical excursion which except a wild fowl expedition is the only event which would have brought me here.

I sent to Poole for the unrivalled James Reade, the Mozart of all the wild fowl men.

I went in the evening to Covent Garden Theatre in order to hear my favourite overture of " Der Freischütz " conducted by the immortal composer himself, Carl Maria von Weber.

to the last most glorious Philharmonic where Thalberg drove me crazy with delight.

toddled into Lymington (in a lobster cart) to the high diversion of ourselves and petrifaction of all the staring dandies and repaired to old Klitz the Clementi of the place. There Langstaff joined in a trio while I went foraging and it came on a determined wet night, for which we were all well armed ; as we brought off a fiddle, a tuning hammer and all the music we could borrow and sat in with a good fire, for a thorough batch of such noise that neither the wind nor the rain was thought of.

I read to-day with tears of the death of the unrivalled Malibran ; and I also lost my beautiful Newfoundland dog, of the distemper.

" Also " is good, but we feel that had he been perfectly honest he would have put the dog first.

Here is a picture of the Colonel and his family at Keyhaven during one of the greatest storms and floods of his time :

We have our punts floating at our door in the street ready to rescue our family in case of danger. What a scene ! Shutter, doors and pails afloat ; birds killed while diving and washed up by the tide ; and in short the best representation I have yet seen of a second deluge. My dear children, instead of being alarmed or ill, were amused with the scramble ; and I by way of aping Nero (who fiddled while Rome was burning) sat at my old humstrum and boggled through a given number of Bach's fugues.

Hawker wrote a book on *Instructions for the Best Position on the Pianoforte*, and invented " hand moulds " for the piano, which he patented, and which were taken up both in this country and abroad. In the intervals of shooting he dashes to France and Holland to recommend his invention. At Haarlem he plays on the gigantic organ and then

took the organist to the church porch, delighted him much with a sight of my hand-moulds for the piano, gave him a prospectus of them, shook hands with him and galloped off.

This musical sportsman was also no mean draughtsman, as some of his illustrations in the volumes show. His varied appreciations are shown in a description he gives of some beautiful scenery in the Lakes :

in a word the view creates a sort of sensation which we feel on hearing Mozart's music, seeing Shakespeare's tragedies, hearing Braham sing or seeing ourselves surrounded by a good evening flight of wild fowl.

His keen zest and interest in life is well illustrated when he describes a day at home alone :

Frost and snow. Alone from morning till night and I have not passed so pleasant a day for these fifteen years ; what with writing, reading, and strapping hard at my long-lost music I could have stayed up till daylight next morning. 'A man ought never to be so little alone as when he is alone.'

He makes notes of functions he has to attend in London, but public affairs, although briefly referred to, he finds too heavy for his diary ; and of course he is perfectly right, they are too heavy for any diary.

As for politics, in his only reference to it he writes of an election in 1832 in which he says the borough of Marylebone showed good sense in " neither being humbugged by the ranting Rads on one hand nor the Joe-Surface hypocrite Conservatives on the other." He wastes no time on sentimental reflections and we should doubt if he ever suffered from misgivings. There are very brief and occasional references to his family. When his son marries, he writes :

Peter was married to Miss Fraser of Stirling. I was married to Peter's mother on the 19th of March 1811. God send him good luck, and less trouble than has, up to the present date, been inflicted on his father.

This entry comes as a surprise, as there is so little grumbling at adversity in the diary as we have it. But we are told that the full diary intact would fill several more volumes, so there are probably many intimate entries which have been omitted.

With his own health he is a good deal concerned. In the earlier years the results of his wound and later other ailments:

> Was nearly tortured to death by a relay of three dentists who failed in drawing a tremendous tooth and finished with breaking my jaw-bone, and complimenting me on the *sangfroid* with which I braved these infernal operations.

> After being four weeks in the very essence of misery with being stewed in hot water, physicked, leeched and butchered, I this day went with Macilwain to consult this most extraordinary old bear that ever appeared in a civilised country, the celebrated Dr. Abernethy.

But his own method of treating illness was probably the best:

> in order to shake off the shivers that I've had for a week I slipped my long water boots and waded up the river. I killed in good style all that I shot at viz 3 jack snipes, 2 of them a brilliant double shot to front and rear with 9 moorhens and 3 divers. I then shifted my boots and beat all the woods and the rows and the only head of game I set eyes on was 1 rabbit which I bagged.

Colonel Hawker shows by his diary how a busy active man can find time to keep a regular record. He ceased writing only a month before his death, in 1853, having begun at the age of 16, in 1802. The portrait of the man stands out very clearly. His conceit must have been rather trying to his fellow-sportsmen, his æsthetic tastes were not of a high order, and there are many commonplace comments on the sights and monuments he visits abroad. But whether he was shooting birds, catching fishes, inventing guns, composing marches, writing books, making drawings, playing the piano, enjoying concerts or travelling abroad, he seems determined to fill and enjoy to the full every hour of his life. He also kept a military diary during the Peninsular campaign in 1810 which he published.

## THOMAS RUMNEY

WHEN a man is occupied all day riding, carting, digging, weeding, ploughing, manuring, ditching, hedging, haymaking, building, quarrying, carpentering, planting, painting or road making, he may have leisure for occasionally drinking tea with his neighbours and playing at cards, but he is unlikely to have much inclination for the literary effort, such as it is, of keeping a full diary. Thomas Rumney was an indefatigable manual worker. We can gather this from the diary he kept in 1805–6 ; and although he made punctual daily entries we can understand that after a vigorous day's toil he was in no mood to do other than just register the work done.

Thomas Rumney was a member of an old Cumberland family. He was born in 1764 and was the second son of William Rumney of Mellfell. He was placed in South Sea House, a London Counting House. His letter-book during the period that he was a clerk shows that he had considerable talent in the epistolary art. When he was thirty-four his elder brother died suddenly and he found himself converted into the Esquire of Mellfell, a small " Statesman " or yeoman farmer. The letter-book was given up and he took to diary writing. By this means we know precisely what he did but very little of what he thought. He becomes far more interested in calves and hogs than in people, although he always mentions the names of the friends with whom he drinks tea, sups or plays at cards and he enters his gains and losses, which were never very considerable.

To show his activity we will take a month in each of the two years. In February, 1805, on the 1st and 2nd, he was carting ; 4th, shooting ; 7th and 8th, stubbing ; 9th, fencing ;

11th, ditching ; 12th to 16th, walling ; 18th, carting ; 21st to 28th, ditching.

In December, 1806. On the 3rd he was painting a cart ; 4th, timber hauling ; 5th, holing posts ; 6th to 9th, carting ; 10th to 12th, quarrying ; 15th to 18th, cutting drains ; 20th, mending pond ; 22nd, killing vermin ; 26th, ditching ; 29th, carting and attending cattle ; 30th, fence making ; 31st, dressing oats and barley.

There are teas, suppers, card parties and fairly regular church going. The company he meets is cheerful and is sometimes "forward in Liquor" ; he himself confesses on one occasion "I was somewhat tipsy," followed the next day by "was very sick this morning." He makes a few health notes and says when he has his hair cut. In these two years there were the important occurrences of courtship and marriage. He does not waste many words about them, but on the whole one is left with the impression that his venture was not entirely successful. The young lady is Miss Castlehow. He mentions meeting her and on one occasion has a "particular conversation" with her. When it comes to a discussion with the father with regard to ways and means which he does not consider satisfactory, he adds :

> I proposed to Miss C that she would give up the matter of our engaging to marry, but she objected to that in her father's presence, and seemed exceedingly affected, and pressed our agreeing about it much but we parted without doing so.

However, he purchases "a marriage license, a gold ring for 6/6" and "16 pairs of gloves, 9 men's and 7 women's" and the following month he makes a bare statement of his marriage with a list of those present and some more about gloves, adding,

> The company remarkably cheerful. Played at cards. The company departed about midnight. No attendance to Bride and Bridegroom upon their going to bed as is customary upon the occasion in this country.

A custom which it will be remembered Charles II took full advantage of on a famous occasion.[1]

Expressions of affection are hardly to be expected in Rum-

[1] See *English Diaries*, p. 138.

ney's diary, but judging by the following entries it seems doubtful whether there were many to record :

Mrs R and I had much talk about housekeeping arrangements in which our opinions did not agree.

I find my spirits the lowest I ever remember owing to domestic matters displeasing me most sadly.

Mrs. R. at midnight screamed out and, pushed the bedclose off her and call'd out Mr R will you leave this place if you please.

Went to Church when I found in my large Prayer Book in the Litany Service a paper wafer'd to the leaf upon which was printed words—"Henpeck'd Husband" and which I then shew'd to Mrs R.

Went to church and to Jos Abbott's in the afternoon to see my charge in Income Papers. Mrs R very much displeased at my going from home at all and renders my return at times truly disagreeable.

Let us hope he found consolation in his cattle and his pigs and in hedging and ditching. He had no children and died in 1835. This diarist also kept elaborate accounts by which it appears that his farm was not a financial success, although he must certainly have improved it by his labour. Thomas Rumney was made the hero of a novel entitled *A Cumberland Statesman*, written by his cousin Barbara Hoyland, and published in 1848.

His letters and extracts from his diary were published in 1914 in *From the Old South Sea House*, edited by A. W. Rumney, who has kindly allowed a full transcript of the diary to be examined.

## KATHERINE BISSHOPP (LADY PECHELL)

SOCIAL diaries are often heavy reading, more especially when they are written for publication. Conscious of a reader, the diarist brings one into the company of the great and celebrated under the impression that the mere mention of their names will suffice to give the pages of the diary the value of history. But when the social activities of a hundred years ago are recorded in a genuine diary which contains domestic details and impressions of the moment, scribbled down without a thought of publication, we get an insight into the life and can breathe the atmosphere of the time.

Katherine Annabella Bisshopp was a daughter of Sir Cecil Bisshopp, who successfully claimed the Barony of Zouche. She was born in 1791 and lived at Parham, a beautiful Tudor house near Storrington in South Sussex. She married in 1826 Captain Pechell, afterwards Admiral Sir George Pechell, Bart., and moved to her new home, Castle Goring, only 12 miles away. When in 1808 her brother Charles died she found a fat quarto notebook of his in which he had written two pages of history notes and "siezed it to scribble in." After very few entries between 1808 and 1812 she settles down to more or less regular diary writing, though seldom for many days together consecutively and often with long intervals. She fills the book up to the last page in August, 1834. On the fly-leaf she discloses her intention of beginning the book "by way of annals (in order occasionally to recall past occurrences)" on her mother's advice. In the following entry, made in 1817, she clearly shows that her journal is kept for herself alone:

I am sometimes tempted to discontinue and destroy it *but I lament so much having kept no account of many happy days I passed from the time I was seventeen until one and twenty* that I will endeavour to persevere in writing this as perhaps I may at some future time (if it pleases God to spare my life) derive some pleasure in looking over even this deplorable remembrancer of my troubles and I now resume it after the interval of nearly a years cessation, as I cannot bear to write at the moment of painful anxiety—if I die I shall be much obliged to the first person into whose hands this Book may happen to fall, to destroy it instantly.

At first sight this may look like a deliberate injunction which has been disregarded. But she was 26 when she wrote this and she lived to be 80.

In 1818 she again has misgivings about writing:

I feel ill and my eyes are very weak. I feel very much inclined to burn all this and leave off writing my journal as it is very accidental when I take it up and I leave long intervals of time un-noticed, which perhaps contain the very circumstances I wish most to remember.

And in 1823 she writes:

How very tiresome it is to write a journal the best way is only to keep to dates which it is sometimes useful to refer to.

And once she calls her journal "this odious book."

These extracts show that although diary writing was sometimes an effort, for the sake of retrospect in her old age and for no other reason she continued it. The careless naturalness of her notes and the frequent unexplained references to events not recorded show indeed that any idea of a possible reader never entered her head. Her mention of her troubles in the first extract above quoted requires some explanation. It is true that the diarist loses her brother in 1813, has a sister Harriet, Mrs. Curzon, who is a chronic invalid, and has to see a great many of the treasures of Parham sold in order to pay for her father's claim to the peerage. She herself also is often ill. But none of these incidents, deeply as she may have felt them, would seem to justify the tone in which she often writes, referring continually to her "great distress," "suffering," "anguish," "dreadful anxiety," "painful melancholy," "vexations," "wretched feelings," "distressing state of agitation and agony" and "the close of another miserable year." But it must be remembered that it was a period in which vapours, self-pity, and lamentation were the *mode* with young ladies just as slang and oaths are to-day. Their power of enjoyment was by no means destroyed. In spite of eyes " swelled with crying " she notes " I was dressed in white and gold and diamonds " ; and in spite of weeping and fainting she dances away till all hours and in the midst of lamentation she tells us of her " green feathers and green and silver body." Nor should it be supposed that the young ladies of that day were languishing and weakly. The energy displayed by Katherine Bisshopp as a girl and afterwards as Lady Pechell is astonishing. It was nothing to go out to dinners and balls night after night six or twelve miles off and sometimes further, not in a smooth-running car on a macadam road but in a chariot or coach on the Sussex roads of a hundred years ago which were proverbial. Nor does she complain of fatigue from constant journeys to London and further afield to country houses. Balls, parties and dinners are the chief topics referred to in her notes. The social life of the aristocracy had not yet become exclusively centralized in London. Much more time was spent in the country and we get a good idea of the society round her home by her accounts of entertainments at Arundel, Petworth and other large houses in the neighbourhood. Sometimes she reacts against frivolity as when after a dinner and ball at Arundel, fully described, she writes :

After it was all over we came home again—the country was in all the splendid beauty of Summer, heightened at this moment by the beautious rising sun. I enjoyed the drive home much more than the Ball although I liked *that* very much while I was there. How infinitely superior are the beauties of nature to the poor little attempts at grandeur made by foolish trifling mortals. What a contrast ! ! to hear the birds singing, to view the glories of the creation, after jogging about on a dusty floor to the sound of a squeaking Fiddle by the light of a thousand stinking Lamps and Candles which only succeed to make darkness and dulness visible.

At home at Parham, which she adored, she was never dull. Here is her day :

I get up at nine and go and see Mama. I then breakfast alone in the end Parlour and afterwards Play on the Harp or Piano Forte till Mama comes down stairs. I then generally write letters for her or my

Father or write to dear Harriet. If it is fine weather I walk with Snugest [her pet name for her mother] or ride on horseback about the Park but it generally rains and then I have time to do my Catalogue or do something of that sort (one winter I painted some velvet curtains for the saloon). We dine at ½ past four. In the evening I read and work and play on the P.F. Dear Paley is always with me. We never see anybody but the Clergyman on Sunday. I am very glad when it is Mr. Cartwright.

She is very much devoted to her mother and there are constant references to "Snugest." In only one entry sometime after her marriage does there appear to have been a little breeze between them:

I went to see my mother and sister at Parham and received great unkindness from them which I thought unfair considering my very bad state of health and my temporary state of anxiety for my Baby then under vaccination.

And there was another occasion on which her mother was "very angry because George (her husband) had requested her to leave her favourite dog at Parham as he disturbed the Goring pheasants."

Parham and its beauties are very often referred to and one day she and her mother hurry from London on hearing the elms were about to be cut down. "We could not avoid making the exertion to save the beautiful trees."

Her father of course is mentioned but seldom with any comment. Judging by the following note he would appear not to have relished the round of festivities in which she and her mother were always engaged:

We dined at Lady Henry Howards and met Miss Petre and George Pechell, a very pleasant party. My Father said coming home in the carriage what an agreeable little party it was which he seldom or never says of any party.

When he dies in 1828 she is unable through illness to attend the funeral. A day or two later her family come over to Castle Goring to see her.

My own family all arrived in a body to see me—I thought I should have died at the entrance of five persons in deep mourning.

Her sister Harriet, who lives at Hagley, she visits frequently and makes continual reference to her illness. She and her sister eventually succeeded as co-heiresses to the estates of Parham, Mrs. Curzon had the house itself and succeeded as Baroness Zouche.

An account of a full day at Hagley will give a good idea of the diarist's style:

I was in a great fuss all morning as Mr. Wilmot was to come and MaMa not having seen him for above a twelve month I was afraid he should come suddenly upon her and agitate her. George Byron was very kind about it and seemed to enter completely into all our feelings he went several times to the town to see if Mr Wilmot was arrived—he did not come till dinner time and I need not have worried myself about it as all went off well. We were all dressed in white and Diamonds for Lord Bagots Ball which was to take place in the evening MaMa had been so good to remain at Hagley a week longer than she intended that I might go to it. . . . We were a party of 17 at dinner and Lord Curzon was not in the least fatigued. Mama and Miss Byron passed the evening with him and all the rest of us went to the ball where I was very much amused indeed. I danced with William Curzon George Byron Mr Hey and Col Greville. Blythefield is an old gothic house and looked very well lighted up. We danced in the Drawing room and supped in the Dining room. The supper was magnificent, Grapes suspended in clusters on branches of Vine were placed alternately all down the Centre of the Table in a very handsome room with a bas relief over the chimney of King John signing the Magna Charta. I persuaded Harriet to dance late in the evening with William Curzon and Mr Key. At this ball Lady Charlotte Leveson's intended marriage with Mr Howard was declared, they were dancing together. I enjoyed this Ball extremely. George Byron told me Mrs Liegh was the most perfectly amiable and agreeable of all human beings, which piece of intelligence amused me excessively. We all came home at five in the morning.

We must refrain from cataloguing a list of the great people she meets. Frequent visits to the Pavilion at Brighton often brought her into contact with royalty, for whom she has a quite undiscriminating adoration, except two Archdukes of Austria, who were "horridly stupid." The Duke of Clarence introduces her to his wife at Windsor in 1818, and shows her over the castle. They talk French, some of his remarks are reported verbatim, but they are not very illuminating. Princess Adelaide is dressed in "a lilac watered-silk Pelisse" and a hat of "white chip with Green Feathers." Katherine is delighted with the Duke's affability and good humour. After he becomes King she often sees him and Queen Adelaide and always refers to him with rapture. We get a different picture of him from those given by Fanny Burney, Greville and General Dyot.[1] Her husband eventually becomes Equerry to the Queen. The King on more than one occasion lends his "sleeping coach" to her invalid sister and when they travel "the apothecary and the maids" follow in the "barouche." They exchange visits with the Duchess of Kent, who is living at Norris Castle in the Isle of Wight, and once or twice she catches a glimpse of Princess Victoria, "a very intelligent, agreeable little girl, not handsome, but very pleasing."

> Thursday evening we all went to an Evening party at Norris, very dull—though a pretty sight to see Princess Victoria take leave of the Company at nine or ten o'clock when she left them for the night—her manner of bowing and smiling to the right and left through the opening people made for her, was very pretty.

But she found the standing in the presence of royalty fatiguing. "The Queen was so kind as to say she hoped I was not tired with standing"—a hackneyed royal remark which has never been accompanied by a command to sit down.

Her future husband's name occurs frequently in the lists of the people she meets before her marriage and in one entry she says, "I have indeed found a brother in him." For various reasons their marriage was postponed more than once. In July, 1824, she becomes engaged. George Pechell has "a long conversation with my mother which fixed my future fate." After a lapse of ten months she writes in May, 1826:

> I find myself still at Parham *unmarried* still enduring the same anxieties and miseries as the preceding eleven years, still expecting that every succeeding week would bring my fate to a crisis, and what is more odd than all, Still alive, and though with spirits broken down and subdued—health impaired and materially injured by anxieties, still laughing and talking and going on with Life and feeling after all that my predominant wish each returning day is that it may be the last and that God will be pleased to release me from a turbulent and painful existence.

This desperate state of mind is accounted for later in the

[1] *English Diaries*, pp. 181, 276, 315.

entry by her referring to her mother having been nearly burnt to death in the previous October. However, she is at last married in August, 1826, but only writes a very brief note of the event. After she has settled down at Castle Goring her social activities continue even more strenuously. But the same unexplained anguish continues, and her capacity for indulging in the luxury of woe is in no way abated. At the end of 1827 she writes, " here closes another year. I part with it without regret. May God help me through the next without illness or discord." We get accounts of her confinements and full details about the children's illnesses. Incidentally events occur which link this purely personal record to the world of public affairs outside. In 1830 she writes:

> During the whole of the month I was distressed with various apprehensions as ricks were set on fire by unknown incendiaries in all directions and the flames I repeatedly saw blazing in the evening while George went out patroling, caused me great alarm as I continually fancied Parham was burning.

She finds " the mob besetting our Door at 8 in the morning " and George goes out and pacifies them. This was the Sussex rising of labourers who had organized a demand for a living wage and became masters of a large part of the county.[1] In 1832 George Pechell accepts an offer to stand for Parliament at Brighton. This entails frequent visits and canvassing. But he is unsuccessful.

> I rather anticipated an unfavourable result being convinced that George's straightforward honourable character was not fit to cope with the ungentlemanlike tricks of those unprincipled *Radicals*, his opponents.

But George has shooting, hunting and attendance at Court to make up for his disappointment. He did not, however, seem to enjoy royal functions as much as she did:

> George and I went to dine at the Pavilion—I was much amused—The King and Queen all kindness—George asked leave for us to go home at ten o'clock which I much regretted it was a very pleasant party. We reached home by 12 o'clock.

These tremendous long drives in the chariot must have

[1] Described in *The Village Labourer*, by T. L. and B. Hammond, p. 247.

been exhausting and on one occasion, returning from a dinner at Worthing, she has a very serious accident which she describes very well and at great length. In a narrow lane they collide with a waggon, the windows are smashed, the coachman in pulling up suddenly breaks the reins, George climbs out on to the box, but falls on the road, and the horses gallop off with no one in the carriage but Lady Pechell. The chariot, however, dashes through the gate of Castle Goring and the horses stop short. She is in a frenzy of anxiety as to George's fate and at last he is brought in on a hurdle with a broken leg. Many entries follow, describing his suffering. His leg was apparently badly bungled by the doctors, as he remains a cripple for a long time. Every symptom is described. Lady Pechell, George's mother, comes to stay, but she does not appear to have been very useful :

> She was always wrapped up in Cloaks and shawls so that she did not always comprehend what was going on nor the full extent of her poor George's suffering.

The diarist now and again makes a note of what she is reading. She discusses a novel called *The Velvet Cushion* with the Dean of Windsor. She dismisses *Mansfield Park*, condemning the characters as " unnatural absurd " and " very nonsensical." She endeavours to study the Bible carefully, but finds it difficult " to remember," and she declares that Wilberforce on Christianity is " consolatory and delightful beyond any other book I ever read." For pictures she has a great appreciation. Not only does she make a complete catalogue of the pictures at Parham, but she describes those she sees at Knole, Petworth, Ashridge and other houses. Her expressions are characteristic of the time : the coronation is " a prodigious fine sight " and weddings are " awful " ceremonies (in the strict sense of the word). She calls a man whom she wishes to avoid at a ball " birdlime " and a lady who calls " bores her to death," of Lady Scarsdale she says : " she was so noisy I was quite stunned." The lady who marries Mr. Edward Curzon, her nephew, makes her very critical :

> rather a missish kind of person and though pretty by no means charming enough to account for the sudden and determined conduct of her little foolish husband.

12

While the diary is of no particular historical value nor the product of a profound mind, it is a natural and quite unaffected chronicle of the doings of a young society lady of the early nineteenth century. It is a good illustration of the diary habit and it is stamped throughout with the personality of the authoress.

The original diary is in the possession of Mr. Arthur Fitzroy Somerset, of Castle Goring, who married Lady Pechell's granddaughter. By his kind permission the manuscript has been examined and the above extracts made.

## J. VINE HALL

A TRACT called *The Sinner's Friend*, originally consisting of extracts from Bogatzky's *Golden Treasury*, was issued in the early nineteenth century by J. Vine Hall, who gradually substituted pages from his own pen until it became entirely his own composition. It reached the extraordinary circulation of three million and was translated into thirty languages. Vine Hall's diary is also a tract relating the author's cure from what seemed hopeless drunkenness. If there had been no cure we should have had no diary and if there had been no drunkenness the diary would not have been worth reviewing. While the references to his drunkenness in early days are very outspoken, he was naturally of a religious disposition and there may well be some exaggeration in his failure intentionally emphasized in order to enhance the triumph of his eventual success. The entries are few, seldom more than three or four in each month, summarizing periods. The diary has been edited in such a way as to give it more the appearance of autobiography, although the dated entries are kept.

J. Vine Hall was born at Diss, in Norfolk, in 1774. He began life as an errand boy to a bookseller. Afterwards he became clerk and traveller to a wine merchant and contracted drunken and profligate habits which were not cured by his marriage in 1806. By 1818, however, he had entirely freed himself from the curse and returned as owner of the bookshop to which he had been errand boy. He absorbed himself in religious activities and was occupied for years with the publication, translation and circulation of his tract *The Sinner's Friend*. He died in 1860.

The diary begins in 1810 and the first entries show that while he is in the clutches of drink he is aware of his failing and the struggle is beginning :

Come J.V.H. listen to me your true friend Conscience : and if you have ever done any good actions do not erase them by indulgence in bad ones. . . . Rouse yourself and I will assist you in the battle. Think of the rich prize to be gained. Think of your affectionate wife and let this day be the dawn of liberty and glory.

This in April, but the next entry, in July, simply records :

" Drunkenness horrible depravity."

The next year, after a few entries, he records in March : " Drunkenness six days drunk " ! " awful ruin," and on two birthdays there is a bout of repentance and confessions of sin, " a strict watch over every thought determined to resist every temptation to evil." He becomes a Methodist. He busies himself with his religious occupations and becomes trustee, treasurer, committee-man and " prayer-man " and refers to himself as a " sinner snatched from the very centre of hell." For eleven weeks he succeeds in abstaining and then after another fortnight failure again overtakes him :

Half mad at having been quite off my guard and by this means falling from a tremendous height into a most dreadful ambush of the enemy. Oh, how mournful for the saints and those who love God ! Soaring too high without the wings of humility I fell into the horrible pit of intemperance while Satan hugged me again with his infernal arms. Horrible indeed I could shed rivers of tears. God have mercy upon me. There is not a greater sinner in existence.

During the next two months he is " fighting desperately " and is " under a dreadful cloud."

Dissipation—a drawing back from God.

Worcester music meeting. Bustle dress singing and dancing and some pleased and some otherwise. Poor Christians ! Vanity fair after all.

A Blessed relief from all the noise and confusion of the week. Find myself by the sole support of my Saviour quietly rising out of the slough of sin : but I am almost afraid to open my lips to anyone, and I go about the house as quiet as a mouse.

He continues to suffer " Very bad still with the bile." " The bile and hell." " O that God would blot out the last week from the sad catalogue of my sins."

Resolutions and lapses go on till May, 1813, when the diary breaks off, and the next entry is in September, 1817 :

> Four years and a half elapsed and no account rendered ! What can have been the cause of this chasm ? Sin ! Yes, sin of the blackest die !

He then describes how 12 months previously he became reformed and for 94 days had not touched any strong liquor, and by prayer and religious discipline had completely reformed himself and corrected his former habits. He describes how he becomes master of the bookshop in which he had been errand boy 28 years before. This is a retrospective fragment, ending with a great expression of gratitude and an exhortation to his children. He has a slight lapse in September, 1818, when

> the weather being sultry in the extreme I drank porter till I became ashamed of myself.

He confesses that porter had been his " idol," but he makes further resolutions when the Minister asks him the simple question, " Do you love porter better than Christ ? "

Next year the last lapse occurs over table beer and from that time onward he confines himself to water or milk and becomes a total abstainer.

There are full descriptions of his symptoms and feelings over the temptations and his visions, his qualms and his conquest. His entries become more general, but as if uncertain of his complete triumph he refers to the period over which he has succeeded. He is asked to come to a pleasant party where wine will be drunk although he need not drink any himself :

> Satan had finely gilded his invitation by the insinuation that my company was so much esteemed that if I would only join the party they would excuse my drinking wine. The snare did not take.

He refuses the invitation. He gives an account of *The Sinner's Friend* and its circulation and he shows that in spite of his victory over drink he has still to struggle with evil thoughts—" a sort of living over again some of the sinful practices of my youth."

He writes many entries about the distribution of tracts, prayer and studies of the Bible. There is a certain perspicacity in his self-examination :

I find a great portion of vanity and self complacency mixed with all my actions ; but if we abstain from exertion till vanity is eradicated we shall become totally useless, therefore we must not allow ourselves to be cheated of opportunities to do good. . . .

He records conversations and chats on religion, talks in the book shop, exhortations to his family and of course a certain spiritual pride was inevitable from the experience he had been through :

My former companions in iniquity, where are they ? Tremendous thought ! Almost all cut down in their sins in early life whilst I remain to tell the wondrous tale of redeeming love.

This sort of refrain recurs page after page. In fact, he says himself, " There is no end of this blessed theme." It shows the great snare of repentance, namely, the enormous satisfaction the repenter finds at having once been a sinner.

As a tract distributor Vine Hall must have been a nuisance. He gave them to prisoners, to passers-by, to people in omnibuses and occasionally dropped a few on the pavement. *The Sinner's Friend* was much appreciated, although sometimes he is snubbed. He hands a copy of *Come to Jesus* to a lady in mourning in an omnibus, but " she would not accept it."

There are occasional references to people, but they are not very interesting (" Dear Mr Williams who translated *The Sinner's Friend* into Tahitian "). He writes in a very devoted way about his wife and constantly regrets the pain he caused her in his unrepentant days. He has a large family of fourteen children and continues to write in his old age up to within a short period before his death. We get a picture of the old man spending his evening alone with his wife :

Dear Mary and self after tea repeated fifty hymns (twenty five each).

Although the theme of victory over drunkenness is far from a dull one, there would seem to be little real edification in Vine Hall's record and absolutely no entertainment such as we get in the diary of Thomas Turner,[1] who has no victory to record.

The diary, edited by his son, Newman Hall, was published in 1865.

[1] *English Diaries*, p. 227.

# WILLIAM KERSHAW

NOT only has this manuscript diary never seen the light of publicity (in this respect it resembles probably the majority of diaries in existence), but the name of the author is not disclosed in its pages. And yet the diary contains an authentic account of a conversation with Napoleon at St. Helena.

The diary is contained in a blue linen bound quarto notebook and covers about sixty pages. It records the voyage of the Honourable East India Company's Ship *Cuffnells* to India and China and the return voyage via St. Helena between August 28, 1814, and April, 1816. On the inside of the cover the following motto is written:

> In mercy spare me when I do my best
> To make as much waste paper as the rest.
> W. K.

These initials were the first clue to the authorship. The only other clue is an amusing account of a very precipitous ride at Penang, in which the following passage occurs:

> finding my horse inclined to have his own way (which doubtless was very right tho' I did not know it) in spite of Curb or Bridle, I slid over his rump and came down upon my own, on terra firma. At this crisis the Party behind had just opened part of the road which gave them a full view of the scene with The Purser sprawling on the Ground and the Horse pursuing his Course with a gentle trott unattended. "A loud Laugh" soon informed me they enjoyed the Prospect before them.

Having the initials W. K. and the fact that he was the Purser, it only required a little further research to ascertain his name. Through the courtesy of the officials at the India Office it was finally ascertained that the diarist was William Kershaw.

The diary is written in a very clear hand with great regularity and tidiness. It begins with pages elaborately ruled in columns headed: Wind, Course, Lat., Long., Knots and Remarks; and while at sea the remarks are very brief. They chiefly concern the weather, the death of Lascars whose bodies are "committed to the deep"; punishments which the Purser appears himself to have administered. "Punished Vincent Cuthbert with 4 doz. Lashes for disobedience"; and frequently on Sundays he seems to have "performed Divine Service." On landing he delivers "the Hon[ble] Company's Dispatches," and he notes with whom he dines or stays. On January 23 they reach the coast of Bengal and writing across the whole page Kershaw gives us an opportunity of getting some insight into his personality and judging his style, which is quite entertaining, as the following entries show:

Feb 6. Bought a horse and chaise for 265 Rupees.

„ 7. Made my entry on the Course after sunset in my new vehicle—very nigh spilt my companion who being rather weighty overballasted the Tilbury in a short time.—*Scandal* says it was *bad driving*.

14. Hindoo holiday—Black gentry wont eat or work—Took a Drive to the Burial Ground—it is large and crowded. Many of its Inhabitants of my own age, perhaps as little expecting to be called to their account as I am now! How soon may this baneful climate undecieve me as it has them?

A little later there follows an excellent description of bargaining in a bazaar. Again, ashore at Madras, he gives details of his pursuits and entertainments:

I went with a party of Gent[n] to a Black Mans Notch, on entering the Ballroom they dress you up in Flowers which stunk to my fancy. Sour wine to drink and burnt nuts to eat and obliged to sit out of complaisance to see *black* Girls dance and stun you with their noise—The natives can't but conceive you must be delighted.

At Penang he has "a most enchanting" jaunt when the incident with his horse, already related, takes place. He stays at Canton from July 16 to December 6, but he only makes a page of notes and proceeds with the brief log-book entries when the *Cuffnells* sets sail again for home.

On July 19 he writes:

> A Dutchman, he says Buonaparte is defeated and that Wellington hung him in the front of the army on a Tree—he don't know where.

And on December 27:

> They tell us we shall find Buonaparte at St. Helena and that a dreadful battle has been fought at Waterloo.

On arriving at St. Helena he seems to be fully aware of the interest and excitement of approaching the prison of the fallen Emperor, whose name for fifteen years and more had been a byword for praise or execration throughout Europe and indeed the world. So Kershaw proceeds to write at great length, describing the precautions and regulations for the safe custody of Buonaparte, telling what he hears as to his habits, his surroundings, and relating how on an apology being made to the ex-Emperor for the house in which he had been lodged, he only said "this is a better place than my mother ever had."

Kershaw seems to have had remarkably good fortune in actually seeing and talking to Napoleon, a privilege which his captain, Robert Welbank, did not share. The entry in which the interview is described, although long and although it contains no sensational disclosures or even particularly striking remarks, is worth giving practically in full, as it is a simple, ingenuous and authentic account of a conversation with the prisoner of St. Helena, which has never yet appeared in print:

> My anxiety to see this man, whose name, some few years ago was a Bugbear to me, a name that prompted a secret shuddering—but my hopes were as few as my anxiety was great—Tuesday Nov. 5th I procured a horse and as I sauntered up the valley, I met a Gentleman known to me last voyage, and who has the procuring and keeping of stores for his establishment. To him therefore I told my wants, and he politely said "I can introduce you per letter to the Grand Marshall Bertrand"—This was not to be refused, he wrote to the Marshall, giving it me and I mounted my horse, with a gleam of hope—thinks I to myself, be content with a sight of Buonaparte, for he has refused instructions to many sent by the Admiral, saying he was indisposed and immediately they had left he comes out in the garden. I was musing on the many events of the man which

pressed upon my mind, and the sure fall of criminal greatness, when my reverie was abruptly broken, by " who goes there," I enquired for the Officer, and passed after informing him of the authority for my visit. The Officer Capt. Nagles went with me, I dismounted and we walked up to the house together. The Marshall came out to meet us, and after exchanging the usual compliments, I was handed into the Countess's bedchamber and had the pleasure of seeing and conversing with her there, for an hour. She speaks very good English and informed me her parents were Irish. . . . The Countess complained of the length of the voyage and the dreary residence allotted them. " What a barren place it is," said she,—" I see " said the Countess " that the Bellerephon is made a Convict ship of, that is the ship we surrendered to, and they have paid us no compliment by its conversion." The Marshall came in, and asked me if I wished to see the Emperor, I said I should be gratified in paying my respects to him. " There then " said he " is an Order to go to Longwood and I shall soon be there." After a little more chit chat with the Countess (for me it was doubly sweet not having seen one of the fair sex for 9 months) I mounted full speed for Gen. Buonaparte's residence.

On entering the grounds at Longwood the officer on guard demands your pass, which I delivered. I rode round the house in hopes of a glimpse, but seeing the officer who had charge of Buonapartes person, he requested me to dismount and walk into his tent which is placed at the bottom of the garden, here I found two or three gentlemen on the same errand as myself. The officer advised us to wait till the carriage was ordered, however my object was to see Lascassas and get introduced. I walked into the garden and turning short on a path came within a yard of two persons in close conversation, this was unexpected, and I observed one of them uncovered, and the other having a star on his breast, I made no doubt it was Buonaparte, but so widely different even at first sight, did he appear, from the representations and portraits I had seen and formed in my mind, that I could not forbear the vacant stare, however to prevent intrusion I moved my hat and passed, Buonaparte took his hat off and bowed *rather politely* (this in general he is not given credit for). Just as I had reached the end of the path I observed the gentleman who was in conversation running after me, I stopped, and when he came up, asked me " who I was, and what, and that His Majesty the Emperor would see me should I desire it." This gentleman was Lascassas, and I apologised for having intruded. He spoke very good English, and we walked up the path together where General Buonaparte was standing, when we came within a yard of him, I bowed and uncovered, Lascassas doing the same, and introducing me to him. Buonaparte took his hat off to his knee, and immediately replaced it, holding it by the top—I remained uncovered.—The General with a sort of half smile on his countenance began by asking if I have made my fortune and how much, this being answered, he placed his hands behind him and commenced asking questions without selection, and as quick as answers could be given—sometimes scarcely waiting for them, before he proposed something else of quite a different nature; he appeared to anticipate the answers of every question he asked. The Grand Marshall Bertrand, Comte and Comtesse Montholen now came up (and as usual with them) continued uncovered, the Comtesse placed herself behind Buonaparte, who took not the least notice of her—a Gentleman (passenger with us) came up and was introduced by Marshall Bertrand as a British Merchant from China returning to England—" Ah ! " said Buonaparte " has he made his fortune," being answered, yes, he said " how much ? £100,000," " No " was the reply, " Mon Dieu," said Buonaparte, " Are the Company's agents at Canton," said he, " diplomatic characters," being answered in the negative he said " then you have no Jurisdiction there ; do the Chinese dread your naval power," we answered yes certainly, but they take great pains to conceal it—he then enquired after the French Missionaries in China and wished to know if we had any, this being satisfied he immediately asked, " if the Chinese doctors use the blister as a remedy," a gentleman present informed him he was acquainted with these things, and explained to him their manner of procuring blisters ; " to an outward sore " said Buonaparte, " they administer many ingredients." " You have not the finest tea on board," said he, " for that goes over land to Russia, but on what account is that do you think the sea air injures it or does it improve by a land carriage." A doubt arose on the subject and Buonaparte asked what we gave in exchange for our teas ? money and some merchandise we replied—" if," said he, " a Chinese asks you to dinner does he give it you after the custom of his country or your own ? " We said the first day after his own but the second day a European dinner, these days succeed each other. " What does their dinner consist of ? " We informed him there were 300 dishes of various descriptions small, consisting of the greatest delicacies to them which they called chow chow, and eat with two sticks of ivory called chop-sticks, very fast,—Buonaparte listened attentively and certainly thought we were *coming the traveller over him*, for he smiled, and asked " where the 300 dishes were placed ? " we satisfactorily accounted to him for what he *seemed to doubt*, by describing to him their manœuvres and the size of the dish which is not larger than a tea saucer, and that every eatable was made into a sort of stew. " Do they drink wine ? ", we said, very little. He then asked whether it was on account of the expense or whether they considered it too great a luxury for health, we told him they had a substitute which they called sham shu. " A wine or spirit ? ", he asked with many other trifling questions of the same nature. " What were your last accounts of population ? ", on being answered he said, " Ah ! they don't lose many in war." On being told the Chinese nation did not like the idea of the British Army in India, penetrating into the North against Nepaul, " I should suppose not " said he—" are there any Chinese now residing in China who have visited England," we answered there were, and Buonaparte immediately said, "With the consent and knowledge of their Government?" We informed him it was entirely unknown to the Mandarins and those who had been to England dreaded the very mention of it, with a quick motion of the head and a large pinch of snuff, Buonaparte signified to us he was aware that such was the case—he now began enquiring about the government, the department of the Mandarins and the duties levied upon merchandise—we satisfied him to the best of our knowledge, although he appeared perfectly well informed himself, as we could perceive by the gestic manner he had, apparently as if to corroborate what he had before heard concerning China. "Can the Chinese," said he, "discover you from nations of the same complexion?" We said they always found out, even between English and Americans (the greatest proximity existing between us) but whether it was by their persevering and sophisticated enquiries, or by instinct we knew not—"Do they covet your trade?" those few who were concerned in it doubtless must, but they pretend an indifference, we said—"but you take plenty of money," said Buonaparte, "to purchase your teas," Merchandise too, we replied, he then wished for an average. We now hoped we had not detained him and bowed to him as we retired. Buonaparte took his hat off, saying "good day gentlemen" after we had gone a few steps, he said "a good voyage to you." His carriage had been waiting at the door some time, for him, to take his usual evening ride, the distance of which is confined to about a mile round and round, in fact there is not much more level ground for a carriage to travel on. He was dressed in a plain green coat with silver buttons (each having a different device on) with an upright green velvet collar, on his left side was a large emblazoned star, the imperial eagle in the centre. Nankeen breeches and white silk stockings with large gold buckles in his shoes. He wears a large cocked hat not mounted—The picture of Isabey with a full length portrait of Napoleon in the gardens of Malmaison with his arms folded has some resemblance, the best of any I have seen certainly, but this is not half stout enough for him, unless since the painting of that, he has greatly increased in corpulency—he is what we generally say of such a stature a little thick set man with a corporation—a most inactive appearance, with a large head, large mouth, the eyes deeply arched and his teeth apparently very good. On approaching him he surveys you from head to foot and then fixes his eyes sternly at you for a few moments—While speaking he takes his snuff box from his coat pocket and at every pause, takes a copious pinch.

One cannot help in contemplating the calm tranquility which reigns about Longwood, now the peaceful habitation of the once mighty agitator of the world, being forcibly struck by the great mutability of human affairs.

On March the 7th the journey home begins and the Purser makes the following reflection:

Not 2 years absence and yet how anxious are we to return to the happy shores of our native Land, but those who are not sensible of the Blessings they enjoy in England ramble over the Globe in pursuit of Happiness and when remote from her fertile land too soon will they be convinced that what they seek is not to be found in foreign climes.

The daily entries are punctually kept, always in the same beautifully neat handwriting. They are concerned with violent gales and squalls which the ship encounters, so that she is left in a " deplorable state " with the pump gear out of order. Many Lascars die and their bodies are " committed to the deep." So dangerous does the condition of the *Cuffnells* appear to be that when the diary leaves off abruptly on April 30 the reader feels uncertain whether she reached port or whether the body of our chatty and observant Purser diarist was not " committed to the deep." But the ship ledger which is preserved in the archives of the India Office shows that whatever was due to William Kershaw of his salary of 40*s.* a month, was paid to him on January 8, 1816, and his signature appears in the receipt book.

The original manuscript was found by Miss Amelia le Pelley amongst " rubbish " when clearing up the papers of her father, Colonel Ernest le Pelley, son of Ernest le Pelley, Seigneur of Sark. The Colonel's sister married Durand Kershaw, a tea planter in Ceylon, which gives the link between the le Pelley and Kershaw families.

## HENRY EDWARD FOX (FOURTH LORD HOLLAND)

THERE are several features in the social diary of Henry Edward Fox which give it more character than is usual in diaries of this description. He has style, great facility of expression, terse and epigrammatic powers of portraiture and gives unreserved disclosure of candid opinions. So we get at the man through the gossip. This does not prevent the gossip of high society being very exhausting, nor does it prevent him from suffering from the common delusion that association with prominent people must necessarily mean gaining wide experience. The smallness and narrowness of social records prevent them from having the same permanent interest as the uneventful life-stories of country parsons and village schoolmasters, because great names and anecdotes rank far lower than human experiences and personal reflections.

Fox is a far better diarist than his mother, Lady Holland,[1] from whom no doubt he inherited the diary habit ; and there is much more colour and bite in his writing than in that of Henry Greville,[2] a contemporary.

He wrote fairly consecutively from 1818 till 1830, and only continued in a very fragmentary way afterwards. He did not write reflections in the quiet days, but only felt the inclination when he was tearing about in the round of social entertainment. There is not a line that does not refer to intercourse with, or descriptions of people who were considered of social or public importance. He recognizes the advantage of writing at the moment and when from indolence he lapses he thinks it " dull and useless " to write up his journal. His object is no more clear than it is with most diarists, but one

[1] *English Diaries*, p. 246.
[2] *Ibid.*, p. 376.

entry seems to show that he looked forward to re-reading the descriptions of the fun he had had.

Now amid the throng of celebrated statesmen, wits, hostesses, beauties, mistresses, dukes and princesses and in the atmosphere of incessant dinner parties, operas, salons, dances, fancy-dress balls, both in England and Italy, and in the maze of tittle-tattle, flirtations, quarrels and sightseeing, let us try and dig out Henry Edward Fox himself. We shall find him because he has a distinctive personality which prevents his observations being purely objective.

Take the following entry to begin with:

> After a debate in which Ld Liverpool made an admirable speech, the Attorney General opened his case lamentably. I did not go to the House but heard that it was really wretched. A violent storm. Drove afterwards to town with my mother. Miss Eliza Fitz Clarence's marriage to Ld Errol declared. I really do not know whether I am glad or sorry, but on the whole I think it fortunate, though I fear it will cost dear Charles a pang. Took a walk in the garden with Rogers and Ld Grey—both out of temper. Amused to see the different manner a haughty, high-minded, fine-spirited, manly man shews his ill-temper from that of a little, narrow-minded, inquisitive, malignant, observant wit.

Here, it will be said, are the shrewd observations of a mature and experienced man of the world. Not at all. This was written in 1820. Henry Edward Fox was born in 1802. He was therefore a boy of eighteen and even earlier entries might be quoted as illustrations of the astonishing precocity of the young worldling who was brought up with people far older than himself and had had little contact with boys of his own age. But he is amusing, not priggish. His opinions are pronounced and even violent. He dislikes the country, he loves town and company, but he is entirely without ambition. At eighteen he says:

> Every day I live I am more and more persuaded not to meddle in politicks; they separate the best friends, they destroy all social intercourse. And why? Is it for power? Is it for popularity? How unenviable they are separately! How seldom you see them combined; and most politicians have neither.

At twenty-two he still shows his disinclination for a political career:

I only possess a little quickness which enables me to disguise my ignorance and to make the most of the little I do know. I have no steadiness, perseverance or application; I seize results and have not patience for details. This succeeds well enough in conversation; but in Parliament more depth and solidity is required which I could only acquire by application and industry—efforts I am not capable of making except for something that deeply interests me. . . .

His father has him elected for the pocket borough of Horsham in his absence and without his knowledge, but he never even took his seat. His religious opinions are very sweeping and emphatic: "No one more heartily despises the mummeries and contradictions of the Xtian religion than myself," but he is impressed by the ritual of Catholicism. His worship of Napoleon is interesting because it cannot have been purely individual and must have been shared by more people than we are apt to imagine. Wellington he calls "the Butcher." When he hears of Napoleon's death at St. Helena, he writes:

Good God! What a melancholy end to so illustrious a life. England will now open her eyes and will see the shame, disgrace and atrocity of his imprisonment. She will perhaps feel how her faith and hospitality will be recorded to posterity; and the paltry gratification of having embittered and shortened the latter days of the greatest man this world ever produced will be a poor recompense for the national disgrace and dishonour.

Fox infinitely preferred living abroad to being in England and often refers with dread to his return home. He admired his father, but was very critical about his mother:

The restraint she imposes on her own family by the caprice of her temper and the fretfulness and contempt she shows at the slightest difference of opinion, drives me to silence in society when she is present; and the exclusiveness of the topicks she allows to be discussed before her makes it altogether very dull and subject to eternal repetitions.

We get the impression of a cynical and worldly man who was evidently a success socially, but he was not dissolute. He did not drink nor gamble much. Cards, he writes, "are dreadful and victorious foes to an agreeable conversation." His various love affairs are touched on in the usual disjointed and confusing way in which these episodes generally appear in diaries, and are not interesting except as showing a certain fickleness. But his warmth of feeling for his sister Mary (afterwards Lady Lilford) strikes a genuine note and is often very touchingly expressed. When she is dangerously ill he writes :

> I could bear many blows and many misfortunes in the world with tolerable fortitude, but that is the only one for which I could feel no consolation. She is so amiable, so sensible, so clever, with such an admirable understanding and such a perfect heart, that she is the pride and pleasure of my existence. About her happiness I am much, much more solicitous than about my own, and she is the only thing on earth for whom I would make any sacrifice.

Fox had great æsthetic appreciations, he reads a fair amount, and his descriptions of scenes abroad are good. But the diary is notable for his comments of the moment on persons. He jots down his own opinion without any regard for reputations. A few instances may be given :

> *Coleridge* (when the diarist is seventeen). In the evening to Mr. Coleridge's lectures. His voice is bad, his subject trite and his manner odious—an affectation of wit and of genius neither of which he has in any degree.

> *Thomas Campbell* (the poet). Campbell sat next me. His voice is sharp and querulous, his ideas vulgarly conceited. He took all my bread and all my glasses, spilt half his dinner into my lap, and then fished for a compliment for his *New Monthly Magazine* which I was determined he should not extract.

> *Thomas Chalmers.* His voice is positively bad, his Scotch broad and vulgar and his doctrines absurd and sometimes odious ; but yet it is impossible to let one's attention flag for one moment, or not to feel deeply interested and occasionally elevated in the scenes he draws from his rich luxuriant fancy.

> *Byron.* Of his faults he has his share like his neighbours and his greatest, in my opinion, is the vanity he has of pretending they are greater than they really are and making a display of what the rest of the world try to conceal. He describes too well the delicate and honourable feelings of the heart to be so devoid of them as half Europe believes.

> *Lady Petre.* Of created bores Lady Petre is the Phoenix with no understanding, an enquiring mind about trifles, an incessant tongue and a stentorian voice. What could be sent on earth as a greater scourge to the exquisites.

13

His account of Hortense de Beauharnais (mother of Napoleon III), whom he often sees in Rome, is very detailed and graphic. From her he culls many Napoleonic anecdotes.

Introspection is not to be expected in a diary of this description. We get a word or two of it, however, in the final entry of the regular diary:

> I look back on life with much repentance. Not for the ambitious objects I have slighted for had I attained them I should not be happier, and had I failed in the attempt, which is more likely, I should have been mortified and miserable. But I have cruelly and wantonly played with the feelings of others, I have never believed any attached to me and I have on that account and on that account only, and not from the fickleness of which I am accused, determined not to be myself attached.

He married, however, in 1832. In spite of his evident powers of expression in writing he never distinguished himself in any way. Indolence, lack of ambition and entire absence of any public spirit held him back. After spending about ten years abroad in the diplomatic service, he returned home in 1846, made a great many alterations in Holland House, and died in 1859.

The diary, edited by Lord Ilchester, was published in 1923.

## ANTONY ASHLEY COOPER (SEVENTH EARL OF SHAFTESBURY)

THERE was a great deal of material for a biographer in the public work of the greatest social reformer of the nineteenth century. But in addition to this no biographer can ever have been furnished with such a full disclosure of personal motive and intention as is afforded by the voluminous diary which Lord Shaftesbury kept. Without the diary the public record of his life would have been very incomplete.

We are confronted here once again with an instance of a man immersed in the frenzied activity of public work finding time to keep a very complete account of his doings and feelings,—another case of a chief actor being a fuller and better diarist than any spectator.

Lord Shaftesbury's pronounced and rigid religious attitude may have induced him originally to embark on a diary for more or less disciplinary motives. However that may be, he kept up to the end of his life a full, faithful and honest chronicle of his career, in which there is no conscious attempt at self-portraiture and therefore we get a very accurate likeness. We see him with his warm affections, his austere severity which never deteriorated into self-righteousness, his fear of deviating a hair's breadth from the narrow path, his intolerant prejudices, his ardent spirit of service, his ambition for achievement, his susceptibility to criticism, and yet his indifference to it, and his unremitting and indefatigable efforts for the causes in which he believed not philosophically but with the ardent zeal of an evangelist.

It is important to note that Lord Shaftesbury never wrote

for publication. When approached by Mr. Edwin Hodder, who was preparing his biography, Lord Shaftesbury at first refused to hand over the volumes of his diary. He said: "They are of no value to anyone but myself; they have never been seen by anybody, and they never will be. They are a mass of contradictions; thoughts jotted down as they passed through my mind, and contradicted perhaps on the next page —records of passing events written on the spur of the moment and private details which no one could understand but myself."

He began writing in 1825, but only intermittently. In 1831 he left off for three years and after keeping a travel diary, which was separate, he settled down seriously to diary writing in 1838, when he was thirty-seven. He continued till nearly the end of his life, filling twelve quarto volumes in a closely written but careful handwriting, with scarcely a blot or erasure throughout. The very first entry gives some idea of his intention:

> Everyone who begins to keep a journal regrets that he did not do so before. I follow the general example and regret the many "fine and apt" things both of fact and imagination that are now irrevocably lost. I had a book, a few years ago, in which I made from time to time some short, desultory entries, but the natural impatience of my disposition and the mischievous and indulged habit of doing nothing consecutively, broke the thread of my record and I now resume a business which will conjoin a head and a tail by the exclusion of all intermediate carcase. Yet an actual journal, a punctual narrative of every day's history would be an intolerable bore—a bore when written and a bore when remembered—at least it would be so to me; the probability is that this book of memorandums will share the fate of all other attempts and go into oblivion unsullied by ink or pencil; but should it be carried on, I will make it a mere cage for light and grave thoughts (the paucity of them will render the task easy) which unless they be caught as they arise, take wing like larks and owls and are gone for ever. . . .

He was not in the habit of re-reading his diaries, for at the end of one or two of the volumes he writes a note declaring he had not reopened the book for thirty-seven years. He definitely made up his mind what should be the fate of the volumes. He bequeathed them to his daughter Victoria, afterwards Lady Templemore:

Never intended for the eyes of anyone but of myself and of that beloved woman now gone to rest, they are the entries of one day after another; and everything may be said against them but the charge that they were not hearty and sincere. Victoria may find them interesting and, possibly, even profitable.

Lord Shaftesbury changed his mind with regard to his biographer's request and allowed Mr. Hodder to have the diaries. On perusing them after his death his biographer found that Lord Shaftesbury had "written his own life." The style of the diarist is rather punctilious and stilted and at times rhetorical. There is of course no flippancy, but there is an absence of humour and a curious cold courtliness. When he speaks of the Queen, whom he sees frequently, it is almost as if he were writing a letter for publication about her, and this is also the case in some of his judgments on his political friends. This entire absence of slipshod or careless language is unusual in a voluminous diary never intended for publication.

The overwhelming stress of his work did not prevent him from taking out his quarto volume and making his daily entry:

Have been in a whirl by night and by day—occupied and anxious all day; sleepless or if sleeping like a drunken man, all night, my head quite giddy and my heart absolutely fainting; too much to do, in quantity, in variety and importance.

Have now, at least, a hundred letters unanswered; and, yet, have not had leisure to do one stitch of private business, enjoy barely an hour of recreation, nothing on public affairs, and two books I have desired to look at still unopened. My mind is as dry as a gravel road, and my nerves are sensitive and harsh as wires.

Surveys of the year and of the past occur on his birthdays, or at the end of a year. He says at twenty-five: "a great age for one who is neither wise, nor good, nor useful nor endowed with capability of becoming so." He complains that "occasionally the question *cui bono?* sours my spirit of application; but generally speaking I have still the passions." In 1851 he sits down on Christmas Day and takes a full and detailed survey of his life under the headings: I. What have I gained for the public? II. What gained for the cause of our blessed Master? III. What gained for myself? and under the paragraph "Then how stands my fame?" makes a searching and probably just analysis of the way he was estimated by his contemporaries:

What I have is *notoriety* not reputation. I have a name that everybody knows, "a household word" writes the American Minister, Mr. Lawrence, to me "from New York to the Rocky Mountains;" but a name that everyone fires at! Some dispute my judgment, some my sincerity, some my courage; some think, or profess to think me unworthy of their notice; some call me "well intentioned but weak;" others "hypocritical and canting;" some hold me to be ruled entirely by vanity, others consider me a mere tool. Now and then I make a speech which produces an effect, and I get some praise; but the speech is soon forgotten and the man only remembered to be treated as before. A few no doubt think of me and speak of me kindly; but they are rare and of small influence in the stirring world. I have been oddly and antagonistically viewed [gives quotations]. . . . But notorious men are good for chairs of dinners and meetings. People come, not through affection and respect but to see the notorious man; and so I serve their purpose.

In a short single sentence entry in 1845 he writes: "At times I quail when I think of the concentrated hatred against me." In another place he says: "my popularity such as it is lies with a portion of 'the great unwashed,' and again, 'I must ever be groping where there is most mischief.'" And in 1869 there is an entry which shows that while he was always aware of public criticism it never deterred him from his work among the outcasts of society:

Debate in the House of Lords on the Criminal Bill. I met as usual from the public with a mixture of praise and contempt. A great majority of mankind assume that if a man be stamped as a "Philanthropist" he cannot have common sense. They hold that it betokens a softening of the brain! Alas poor Yorick.

Last night at Wellclose Square went to a gathering of thirty thieves. What a spectacle! what misery! what degradation! and yet I question whether we fine, easy, comfortable folks, are not greater sinners in the sight of God than are these poor wretches.

As Lord Ashley he sat, except for a brief interval, in the House of Commons until he was fifty. The fullest account is given in the diary of the debates in which he took part and of all the political changes and controversies. From the time of his maiden speech in 1828 when he notes "I did not utterly disgrace myself" his enthusiasm for the particular work to which he was devoting his life predominated over all other considerations and he grew more and more to hate party politics. So sensitive, however, was his conscience that as a convinced Protectionist he refused to follow Peel in 1846 and resigned his seat in Dorset:

> I shall resign my seat and throw up all my beloved projects ; all for which I have sacrificed everything that a public man values ; all that I had begun and all that I have designed. Nearly my whole means of doing any good will cease with my membership of Parliament.

He was, however, elected for Bath in the following year. He always speaks disparagingly of his own powers:

> I am always cast down when I estimate by comparison with others my Parliamentary capacity of doing service *Je manque de profondeur et de suite.* My memory is deficient, my knowledge scanty ; I have no readiness for impromptu speaking ; all must be prepared and the greater part even to language, but nevertheless I must do my best, and commit the issue to Him in whose service I am labouring.

Many are the entries which show that his philanthropy was not a matter of abstract study but of personal investigation:

> Perambulated many parts of Whitechapel and Bethnal Green, to see with my own eyes the suffering and degradation which unwholesome residences inflict on the poorer classes. No pen nor paint brush could describe the thing as it is. One whiff of Cowyard, Blue Anchor, or Baker's Court outweighs ten pages of letter press.

His reply when approached to withdraw an amendment on the Factory Bill so as not to embarrass the Government, in 1844, is a good example of his uncompromising persistence:

> if my perseverance involved the repeal of ten thousand Corn Laws and the dissolution of as many Governments, I would go on with all the vigour I could command ; that were I disposed to hold back, I could not do so in the smallest degree ; that even in a mere question of politics a man would be regarded as a sad specimen of faithlessness who retired simply to gratify the convenience of his Parliamentary friends, but that in this case when I had toiled for so many years and placed the whole matter on the basis of duty and religion, I should be considered and *most justly so* a hypocrite almost with parallel.

In such a nature as Lord Shaftesbury's there was far more room for depression than elation. The standard of accomplishment he set himself was almost beyond human power. At the same time he could not but gain some satisfaction from the actual passage of measures and introduction of reforms which were so largely due to his untiring efforts. A couple of entries may be given, the one showing him in a downcast mood, the other more encouraged:

A great deal of melancholy over me both today and yesterday and the day before. Truth is I am a little tired and a little disheartened; men are untrue and luke warm. I am endeavouring to pile Pelion on Ossa, the work of the Titans, with the force just sufficient for an ant hill. . . . Talk of the dangerous classes indeed! The dangerous classes in England are not the people! The dangerous classes are the lazy ecclesiastics, of whom there are thousands, and the rich who do no good with their money! I fear them more than whole battalions of Chartists. I am as much fretted by anxiety as worn by labour. I cannot feel by halves, nor only when the evil is present. I take it I suffer very often much more than the people themselves.

Harassed by public and private business. My heart goes so completely into every question, that I fret like one possessed. Chimney sweepers, juvenile mendicants *et hoc genus omne*. Speeches and chairs without end. But all is not vain; I am reaping a harvest. Is it because in God's mercy, I have not fainted? The working of the Ten Hours Bill is peace, wealth and happiness, social order and moral improvement.

At the age of seventy he is still making his retrospect and estimate of his work, lamenting his want of self-confidence and ineffectiveness as an orator, condemning himself for being "over-anxious for success" and "over-fearful of failure" but obliged to admit that he has had "great successes." His unflagging determination to continue work with whatever power and influence he had, carried him to the age of eighty-four, still making entries of his public engagements.

Shaftesbury's religious zeal was not only disciplinary, it was dogmatically orthodox and often intolerant. "To all subjects I prefer theology," he writes on one occasion. He abhorred Rome or anything that even savoured of High Church. He inveighs against the monasteries in the fiercest language, calling them "dens of hypocrisy," where "oppression, vice and violence" reigned and "degradation of soul and body for time and eternity." His austere severity in this connection permeates his politics and his views on life. Seldom does he allow himself to relax, but we catch him once in a livelier mood when he writes: "I have been in good spirits since my arrival in Scotland, and have laughed a great deal, perhaps too much."

A legitimate pride and a proper estimate of his capacity and influence made him refuse office on more than one occasion. The offer to him of a Court appointment he regarded almost as an insult and records all the circumstances in very great detail. His disappointment, from the point of view of career, at these offers of minor office he does not conceal. To his diary he confides all his feelings on the subject.

Shaftesbury was no mild critic, at any rate in his diary, of those who opposed him politically; and his estimates of those with whom he was in political association are penetrating, although they undergo changes as all personal estimates in private diaries almost invariably do. His notes on two Prime Ministers may serve as illustrations:

> Sat next to Peel at dinner last Saturday. What possesses that man? It was the neighbourhood of an iceberg with a slight thaw on the surface.

> He has abundance of human honesty and not much of Divine faith; he will never do a dishonourable thing, he will be ashamed of doing a religious one; he will tolerate no jobs to win votes, he will submit to no obloquy to please God; a well-turned phrase of compliment, and eulogy from Lord John or Macaulay will attract him more than "Hast thou considered my servant Job?"

Yet a sense of loyalty makes him also say: "I cannot forget ancient friendships, ancient hopes, ancient co-efforts with Sir R. Peel." The most caustic of all his personal comments is directed against Disraeli when he succeeds Lord Derby as first Minister of the Crown:

> D'Israeli, Prime Minister! He is a Hebrew; this is a good thing. He is a man sprung from an inferior station; another good thing in these days, as showing the liberality of our institutions. "But he is a leper" without principle, without feeling, without regard to anything, human or divine, beyond his own personal ambition. He has dragged and he will continue to drag, everything that is good, safe, venerable and solid through the dust and dirt of his own objects.

Disraeli's spectacular triumphs did not move him. At the time of the public ovation after the Congress of Berlin he writes: "I had rather, by far, be George Holland, of Whitechapel, than Benjamin D'Israeli, Earl of Beaconsfield." On

Beaconsfield's death, in 1881, there is an entry admitting his astonishing powers and success and ending " he was a wonderful man in his generation ! But was he a useful one ? "

The diary with its critical references to political colleagues and opponents makes one realize what an isolated figure Shaftesbury was. He shows himself incapable not so much of friendship as of fellowship, obviously by his own confessions a difficult man to work with. His religious intolerance it would seem from his own record had a good deal to do with this. He appears happier discussing the second Advent with the Duchess of Bedford in a country house than talking over the reforms to which he was devoting his life with people who did not share his religious views. Nevertheless he was intensely domestic. Of his devotion to his wife there is proof in numberless entries. It is the one subject on which he lets himself go without misgiving, without reservation and with a rapture which he is never tired of repeating. Her death is a blow which shatters him and the fact that he pours out his inmost feelings in his diary would seem to give additional evidence of his loneliness. He had no one else in whom he could confide. His oft-repeated eulogies of her are written in simple and sincere language, not perhaps so perfect in form as the one entry on the same subject by his diarist ancestor the first Earl,[1] but just as heartfelt and moving. There are many affectionate references to his children and to his home life and full accounts of their travels abroad. These form a contrast to his early life which had been miserable and to the strained relations between himself and his father. Of his health he speaks occasionally like all diarists and in his old age he analyses with extraordinary minuteness his declining powers and describes his failing voice as though he were " speaking through all the cotton in Lancashire."

There are no jokes and epigrams to extract from the quarto volumes, no frivolities or descriptions of food, no discreditable backslidings, no piquant morsels of scandal which give so many diaries their fame.

It is the sum total rather than any special entries which makes the diary remarkable. It is not a good one, therefore,

[1] See p. 68.

for quotation. You may like Lord Shaftesbury or dislike him; you may agree with him or disagree with him, admire him or not, but at any rate you have before you in as complete a picture as ever a diary made of its author. The honesty of it comes not only from the fact that he never wrote for publication, but also because he was himself incapable of dissembling. Even his rigid religion never leads him to any excessive and abject self-disparagement. His self-depreciation is temperate, obviously sincere and to a large extent true. It is not exaggerated with a view to eliciting external sympathy. So also his elation is very restrained, showing a nature never given to exuberance. His journal could not make popular reading any more than he himself could get cheap popularity while he lived.

A note jotted by a contemporary is sometimes better than volumes for bringing a personality before one's eyes. A contemporary, also a diarist of a very different character, makes a couple of references to young Ashley at the age of about twenty. Henry Edward Fox, afterwards Lord Holland, writes in his diary[1]:

> Ashley's character seems to me quite unintelligible and can only be accounted for by a dash of madness. From having a dislike that almost amounted to hatred, I have grown insensibly to admire and like him.

> Ashley came for me at about two. We had a very pleasant journey and I got from his conversation a much better opinion of his heart than I ever had before. His understanding is so warped by the most violent prejudices, that he appears quite ridiculous whenever he finds an opportunity to vent them.

Throughout his life Lord Shaftesbury's character was very deep cut, deeper even than the admissions in his diary would lead one to suppose. His intolerance was his strength; his severity his weapon; his religion his inspiration. His place in history is a great one but an unusual one. His service, as has been well said, was " not the service of a statesman with wide plan and commanding will, but the service of a prophet speaking truth to power in its selfishness and sloth." [2]

[1] See p. 190.

[2] *Lord Shaftesbury*, by T. L. Hammond and Barbara Hammond.

# EMILY SHORE

THERE are several instances of lifelong diarists beginning at an early age with childish notes, Fanny Burney began at fifteen and Queen Victoria at thirteen, Emily Shore began when she was eleven, but she died before she was twenty. It might be supposed, therefore, that hers is a child's diary. But one may look almost in vain for a childish expression or even childish grammar. It is the diary of an infant prodigy whose extraordinary capacity for absorbing knowledge charged her with an abnormal amount of erudition, but at the same time evidently extinguished in her all traces of childishness or even youth. This fact makes the diary unique in its way, as it presents an almost ludicrous contrast to the social diary kept by young ladies of her age. But the entire absence of frivolity or of any lightness of touch, the immense scientific disquisitions, the unceasing record of reading and study are seldom entertaining and make one somewhat impatient with the parents who allowed her frail physique to be undermined by such wearing intellectual strain. However, it was her own inclination ; she needed no driving and her father, who was a tutor, was only too ready to fall in with her wishes. But she herself admits overworking her mind and overtaxing her strength.

Emily Shore was born in 1819 and died of consumption in Madeira in 1838. In her nineteen years of life she mastered Latin, Greek, French, Italian and began Portuguese and German ; she had a profound knowledge of history ; but it was in botany and natural history, more especially ornithology that she excelled chiefly and showed the powers of a patient and remarkable investigator. As, however, her notes necessarily lack the authority of a mature expert, but at the same time show none of the *naïveté* of a child, they are only valuable as illustrating her extraordinary powers of application. Even her descriptions of journeys and places, detailed as they are, will not arrest a casual reader's attention. It is all very conscientious and elaborate, but only here and there do we get the lighter touch of the girl apart from the student.

Emily Shore became from the age of eleven a confirmed, methodical and inveterate diarist. No diarist, not even Amiel himself, can have examined more profoundly the whole psychology of diary writing and faced the problems of the honesty of introspection and the questions of motive in writing and the eventual fate of a diary with greater perspicacity than this girl writing at the age of eighteen after keeping a journal for seven years. The entry in which she discusses the whole subject is a long one and only some of the passages can be given :

> I am sure it (her journal) is a memoir of my character and the changes and progress of my mind—its views tastes and feelings. But I am conscious that, at the same time, it is far from being as complete as with this end it ought to be . . . it has become to me a valuable index of my mind, and has been the record of faults and follies which have made my cheek burn on the reperusal. I have poured out my feelings into these later pages ; I have written them on the impulse of the moment, as well as from the coolness of calm deliberation. I have written much that I would show only to a very few and much that I would on no account submit to any human eye. Still even now I cannot entirely divest myself of an uncomfortable notion that the whole may some future day when I am in my grave be read by some individual and this notion has without my being often aware of it, cramped me, I am sure. I have by no means confessed myself in my journal ; I have not opened my whole heart ; I do not write my feelings and thoughts for the inspection of another—Heaven forbid !—but I imagine the vague fear I have above mentioned has grown into a sort of unconscious habit, instinctively limiting the extent of my confidence in ink and paper so that the *secret chamber of my heart* of which Foster speaks so strikingly, does not find in my pen a key to unlock it.

She then describes how her family find entertainment in the passages she reads to them and discusses the " remote consideration " that one day her records may be " instructive and interesting " to her children. Finally she resolves to keep a second journal into which she will pour out all her secret feelings and inmost thoughts :

I know the task will be most painful and humiliating. I know I shall seem to be cutting across every sinew of my self esteem with a blade of caustic ; but do it I must. May God give me grace to persevere and to do it honestly ; for if either of these two requisites are wanting, it will be useless. Let me do it feeling certain that it will never be seen by human eye and let me take effectual means that this shall be the case.

Her project was not carried out because within a year she died. In the Journal as published the Editor tells us he has abstained from any " violation of what are felt to be the sacred privacies of the soul," so the deeper interest is impaired by this compunction. At the age of sixteen she declares that she finds keeping a diary a useful and entertaining practice and she is resolved to continue it all her life. " I have been long convinced that the use of the pen is amongst the most valuable means of improving the mind." On the other hand, towards the end when her health is failing, she notes " Journalizing has lost its interest with me. I am dreary, dispirited and ill." However, she continued to write as long as she had strength, to within a fortnight of her death, and filled twelve octavo volumes, every page written in a wonderfully neat *printing* hand.

On her birthdays she makes introspective meditations. At the age of sixteen she writes :

There is completely a world within me, unknown, unexplored by any but myself. I see well that my feelings, my qualities, my character are understood by none else. I am not what I am supposed to be ; I am liked and loved far more than I deserve. I hate—yes, I truly hate myself ; for I see the depths of sin within me which are hidden from all other eyes.

But before quoting more of the cogitations of the student philosopher let us turn to the early pages and try and find the child.

There is an exactness of detail in her descriptions in which her age may be detected, but the phraseology is grown-up, and there is not a word—except it be " unmeaningless "—which is ungrammatical or wrongly used. She has much to relate about her pasteboard steamer and her stuffed birds. Her father offers her a shilling for every stuffed bird she would throw away, " but I would not for a guinea." Her parents present her on her twelfth birthday with what sounds rather a dry work, Babbage's *Economy of Manufactures*, but she thinks it beautiful and interesting. She and her brothers and sister speculate on what they would do were every flake of snow which fell a piece of gold. At the end of this entry she adds "I should like also to have a tame elephant." But except for this there are no amusing childish remarks to be culled. She is already beginning her natural history studies and her investigations are from the first carefully scientific. She watches birds closely until there is little about them she does not know. She makes the most elaborate notes of the progress of vegetation and one day she watches the proceedings of a mason wasp which is hoarding caterpillars in the lock of her dressing-table drawer and with the patience worthy of a Lubbock she notes precisely what happens minute by minute as it makes thirteen visits to and fro through the window. She memorizes chapters of the Bible and repeats them on her walks, she reads Gibbon while she curls her hair, at meals she thinks of arithmetic, history, and geography, she collects birds' eggs, ferns and mosses, she makes gigantic chronological tables, she teaches other children and she has unrivalled capacity as a story-teller. At twelve years old she says, "I think by this time I must have told them many thousand stories." She paints and draws, discusses politics, music, and literature. All this we find out from the full account she gives day by day of how she spends her time.

It was inevitable that Emily Shore should be a bit of a prig. In a conversation which she records in her fourteenth year with a Miss Caroline who is staying with them, she deplores that people at balls do not talk about "science and natural history," and when Miss Caroline declares she likes going to balls very much indeed:

> Like it!—(cries Emily) How horrid! How can you like it? What a very great waste of your time, when you ought to be learning and improving your mind to go to balls and talk nothing but nonsense! Where is the pleasure of it? Do you not think it a waste of time?

But Miss Caroline is not persuaded and even confesses that sometimes she goes to three parties in one night. "What a waste of life" sighs Emily.

In a minute description of her room in a house in Devonshire to which her family moves she describes each piece of furniture, her pictures, collections, birds, drawings and incidentally refers—as if it were the most ordinary form of wall decoration, to "a set of arguments against dissipation fastened to the wall with tin-tacks." In addition to her reading and writing she has the advantage of listening to her parents' conversation and notes it with the fullness and accuracy of a reporter. Her father was advanced in his views. Although he had been a curate he abandoned the Church because he could not conscientiously sign the Thirty-nine Articles. She is twelve when she notes this extraordinarily well-expressed epitome of a conversation:

At tea papa and mama always sit at the fire by themselves and we listen to their conversation; this evening it was peculiarly interesting. Papa began by condemning the idea that the Duke of Wellington's military prowess ought to exempt him from dislike on account of his political opinions or anything else. He instanced Mr. T. Quinton, who would call it quite a shame that after all he had done for England he should be so unpopular; but if a man who had been eminent in science, and had made useful discoveries should fall under general odium for his after conduct or opinions he would think nothing of abusing him. And yet this man would be much more deserving of public esteem, for he would really have been a benefactor to his country; he would not have been employed in cutting throats, in war and massacre, in which men nevertheless glory instead of considering the business of a soldier a painful necessity. Soon after Mama remarking that the Conservatives had still a strong party in England, papa assented and then said that the late election cost Mr. Stuart, the Tory member £20,000. This was chiefly spent in indirect bribery by entertaining people in public houses, "a beastly way of spending money."

Her style is staid and sometimes sentimental, but there is nothing remarkable in her long accounts of places and scenery except always that the tone is almost middle-aged. Flights of fancy and humour she seldom allows herself, but there is a picture of a young preacher at Vere Street Chapel which is amusing:

His manner was such that it would not have been surprising if the whole congregation had burst into a laugh. He bowed; shook his head; sailed backwards and forwards; sank, rose; held one hand on his heart and stretched the other over the congregation or clasped them both together; waved his handkerchief; closed his eyes; smiled sweetly; shook his voice; assumed a ludicrous sentimental tone, even when quoting a text; jogged his sermon up and down; leant over his cushion; grinned; sighed;—in short, did everything that he possibly could to make himself offensive and ridiculous.

As Emily is undoubtedly an honest diarist, a reader may be tempted rather mischievously perhaps to seek amidst the books and grammars and charts and stuffed birds some trace of romance. And he will find it; very delicately sketched, it is true, and probably the Editor's scissors makes it still fainter than it is in the original manuscript. There is a Mr. Henry Warren who tells "remarkable stories about apparitions" and was forward enough to hold a parasol over Emily while she sketched and "is more employed in talking to me than in looking at the views." But, we are told, the parents intervened and the episode passed.

Towards the end Emily Shore quite realizes what her fate is to be and when she visits the cemetery at Frendeal, "I felt as I looked at the crowded tombs that my own might not long hence be amongst them." But the young philosopher with stoical courage abstains from morbid reflections and finds refuge in the many resources of her well-stored mind up to the very end, with death staring her in the face.

The diary was published in 1891, together with some little plays and poems by Emily Shore.

## WILLIAM CHARLES MACREADY

THE diaries of Macready, the celebrated actor (from 1833 to 1851), have been published in two large volumes. He wrote fully and regularly, he was intimately associated with many interesting people, his devotion to his art is apparent in almost every entry. There are many passages which disclose his attempts at self-correction and many particulars with regard to his family ; from time to time also he indulges in prayer. It is in fact a typically full diary of a man who is interested in life and interested in himself. It is written almost daily and although what he does and says predominates largely over what he thinks and feels, it probably gives a very accurate picture of his character. It is curious, therefore, that such a good diary should not be more arresting than Macready's is. We are inclined to think this is due chiefly to two causes. His profession was absorbing, but at the same time very narrow and confined, and he himself, although attractive on the stage, appears personally to have had a somewhat harsh and touchy disposition and to have been devoid of the particular form of humour which would have made him laugh at himself.

He was cultured, well read, interested in much beyond the stage, especially politics, but he was incapable of imparting to the review of his daily pursuits, to his struggles and adversities, to his triumphs and achievements or to his criticisms the particular spirit of sympathy and pleasure which far less notable writers in briefer diaries have been able to instil into their records. We are left with the impression that Macready, the man, was devoid of charm. This was not due to his bad temper, which caused him so much trouble and with which he continually struggles, but rather to his conceit, his censorious and rather spiteful attitude towards his colleagues and to the predominance of his love of disparagement which becomes almost monotonous in its constant recurrence. The diary, therefore, may be claimed to be good from the point of view of its value as a faithful picture of the author, but while it has interest, it has little entertainment. One can at once recognize his distinguished abilities and his high character, but somehow neither in his virtues nor in his faults is there much that endears him to a reader. When the diary begins Macready was forty and with the exception of Edmund Kean, foremost among English actors. Illustrations may first be given from throughout the diary of his remarkable conscientiousness as an actor and of his self-criticism :

> I played only tolerably. I want to consider every line, and test each by a natural standard.
>
> Acted Lear ; how ? I scarcely know. Certainly not well—not so well as I rehearsed it ; crude, fictitious voice, no point ; in short a failure ! To succeed in it I must strain every nerve of thought, or triumph is hopeless.
>
> I acted Lord Hastings well—really well, I almost satisfied myself ; a little more truth in part of the last scene would have made it a very commendable performance.
>
> I acted disgracefully, worse than I have done for years.
>
> I was most attentive to the necessity of subduing my voice, and letting the passion rather than the lungs awaken the audience. In consequence I acted well.
>
> My performance in the first two acts was so unlike my rehearsal that although I goaded myself to resistance by suggestions of my own reputation, of my wife and children's claims upon me—still I sunk under the idea that it was a failure.

Towards the last years of the diary he is often very well satisfied with his performance :

> Acted Iago with a vigour and discrimination that I have never surpassed if ever equalled.
>
> Acted Brutus as I never—no never—acted it before, in regard to dignified familiarity of dialogue or enthusiastic inspiration of lofty purpose.

Favourable or unfavourable, these comments occur almost every time he acts.

References to his ungovernable temper or "violent passion" as he calls it, are very frequent. A few instances may be given, showing his continual struggle at self-mastery:

What an irascible disposition I must have *had*, when even now I have such frequent occasions to rebuke my waspish impatience and pettishness at the various trifles that happen to cross my mood as I sit here alone.

I must not omit to notice the temper I displayed on the occasion, which calls up my bitter regret as it merits the heaviest censure. What would I not do, or give, to cure myself of this unjustifiable, dangerous, and unhappy disposition. Regret is no expiation of a vice that injures others and degrades myself.

The best thing in the play was the grave scene, I played it well, the rest was effort and not good. Still worse, I was morose and ill tempered. Fie! fie! shall I never outlive my folly and my vice? I fear not.

My ill-conditioned nature, my ill-disciplined mind is a constant cause of self-infliction. God send that I may so instruct my blessed children as to save them the loss of quiet and of time that my evil propensities induce! Amen!

Rose with very unhappy reflections upon my wretched temper which makes so much of what is unhappy in my life. I know its sin, its folly, its unamiable effect, its terrible punishment, and yet I cannot—exposed as I am to these excitements—I cannot subdue it to my will.

Owing to his temper the performances arranged in which both he and Edmund Kean were to appear had to be abandoned. This was before the diary begins. In 1836 a furious outburst on his part against his manager Mr. Bunn led to very unfortunate results. However much Bunn may have been at fault, from Macready's own account of the incident, written, as he always wrote, on the day, it must be admitted that he completely lost control of himself:

As I came off the stage, ending the third act of *Richard*, in passing by Bunn's door, I opened it, and unfortunately he was there. I could not contain myself; I exclaimed "You damned scoundrel! How dare you use me in this manner?" And going up to him as he sat on the other side of the table, I struck him as he rose a backhanded slap across the face. I did not hear what he said, but I dug my fist into him as effectively as I could; he caught hold of me, and got at one time the little finger of my left hand in his mouth and bit it. I exclaimed: "You rascal! Would you bite?" He shouted out: "Murder! Murder!" and after some little time, several persons came into the room.

This led to a lawsuit in which the verdict was given against Macready who had to pay £200 damages. His remorse continues day after day for weeks after the incident. But it is remorse at his own loss of self-possession, not at the injury done to Bunn. Whenever Bunn's name occurs in the rest of the diary, he is invariably referred to in the most violent language.

For his fellow-actors, with whom he has continual altercations, he hardly spares a generous word. He refers to nearly all of them in disparaging terms, partly out of irritation, but partly, too, out of jealousy:

Kean's death scarcely awoke a passing thought; he has lived his own choice of life; even his very indecencies have found eulogists, as the worst parts of (often admirable) acting have had loud-throated admirers.

(Fanny Kemble) I think her a shallow instead of a clever imposter.

(As Lady Macbeth) was occasionally disconcerted by this monstrous pretender to theatrical art who to me is most unnatural and bad. I do know her effect on the audience but cannot think it good.

I cannot believe that the sense of the audience could be in favour of paying a compliment to the worst among the leading actors of the play and for such a miserable performance as is the Mark Antony of Mr. C. Kemble.

So he refused to respond to the call of the audience because Kemble was called before him.

Poole called, and in the course of conversation alluded to some persons talking of myself and Mr. C. Kean as actors!!! Now really it is almost an excuse for expatriation, for anything in the shape of escape short of suicide, to think that one has lived and *had a mind* and *used* it for so many years to be *mentioned* at last in the same breath with Mr. C. Kean! Particularly offensive!

Charles Mathews, Helen Faucit and others are mentioned in the same way. But his fellow-actors come off cheap as compared with his critics. Writers in *The Times* and other papers exasperate him beyond measure. No doubt on reflection he would in many cases have written differently, but as a real diarist he is spontaneously recording the angry impressions of the moment. But the atmosphere he thereby imparts to his diary of unceasing quarrelsome recrimination is exhausting for a reader. His touchiness and the ease with which he took offence is illustrated by a correspondence with C. Kean about a command performance at Windsor. The communication he describes in his diary as "most inane and senseless bluster" is reproduced by the Editor, in a note, and is a perfectly courteous, mild and dignified letter.

He had, however, good cause for annoyance during his American tour in 1849 when the American actor, Forrest, organized opposition against him. In addition to interruptions on one occasion, half the carcass of a dead sheep was thrown on the stage and in New York matters became so serious that, after chairs, eggs, fruit, etc., had been thrown on the stage, there was a riot, the military were called out and several lives were lost. Macready's long descriptions of these scenes are very graphic and dramatic and we can hardly blame him if his references to Americans subsequently are far from complimentary. He is obliged to leave America, and on his return home he has a command performance at Windsor and a great triumph at Birmingham which he describes very well:

Delighted—constantly did the thought, the sense of *delight* recurr to me—to find myself in *England*, to find myself under the security of law and order, and free from the brutal and beastly savages who sought my life in the United States. Thank God!

Rested. Thought much of my character of the night. Acted Macbeth—yes *well*. The audience, the Birmingham audience, gave me a reception such as I have never witnessed out of London, *very, very rarely even there*. They stood up all through the house, waving hats and handkerchiefs, till I was anxious to proceed. I thought to myself "Will I not act for you!" The stillness—the rigid stillness that followed—every word ringing on the ear—was really awful, but I felt it was my last night of Macbeth in Birmingham, and I resolved to *do my best. I did.* The applause was fervent, the attention deep, and the reception when I was called on, equal to the first appearance. And the conceited prigs of America talk of the education of their *masses*—the dancing bears! They are *brutes and savages* compared with the galleries of our manufacturing towns.

Macready was a great Radical and in his constant references to politics, royalty and the aristocracy, with whom he is always " disgusted," he often lets himself go in just the same characteristic way :

Sent to the theatre about the rehearsal, and after looking at the newspaper to ascertain the state of the Kings health—what an absurdity that the natural ailments of an old and ungifted man should cause so much perplexity and annoyance !—went to the Haymarket and rehearsed, with some care, Othello.

The Morning Post mentioned as a marvel that the Duke of Nemours " was exposed to a raging sea for nearly twelve hours, and we understand was seasick nearly the whole voyage ! " Mighty Heaven ! would it not be better that the Duke of Nemours, and all the fools and sycophants that make up their mob of idolaters were buried fathoms below the surface, rather than that the reason which God has given man should be prostituted and abased to such vile purpose as communicating or reading such disgusting absurdity ?

Looked at the newspaper and thought what a world of utter deceit, delusion and falsehood it is. Great God ! where is there truth ?—where will it be found on earth ? *It never will.* The world is one great lie. Bishops, statesmen, lawyers, soldiers, lords, chartists, all unworthy to be *men*—I sicken at the contemplation.

Read a paragraph of Peel on his knees at prayer ! ! Let him do right and justice to his fellow men and then *stand up and thank God.*

(at the House of Commons) I sat from six till twelve o'clock listening to the vilest stuff and poorest trash of words that ever dulled or tormented the ear of man . . . weary and disgusted I returned home about one o'clock.

On political matters I have been thinking much, and I think I see, and with true and deep regret, reasons for apprehending the decline of English greatness. It is in our Government. I really wish now to divest myself of passion and of prejudice. The Government of *a* class must be selfish—a part for the whole must have an interest in maintaining its ascendancy.

Disraeli, " miserable *soi-disant* Christian," " mountebank," etc., makes his " gorge rise." He not unnaturally refers to Louis Philippe as " a shabby dog " when he discovers that the gold jewelled dagger with which he had been presented in Paris was only gilt and the jewels were sham.

With authors and playwrights he is much more tolerant and considerate. He is sorely tried by Browning, of whom he has not a high opinion. Bulwer Lytton he is thrown with a great deal. But from the day in 1837 when he notes in his diary " Forster came into my room with a gentleman whom he introduced as Dickens, alias Boz—I was glad to see him " his references to his great friendship with Dickens are always filled with warmth and affection.

It would be a mistake to suppose that Macready was never anything else but harsh and truculent. He was exceptionally domestic and very many of his entries are concerned with the enjoyment of his family life at Elstree and elsewhere and appreciations of the country. The loss of one of his children causes him the acutest anguish and he makes an annual reference to the child for many years afterwards. The rehearsals for the first performance of *Money* coincide with the severe illness of a child and his distraction and preoccupation in the two different directions is brought home to one in the daily entries. Like Byron and Haydon, the last thing he wanted was for any of his children to follow their father's profession. He expresses the fear " lest they should imbibe a liking for the wretched art which I have been wasting my life upon. God forbid."

He reads a great deal and often with pleasure both classical and contemporary authors. When *Vanity Fair* appears he reads it in two or three days and ends his criticism with the following comment:

> . . . the book is an extraordinarily clever one, and, differing in its kind, is second to none of the present day, which is an admission I make almost grudgingly for Dickens' sake ; but the truth is the truth.

Of his health he complains very little, although he is occasionally tired and off colour when he acts. This reference to a tooth is like a comment on one of his colleagues :

> A paroxysm of pain with this treacherous tooth—an old ally turned corrupt and traitorous.

In the course of his travels in the provinces and abroad he sometimes falls on stock companies which are very inferior and on audiences which are bad. As may be imagined, he expresses himself freely on both subjects :

> (Dublin) It is not fancy or humour that makes me assert it, but my work is heavier here than in any other theatre in which I have been. The actors are *so bad*—so very bad—my friend Calcroft so inexcusably bad, the stage manager so utterly—utterly incompetent,

that I am in despair ; the time and suffering a rehearsal costs me is only equalled or exceeded in acting.

Several accounts are given of women falling in love with him. He wards them off kindly and successfully. In these entries there is no vestige of conceit. They display the genuine embarrassment of a high-minded man who realizes the temptations to which he is subjected, but in his devotion to his wife and family finds a strong bulwark against any moral catastrophe. His depression at the " disgusting world " are frequent and while devoted to his art he loathes and detests all its surroundings. He only goes on with it in order to make sufficient money to be independent. When not under his own management, he notes getting £100 a week and later £120 for three performances a week. In 1844, although only fifty-one, he begins to note that he is " far advanced in life," and in 1849 " For the first time I saw in the glass today that I really am an old man." He definitely retired in 1851, at the age of fifty-eight, and gives a full description of his last performance and Farewell to the Stage.

Like many regular diarists Macready often makes reflections either on his birthday or at the end of each year, sometimes accompanied by prayer. Two instances will suffice :

1835. Dec. 31. The year is gone, and with it much of happiness, of care and fear ; I am so much older, and lament to say not much better, not much wiser. Let me offer up prayer to God Almighty, who thus far has protected me and mine, to continue His gracious blessings on the dear heads of my beloved family, and to grant me health and energy to make them worthy disciples of Jesus Christ and happy denizens of this our mortal state. Amen.

1848. Dec. 31. A year of awful, stirring, fearful and afflicting events is this day brought to a close. Many friends, some most dear, and one among the very dearest, have been taken from earth, and I have been taught to feel the truth of my own mortality. The income granted to me has been very great, but the expense of the year has been great in proportion and I have not added so large an amount to my capital as I could have wished. For all, however, I am most thankful, most grateful, O God, and bow down my heart in earnest and devout acknowledgement of Thy mercy to me.

In conclusion, in order to illustrate more fully his style, three complete entries may be given :

After rehearsal went to Garrick Club, where Captain Williams, Fladgate and Mr. T. Hook were in the room—the latter saluted me and advanced with one finger; I met him with one finger and he perceived that I was not disposed to acknowledge his title to be impertinent, for he soon took Captain Williams upstairs. He is an object of disgust—physically and morally—a puffed out mountebank. Went to theatre and acted Lord Townley in a very mediocre manner, occasionally with spirit but with an utter absence of finish and high deportment. Spoke to Cooper on hearing of its intended repetition on Saturday and told him that I could not do Othello on Wednesday if my time were thus taken from me.

Called on Dickens and gave him Darley's first copy of *Ethelston*. We walked out, called on Rogers ; I told him that Chantry was to see him and mentioned the proposal of my setting the subscription on foot ; he readily approved all. Asked Dickens to spare the life of Nell in his story (*Master Humphrey's Clock*) and observed that he was cruel. He blushed and men who blush are said to be either proud or cruel ; he is not proud and therefore—or as Dickens added the axiom is false. He invited me to dine on Sunday sennight.

Rehearsed *Every one has his fault*. Incessant business until nearly half past four o'clock. I was fearful I should not have command of the words of my part. Note from Sir H. Wheatley wishing to see me about the Queen's box. Read over *Harmony*. Acted it tolerably well. Was not known by the audience at first. Called for and well received. The play seemed to have made an agreeable impression, about which I was very anxious as being a comedy. Mrs. Carlyle was in Catherine's box and very pleased to see me.

Macready lived for thirty-three years after the close of his professional career when the diary ends. His residence as a country gentleman at Sherborne was not very successful, but in the last ten years he married again, settled at Cheltenham and had a calm and peaceful close to his life.

The diary was probably not written for publication, but it was certainly written to be read. However, the daily diarist who lets himself go often forgets to visualize any eventual reader. If Macready's diary cannot be classed among the very best, it is not because of his method or his style, but because of the limitations of his own personality. For this very reason, however, it ranks high as a human document, because whether you like it or whether you do not, it is Macready the man, to the life.

The two volumes, edited by William Toynbee, were published in 1912.

## MISS J.

THE correspondence of the Duke of Wellington with Miss J. was first published in New York. In 1889 it appeared in London. The authenticity of the letters was at once challenged and most people regarded them as an ingenious forgery and a hoax. Ten years later Sir Herbert Maxwell, the author of the *Life of Wellington*, declared that there was not a shadow of doubt that they were genuine. He had found and examined the original letters and also the diary of Miss J. A new edition of the correspondence was published in 1924, with an introduction by Mr. W. R. H. Trowbridge, who refers to Miss J.'s diary as having been " so to speak, the key to the cipher."

It is necessary to make these preliminary statements, otherwise many may still believe that this amazing correspondence is a work of fiction, and Miss J. a creature of the imagination of Mrs. C. T. Herrick, who was responsible for the editing and publishing of the book. Of course the correspondence, not the diary, is the sensational part of the published book.

The Duke's letters must be read in order that this extraordinary episode in his life may be fully appreciated. Neither Miss J.'s letters nor indeed her diary entries would have the smallest value were it not for the personality and position of her correspondent. There is, however, a certain psychological value in the confessions of the person who was instrumental in throwing a peculiar sidelight on the personality of a man who was more prominently in the public eye than any of his contemporaries.

The bald fact to be borne in mind is that the Duke of Wellington at the age of sixty-five began a correspondence with an entirely unknown young lady called Miss Jenkins, and kept it up with breaks and intervals for seventeen years.

We must desist from entering into any disquisition on the Duke's views with regard to women, and the correspondence itself, entertaining as it is, cannot be quoted here, although Miss J. copied most of it into her diary. It is with the diary itself that we are concerned. This was kept by Miss J. in a locked book from a very early age. She was a very beautiful young woman of twenty, of good English family and well educated. But she was also a religious zealot fanatically anxious for the conversion of those about her. An early love affair, about which she writes, came to nothing, as she could have nothing to do with one who had "never known a new birth unto righteousness." She undertook work quite after her own heart, which was visiting prisoners, and of this she gives some account in her diary.

But she was always looking out for new fields for conversion and at last her attention was drawn to the Duke of Wellington. She wrote her first letter to him on January 15, 1834, when he was sixty-five years old, and had been a widower for three years. Her first interview with him, after sending him a Bible, took place in November of the same year. She only notes the bare facts in her diary. She was dressed in an "old *turned* dark green merino gown, *daily* worn," and after reading a passage from the Bible to the Duke, he exclaimed, "Oh *how* I *love* you," and then appeared struck dumb. She writes up the incident more elaborately at a later date. The following month the Duke called on her and this is the account she gives of the visit in her diary:

During the next visit from the Duke he exclaimed, speaking of his feeling for me, 'This must be for life!' twice over successively. He then asked me if I felt sufficient for him to be with him a whole life, to which I replied: 'If it be the will of God.' I observed much excitement about him, and he in a very hurried manner told me that he was going on a visit to the King. This led me to reply, 'I wish you were going on a visit to The King,' which he evidently interpreted to mean The King of kings. He left me hastily, saying he purposed returning in a short time. In the interim I locked my door and knelt down, beseeching God to be with me and protect me, showing me what He would have me do under such marvellous circumstances. Forgetting that the door was fastened, I was obliged on the Duke's return to explain wherefore, stating that it is written, 'When thou hast shut thy door, pray to thy Father which is in secret, and thy Father which seeth in secret shall reward thee openly;' adding,

'Therefore I locked the door when you were gone, Your Grace, to kneel down and ask God to take care of me.' On hearing this his eyes dropped, but he said nothing. On his asking me why I had not written to him during his absence from town, I replied, 'Because God would not let me;' when his eyes again fell, and he was silent.

This led subsequently to a tiff. She became enraged at the idea that the Duke was trifling with her. She asserts openly in several places in her diary that she believed it to be the will of God that she should become the wife of the Duke. "I should have considered, I conferred as high an honour on the Duke in bestowing my hand as he would in receiving it, of which he was well aware." In fact, Miss J. developed a grand passion founded on "the glory of God," and her friends declared that never, till the Duke's death, did she resign hope of becoming Duchess of Wellington. The Duke's attitude is more difficult to understand. What must have been at first simply a flirtation with a pretty girl was continued for so long and in such extraordinary circumstances. For instance, a series of entries in September, 1835, show them in constant intercourse, and such intercourse!

I have been here (in London) nearly a fortnight, yet have seen the Duke only twice, but receive letters daily,—and last night a particularly kind one. I have been expecting him, but he comes not, being so occupied with his Parliamentary business. What can I say to such things but this,—'Shall not the Judge of all the earth do right?' and, 'Has HE not a right to do what HE will with His own?'

September 10th. I wrote to the Duke to-day and hope the Lord will permit him to receive and answer it kindly. The Subject on which I addressed him was on Christ becoming sin for us and bearing the wrath of the Father. O Lord, I pray Thee, have mercy upon his precious soul!

September 14th. I shall have been here three weeks tomorrow, during which I have seen the Duke four times, and will just allude to the subjects introduced during each visit.

The first brought with it remarks on True Nobility, obliging me to declare it is to be found only in Christ and His Righteousness in man. I mentioned what St. Paul said when contrasting the Bereans with the Thessalonians, namely, 'These were more Noble than those in Thessalonica in that they received the word with all readiness of mind, and searched the Scriptures Daily, whether these things were so.'

During the second visit, I read to him the 49th Psalm and particularly called his attention to the last verse thereof thus written—'Man that is in honour and understandeth not, is like the beasts that perish,' reminding him they were God's Words.

During his third visit I told him I should like to be hated of all men for Christ's sake! and during his fourth and last that he did not believe Christ to be The Son of God! since which I have written to him daily and the first reply I receive is one calculated to produce another check to my feelings, all of which I give up entirely to the Lord, imploring Him to govern and actuate them just as HE sees His own honor and glory require, causing me to make nothing a consideration in comparison therewith.

The next quarrel arose out of the fact that the Duke used a *plain* seal on his letters, which she regarded as a want of respect, and she discusses at great length in her diary whether she shall return all the Duke's letters. For a while the correspondence ceases.

My disinclination to write to the Duke continues. O may the Lord bless him by quickening his dead soul and call him forth to glorify Him mightily for Christ's sake.

But she soon begins again and encloses a poem. The correspondence continues and we find the entry at the end of the year after a summary of the various letters:

Letters received from the Duke during the year 1835. SEVENTY EIGHT.

The Duke finds Miss J.'s handwriting difficult to read. Of course she is offended, although she confesses to her diary that her pen could not keep pace with her feelings. At the end of the year the Duke comes to see her and talks "without any reference to God's holy will" and when she asks after his knee which he had hurt:

he appeared delighted, brushing up his chair nearer to me which of course met with the withdrawal on my part *due* to *Christianity*.

The score for 1836 is entered as "56 letters." There is a drop in the following year to fifteen, during which period they communicate with one another in the third person. And again to eight in 1839. Then comes a long silence lasting from August, 1840 to June, 1844. Here was an opportunity for the Duke to drop the correspondence, but Miss J. tells us:

> The Duke's last letter had decidedly declared he would write no more, and his character is too well known by the World for such to conclude he would not act up to his word and determination. But since 'It is written "The King's Heart is in the Hands of the Lord as the rivers of water, He turneth it which way soever he pleaseth," so likewise ALL hearts. Consequently when The Lord's time came for proving to him the folly of forming such a rash resolution, he writes accordingly, and that too at a moment when I least expected it, so long a period having elapsed in silence. Nor do I, as he therein specifies, recollect requesting him to answer that any more than other letters from time to time forwarded as the Lord condescendingly influenced me, however solicitous I was for their safety. I continued to hope that their contents would eventually be permitted to lead him to feel the emptiness and nothingness of all earthly grandeur, in comparison with the enjoyment of a Crown of Glory.

And the correspondence continues as regularly as ever, the Duke good-natured though sometimes rather abrupt, Miss J. never realizing for a moment the duties, position, and enormous correspondence, of the object of her adoration. But in 1846 comes a serious misunderstanding on the subject of "a loan." The diary entry shows how offended she is:

> Friday, September 26th, 1846. O my God, Wherefore hast Thou thought proper to let Satan try and distress me in this unanticipated manner?
>
> I did not ask Thee to bestow the Duke upon me! I did not think of ever writing to him until Thou madest me do so! and therefore I marvel at his being allowed to torture me first in one way and then in another for the last twelve years of my life, and above all by what he has now so insultingly done in pretending to think that I have written to him for a Loan, which Thou knowest, for Thy honor and glory I would not do under existing circumstances, for a thousand worlds!

The Commander-in-Chief of the British army, the most famous soldier in Europe and an ex-Prime Minister, was now subjected at the age of seventy-seven to a series of indignant epistles from this fanatical young lady and *he answered her*. Her indignation boils over in her diary:

> I have written another indignant letter to the Duke, in which I purpose enclosing his hair and picture, which last being made of sealing wax is of course of no value. These being the only things ever received or required by me, I am solicitous to relieve myself from the

burthen they necessarily become under present circumstances. Consequently, after considering or reflecting that it may perhaps be more for the honor and glory of God to return them in silence, I have enclosed them in two blank covers, waiting now only to ascertain their weight in order that they may be stamped accordingly and reach him in safety.

They make it up, but in 1848 the correspondence on the Duke's side falls to three letters. During Miss J.'s illness the Duke writes kindly to her, but there are more rows over the Duke's offer of pecuniary assistance, and while his letters become less frequent, hers in length and number continue the same.

In February, 1851, she writes in her diary:

I have been pondering over the account given in the Times paper of this day wherein the Queen's visit to the House of Peers is noticed and among other things the following remark in reference to the Duke —' His Grace appeared to shrink from the attention and respect of which he was the object.'—This induced me to marvel whether The Great Lord of Lords has not at length begun to exercise His Godly Power over his precious soul, making him consequently feel the nothingness of all things in comparison therewith!

His last letter is dated March 10, 1851, and brings up the final score to the incredible number of 390. Miss J. gives the following account of her reception of the news of his death:

November 28th, 1852. I dare not trust my pen to refer to the unanticipated dreaded end which has caused me so much deep sorrow although nearly three long months have rolled over my head since that awful blow was given and which, had it not been for divine support would I fear have deprived me of my reason, for it was so unexpected that when my Physician called to acquaint me thereof, I said, pointing to a letter on the table: ' That is for the Duke,' intending to ask him to put it into a Post Office, being sealed and ready.

On perceiving my doctor silent, instead of offering with his usual kindness to post the letter, I enquired wherefore? he replied that he thought it had better be postponed. This made me still more anxious, eagerly asking, if he were ill? when Dr. P. said he had not been well, and thus by degrees unfolded the awful truth that he was indeed No more.

O I can never forget my feelings! continuing after his departure as if riveted to my seat and speechless.

To the end she is uncertain that the Duke had known a "new birth" but hopes that even at this the eleventh hour his precious soul may through a Saviour's righteousness have been permitted to wing its flight to Mansions of eternal glory.

Miss J., we are told, became more bigoted as she grew older and even her sister found it impossible to live with her. She died in New York in 1862.

# FORD MADOX BROWN

BIOGRAPHERS devote a great part of their books to an estimate and criticism of the achievements of the persons whose lives they are writing. In the case of the creative arts, books, pictures and compositions can be examined in order to illustrate not only the genius and talent but the personality of the artist ; and letters and impressions from friends help to fill in the details of the portrait. When there is a diary which can be quoted an entirely different and very valuable element is introduced which immediately brings us much closer to the subject and makes that which may often run the risk of being an elaborately dressed lay figure into a living person. Of course the diary must be more than dry memoranda of engagements for it to be worth introducing at all. But if it chances to be a good one, it becomes for those who are seeking the man or the woman the most interesting part of the book.

The extracts from Ford Madox Brown's diary are not all contained in one book. Only a few after 1856 are given in the biography by his grandson, Ford M. Hueffer, and the earlier quotations, which are the best, are published in W. M. Rossetti's *Pre-Raphaelite Diaries and Letters.* What we get of the diary, cut, trimmed and incomplete though it be, gives us something of Ford Madox Brown which we could not extract from his pictures or from his association with the Pre-Raphaelite movement.

In early years he was certainly a fresh, very natural writer whose chief motive would seem to have been a desire to keep a record of his work. There is a natural spontaneity and unconventionality in the style which is particularly attractive. Brown, who was born in 1821, married at an early age, and after living in Paris for a while, came to England in 1844 and took a studio in the Campden Hill district. He begins his diary in 1847 very deliberately. After a long description of a picture he is working at he ends his first entry, "I have long intended beginning this journal; praised be God it is begun at last." An entry seven years later, on beginning a fresh volume, shows what importance he attached to diary writing:

I hope I shall keep this one more regularly up than hitherto. Having now recommenced I must be in earnest one would think, after such a pause. Should everyone keep a record of his daily acts and sentiments, the history of the world would be made out in a way no historian could distort. However illiberal or enthusiastic in his nature, however stupid a man might be, could he be persuaded to set down what he thought and did, something would accrue from it.

And a passage in one of his entries in 1857 shows how accurately he recognized both the peculiar value and at the same time the limitations of a diary:

What I am now writing wants the freshness and force of incidents noted down diurnally while at the same time it is too hasty and careless to be readable history.

Yet, like so many diarists, he sometimes has misgivings as to the why and wherefore of his writing. "Emma has just gone to bed and I am writing God knows to what purpose (but vanity)." At any rate he went on with it for at least eleven years with long breaks and short breaks, writing often daily and regularly, describing in detail his work, his mood, his opinions and the most trivial incidents, sometimes in a few lines, at other times in a page or more. This is quite a different form of diary writing from the punctually kept daily memoranda inserted in the ruled spaces of a printed diary book and of course it is infinitely better from a reader's point of view. He writes not from habit or from discipline, but from inclination—when the spirit moves him—and one is glad the spirit moves him so often.

A few consecutive entries in the first year will illustrate his absence of restraint and easy natural style:

1847. Got up at seven worked pretty well all day. The Lucys come in and in the night the rats ran away with a mutton chop—could find no trace of it, not even the satisfaction of seeing the bone.

Got up late—painted till five. . . . Find that when I have painted some hours, I get tired and cannot see the colour, but can see the shape. Memo, ought not to paint too long if I want to do good.

Got up early—and got to work late. Fumbled till twelve o'clock over the hood of the left-hand corner figure of the knight; made a liripipe for it. About twelve set to work at a small drawing, had not finished it by dusk. Am a very swine—shall never get the painting done in time—am a beast and a sleepy brute.

Brown's first wife died before he began keeping a diary. Her death was a great blow to the young man, but in retrospect he does not allow himself to indulge in morbid ruminations. " These are thoughts that I must banish; it unnerves me," he writes, and except for noting an occasional visit to the cemetery he says no more. In 1849 he married the daughter of a farmer, Emma Hill, who remained with him till within five years of his own death, which occurred in 1893. There is a gap of six months in his diary at the time of his second marriage, but when he resumes writing he makes a long retrospect with regard to his work, but says nothing of his marriage.

The salient feature in the early life of Ford Madox Brown is his bitter struggle with poverty, not just want of comforts, but actually want of sufficient food. He works till he almost drops, and very naturally at times he is overcome with depression, but his good nature, his buoyancy and his sense of humour carry him along and carry him through. A series of entries may be given in 1854 and 1855 which show the artist continually struggling for a few shillings:

Terribly warm, could do nothing after I came back headachy and feeble. . . . After dinner no work; stupid and lazy—unwell and disgusted. . . . Funds reduced to £1. 9s. 6d.

Off to the field; rain; worked about one hour and a half under an umbrella, at the swedes. Rain drove me off; came home and dined. At half past three prepared all our plate (six teaspoons) all the jewelry, my watch, opera-glasses and bronzes, to take into London to the pawnbrokers. Stayed unconsciously too long at dinner. After dinner it rained so furiously that I hestitated, and finally remitted the expedition so I have the pleasant task for the morning. Funds reduced to three shillings and two more that Lucy has left behind.

Walked into London. Raised £11; bought Lucy some things and self a pair of shoes.

Today one of fearful idleness self abasement and disgust. Emma got up ; I went down to breakfast with her, unwashed and only half dressed. I intended working at the coat, then walking to Hampstead to purchase flannel for Emma and babyclothes. I sat down to write to Gabriel (Dante Gabriel Rossetti) a few lines about his calf, and like an ass must write in verse—bad rhymes. Spent till one o'clock and lunched—still unwashed—then read the paper—still unwashed till half past four " Oh that it should be so ! " Then dressed and took Katty out—then we dined—then read the paper to Emma ; the dear is poorly and nervous. This is the true and particular history of a day —a piteous thing to tell.

A complete blank. Have done nothing all day but sit by the fire with Emma and try to think of ways towards means, ineffectual. Could think of anything else but that ; romped with Katty. A pitiable day.

A day without work, however, was a very rare occurrence. He generally worked at least 5 hours and 10 to 12 and even 15 and 18 are recorded.

Reflected seriously on my money position. Found I should have four weeks money and the same credit ; after which something must be done if White (the dealer) does not come.

Some sort of tin tumbling in and the old saying of an ill wind very truly exemplified (five hours).

After dinner tried to think of ways towards means ; could not think of anything else—fell asleep. No decision as yet : £8 left (two and a half hours).

Made up my mind to make up a parcel of Emma's shawl, some papier maché ornaments, and two engravings after Claude with the large *Shipwreck* of Turner to send by the carrier to old Williams to-morrow, for him to pledge, if we do not have a letter with Ritchie's money before the carrier calls. Something must be done as there is only $3^s$ $3^d$ in hand and Emma about to be confined. . . . I am getting a regular Hayden at pawning. So long as I do not become one at cheating my crediters, it matters little. God help us. I see nothing but ruin by progressive stages. No work today.

I did the cradle and painted at the cloth but it looked wrong. Dreadfully nervous. Anxiety about immediate money-wants and the melancholy prospects of future ruin, I suppose cause it ; but I do not *much* worry about it neither, only when I wake up in the morning I feel it rather. Emma is very well and the boy getting fat. Funds £3.2 nearly all owing.

Got Seddon's £50. . . . Heard that Windus had bought four of my pictures from White; the cunning old rogue never told me this. I consider this may save me from going to India.

Here is one of a series of days of overwork:

Got up at six, to work by seven. Till ten at the shoes of Gower and the steps; from half past ten till half past one at the head of Wiclif from Krone; eyes so dizzy obliged to leave off. Went for a walk bathed my eyes; began again at three till six—not the thing. Dined went to sleep. Mr and Mrs Lucy called in. Set to work at ten at one of the cinqfoil ornaments. Have not finished it, twelve o'clock; must finish it before I go to bed—finished it by one (twelve and a half hours).

He must have had his diary by him as he worked. The occupations which keep him from his work are sometimes amusing, sometimes trying:

Wasted one and a half hours cleaning a damned pipe.

Cleaned the dog and shaved his head and paws.

Tooth all day.

Painted lilac leaves till four o'clock dinner, then toothache on the sofa till six then work till seven and toothache drove me in.

We get a full description of his work on each picture, the doubts and misgivings, the alterations, the enthusiasm and the prodigious amount of work. Here is a day in which, in spite of interruptions, he is at work on two pictures:

To church with Lucy; then worked at Peter's green mantle improving the colour, for since 1851–2 I have improved at that, but Hunt and Woolner and William came in and stopped me. They went off to Browning's and Hunt stayed and told me about the B—— of Jerusalem who seems to be one of the meanest scoundrels not yet in h——; then about his sale of the *Scapegoat* to White for 450 guineas at three months' date. . . . Painted at Peter's Cloak till dinner then the leaves. At eight last night I set to work on the proof of Dalziel's Prisoner of Chillon and worked till three at it.

It is noticeable that whenever he refers to colleague Pre-Raphaelites, Millais, Holman Hunt or Rossetti, so far from there being an atom of jealousy in his remarks, he has nothing but unmeasured praise and appreciation of their work. He constantly refers to the beauty he sees in nature, but he makes this reflection:

How despairing it is to view the loveliness of nature towards sunset and know the impossibility of imitating it !—at least in a satisfactory manner as one could do, would it only remain so long enough. Then one feels the want of a life's study, such as Turner devoted to landscape ; and even then what a botch is any attempt to render it ! What wonderful effects I have seen this evening in the hayfields ! the warmth of the uncut grass, the greeny grayness of the unmade hay in furrows or tufts with lovely violet shadows and long shades of the trees thrown athwart all and melting away one tint into another imperceptibly ; and one moment more a cloud passes and all the magic is gone. Begin tomorrow morning, all is changed ; the hay and the reapers are gone most likely, the sun too or if not it is in quite the opposite quarter and all that *was* loveliest is all that is tamest now, alas ! It is better to be a poet ; still better a mere lover of nature, one who never dreams of possession.

He describes going off to try and sell some of his pictures.

Packed my five pictures in a cart and at 10 a.m. started on my way to London down the new Finchley Road—I driving because it was too heavy to sit both in front and perched up behind was anything but comfort. However the pony being a mettlesome beast, had no idea of going unless his own master thrashed him and seemed to despise my attempts in that line ; so we had to change seats. It is Barnet fair and we were taken for return Showmen on the road.

This expedition (in 1855) was more or less successful, as he got £150 for one of the pictures. Of domestic details there are plenty, including a full account of trouble with a maid. His son, who was born in 1855, arrived when he was in rather straitened circumstances.

This morning at half past 12 a.m. dearest Emma was delivered of a son, my first. He is very red, a large nose, eyes and shape of face like a Calmuck Tartar, shape of head like a Bosjesman. . . . Emma, dearest, pretty well feverish. Thank heaven it is comfortably over. The surgeon . . . turned out a very pleasant clever fellow well informed and this was because he was a Scotchman ; knew all about my grandfather (Dr John Brown) says his doctrine is every year coming more into practice. A cheque from Ritchie come for £9 and I went and paid the butcher and baker and got a bottle of whiskey. Today sent money to get the clothes and pictures back ; item to Emma's mother in arrears : net result £1. 16 in pocket. Shoes leaky.

There is one account of a serious misunderstanding with his wife, which covers four entries :

Emma began the day with quarrelling.

Emma started off to London this morning without letting me know before I was up.

As Emma was still not returned, I wrote a letter to her the answer to which our fate seems now to hinge on. I am writing I don't know what scarce, because the moment is heavy with dread thoughts and I must occupy myself. When I was young a disappointment in painting used to give me a dreadful pain in my throat; now other miseries take the place of these, and the nervous system feels most acutely about the heart and chest—no pain is like this. What would become of my children if I were to finish my wretched existence and what is to become of me if I do not. O God! have mercy on me and save me.

Emma gives in so we are all happy again. Thanks to God if He did it.

His brother artists are of course frequently mentioned, more especially Rossetti, of whom he often speaks with warmth from the day on which he first mentions him in 1848 as "my pupil":

Really Gabriello seems bent on making my fortune at one blow. Never did fellow, I think bestir himself for a rival before; it is very good and very great to act so. Ever since he felt he had hurt me some little time ago he has done nothing but keep on making amends to me, one after another.

When the diary leaves off he is talking of a hundred guineas and even four hundred guineas for his pictures. He was launched. In later years and in his old age, his grandson tells us, he retained his same *naïveté* and his zest for living. His early experiences left a deep impression on him and he was always anxious to help and encourage struggling workers. "Of his open-handed unconsidered charity," says his biographer, "I have already spoken; in no case could any terms exaggerate this side of his character. With open eyes he would assist people who had again and again imposed upon him, having constantly in his mind the thought that however unneedful his help before had been, it might now be really needed."

Both the illusive beauty of his successful pictures such as *Jesus washing Peter's Feet* or *The Last of England* and the rather laboured unconventionality of some of his other works might well give one the impression of a precious learned elaborate personality. But his diary, even more than his letters, shows him as he really was, entirely without pose, very human, rash, impetuous, enthusiastic and charming. He wrote without a second of premeditation, with curious grammar and at times using words wrongly (as, for instance, more than once he writes *seriatim* for seriously). But his lack of intention and forethought is one of the factors which makes his diary a good one.

William Rossetti also kept a diary, extracts from which (1862–1870) are quoted in *Rossetti Papers*, published by him in 1903. It is a purely objective journal describing the intellectual and artistic pursuits of his brother, Christina Rossetti and himself, with notes of travel.

## CHARLES RUSSELL

A COMMENT was made in the Introduction to *English Diaries* with regard to the fact that diaries in the past have been comparatively few, as they were confined to the educated or literate class. But it was also remarked that ability to write, that is to say, form letters with a pen, was the only prerequisite of diary writing; further equipment was superfluous. No diary of a professional manual worker, however, was discoverable at that time. The effort of writing acts as a deterrent for anyone who is not in the way of using a pen since he left the elementary school.

This omission, however, can now be rectified by the inclusion of the diary of a foreman riveter. Charles Russell was employed on the Uganda Railway from August, 1898 to October, 1901. We are told in the preface to the diary, which was privately printed, that he was a typical Cockney and a remarkably good workman. After his departure the diary was found amongst other papers in the tin shanty in which he had lived. It covers the short period from June 29 to August 1, 1898, that is to say, just before he took up his work on the Uganda Railway. It was written on many kinds of paper, sometimes in pencil, sometimes in ink of varying colours and qualities, and each day has its entry.

One might suppose that Charles Russell intended it for some one with whom he was corresponding at home but never despatched it. The style is epistolary and he seems to be addressing some one when at the end of some entries he writes "Good Night" and uses expressions such as "I can tell you." But that some one was perhaps only the shadowy unknown being whom all diarists address,

The probability is that in the uncertain period before he got regular work it amused him to write down all his experiences and defective spelling and grammar offered no obstacle. At the same time he must have been able to write easily and quickly, as no laboured effort interferes with the flow in which lively dialogue often finds a place.

As a human document this diary is certainly without any parallel. In the graphic outspoken entries which run on without any stops to speak of, Russell may be unconsciously humorous, but he is also intentionally comic in his Cockney way.

In the first half of the first entry he compares Beira as he finds it with Beira as he knew it six years before and he then falls into a detailed account of the events of the day. He gets a job under a boiler-maker, but he is very uncomfortable:

6 of us in One Room A Room about 16 Ft. by 18 Ft. and no bed Clothes Only A Stretcher and one Dirty Rotton pillar and Water was that Brackish that you could Hardly wash Yourself. Comb and brush was out of the Question. At night Each Room was allowed half a candel, size 3″ and so the first Man that went To bed was sure To burn all the Candel and the Rest of the Chaps Had To go To bed in the Dark, as to the Food it was very Rough being Nearly all Tin stuff. There was always Plenty of Rice and Curry. Tea was simply Water and Milk and if there was Pastrey, you always wanted a Hammer and Chisel To Cut it Knife and Fork was no use, Bread was always a Week Old in Fact I always Got up From the Table more Hungary than when I sat Down so I was just about Full up with the Point Hotel.

He hates Beira and is "sick of seeing funerals every day of the week":

*Tuesday 5th.* Turned Out and Had Coffee and Went Down To The Yard and started the Men To Work. I Do not Feel very well somehow I Am Getting Damm sick of Beira something Tells me to clear out as soon as i can, every time I see a Funeral I keep on thinking that I shall be the Next. Now I Have Got a Great objection To Die in Beira this Makes my 4th Time in Beira, I Have Left safe the other 3 times Although I Have been in the Hospital 4 times with the Fever, But I Have Got over all right. it is a Very Nasty Fever To Have, You May Got on all right and you may Go under very Quick. Hospital Dues is £1–0–0 Per Day, and For the Doctor to Visit you in your own Place is £2–0–0 Per Visit Without Medicine, and I Recon I Have Had My Share of Fevers Doctors and Hospitals if I Never

Have Any More, so as soon as I can Get the Money Together I should Like To stop Up Till Next January, But if I am Going To Have the Fever before then I shall leave Beira as soon as I Get Better, anyhow it is no good thinking about that, But it is seeing Funerals Every day Makes you think about such things.

He quarrels with the engineer and throws up his job:

*Saturday 9th.* Had Coffee and Went and started the Men To work About 8 O'clock the Engineer and Boilermaker Came and Had a Look at the Work and Found Fault with the Rivits, But I Fully Expected that the Engineer Whould Tell the Men To Finish at 11 O'clock But He Turns Round To Me and started To Growl and God Damm it, I was not Going To stand and Let Him Curse me up Hills and Down Dales Before all the Men without shoveing in a Word or two, so I Done a Bit of Cockney swearing. But He did Not Like My way of swearing and so He Told me so, so I Gave him a bit of Uncle sams Lingo Guessing and God Damming Him From New York To Frisco But He did not like that Half as well as the Other I could see that. Well the up shot of it was I Told Him He was a God Damm B.F. and that I would Trouble Him For My Money on Monday First Thing, Put my Tools away and Gave the Keys To the Boilermaker and Went Back to the Hotel and Had a Bottle of Beer on the strength of the Pow-Wow.

He is recommended for a job with a Mr. Lind 23 miles off. He gives one or two technical entries about boiler repairing, but he cannot get enough to eat, and on this subject he enlarges in several long entries. Few people can write exactly as they talk, but Russell could. One entry may be given in full:

*Saturday 16th.* Turnes Out Hungary as the Devil been thinking all Night if I should Get anything to Eat. To Day Goes to the table and sit Down and wait For the Boss To Come and sit Down by and By His Girl Come and Told me not to wait but Have My Breakfast. But Damn Me there was Nothing To Eat Only Dry Bread and Tea. saw his Girl Take some Eggs and Toast in the House so I Waits thinking some was Coming my way, I must Have Been waiting about an Hour when the Girl Come and ask me what I was waiting for I says I am waiting for something To Eat so then Mr. bob Comes Out and says I was Not To sit all the Damn Day On Breakfast, But to see about Doing some work For the Money I was Getting. Well I thinks this is all Right so I has Breakfast of Dry stale Bread and a Cup of Tea and Goes To work 10 O'clock Mr. Lind comes and Wants To know what I am Doing of, Tells Him and away He Goes. 12 O'clock and the servant Comes and Tell me To Come To Dinner, washes my Hands and Goes To the Table and sits Down we Has salt Herrings and Bread there was Only 1 Herring on the Table so He Cut the Herring in Half, Gives me the Head Part and He Takes the Other, 2 Cups of Tea and that was Dinner, so I thinks if this is Dinner God send Tea as Quick as Hell Allows Him so up he Jumps and Goes in the House and away I Goes To My Room. Well about 3 o'clock Mr. Lind Comes Down to the Engine and began Working. By and By He says Oh ! Russell You Might Go up to the store Room and Get Me a few Copper Nails so up I Goes To the store Room and Oh ! Dear it Made Me Quite Hungary To see the Tins of stuff in Boxes and Shelves. Oh ! Damn it I says Here Goes I Going To Have some so I Collars a sack and Puts in a 2 lb Tin of Biscuits, Tin of Jam, 2 Tins Salmon, Tin of Milk and 2 Tins of Preserved Apples and Runs away To My Room and Plants them, Comes back Takes the Nails To Him and Gives Him the key of the store Room. By and By He knocks off and Tell me To Finish as soon as I Like so I Puts away the Tools and Goes to my room Have a wash and waits To be Called To tea. 6 O'clock servant Come and Calls me To Go To tea and away I Goes, it was just the same Old thing Over Again salt Herrings and Bread so I says To the Boss What's For Tea To Night, Can't you see He says Well I says You Not Going To stuff Me on Bread and Herrings so Trot something Out To Eat. with that He Glares at me and said if this is Not Good Enough For You its Good Enough For Me and You Gets nothing More at My House, Oh Well I says its Not Worth the Trouble of Comeing to the Table as there is Nothing To Eat on it and as I've Not Been used To this kind of Grub I'll Trouble You to send My meals to My room in future for I'm More Hungary when I Gets up than I was When I sat Down. Oh Lor I thought he was Going To Choke with Rage so I jumps up and was Going To My Room, He Calls the servant and Tells Her To send My Tea To My room Just what I wanted so she Brings the Jug of Tea some Bread and Fish To me. I sent her away and then I Haves A Feed. When she Comes again I sent back the Fish and Told Her to Tell the Boss I should like an Egg for Breakfast if He did not Mind so I has a smoke and Turns in. Fair sick and Tired of it.

His description of Mr. Lind's " Fancy woman " is a little too broad for reproduction. The food controversy continues. There is a real bit of Cockney sarcasm in his saying to " the Boss " " Many happy return of the day " when he sits down to breakfast. " What do you Mean he says Aint this Your Birthday No he says What Makes you think so ? Oh Nothing only I thought it was by the Breakfast you sent me."

Minnie, the maid, whom he refers to as " Miss Pretty " and " Darling," befriends him and gets food for him between meals. There is a very amusing entry describing how

Lind tells Minnie to make a hash for tea out of one potato and a small bit of salmon:

Bring the Tea Minnie He said On Come A Big Dish I thought Minnie Must Have something Very Nice so When the Cover was Lifted off I thought I should have Died with Laughing I Farley Roared Fancy A Big Dish and in the Middle was Just a spoonful of Hash What is this says Mr. Lind the Hash You Told me To Make a hash of What was Left From Dinner and I Made it. Well Bob Lind Look at the Poor Girl as if he was Going To Kill Her Oh well he says there is not Much any How, Well says Minnie What Can You Expect Out of one Potato and A spoonful of salmond, Well Well we shall have To Make it Do, Russell Help Yourself After You Mr. Lind I said, Nellie a small bit He says Just a small Wee Bit Bob she says Realey I am not Hungry at all. A small Bit Mrs Lind I said Do Have a small Bit I sure it Looks Very Nice I said, she Takes A Very small bit with Her Fork and He Passes the Dish On To Me. Oh Miss Minnie I says Whould You Mind Going To My Room and Fetching Me a Pair of spectacles What Do you want specks For says the Boss Well I Replied I shall be able To see What I am Eating and Make it Look twice as Large and then I shall Fancy I Have Had something For Tea, Oh Lor Oh Dear Dident He carry On I was Never satisfied With any think, anybody To Hear You Talk whould think you was being starved He carried on For about 10 Minutes so I said Well Mr. Lind I'll Toss You Who Have the Lot sudden Death or Best 2 out of three Well that upset His apple Cart altogether.

The food improves, but Russell does not restrain his sarcasm:

Had Dinner About 12, For A Wonder we Have Tin of Roast Mutton Potatoes and Beans and Bread and Jam so After Dinner I said To the Boss I supposed they Must Have Lost the Train or Else they would Have been Here By Now, Who Lost the Train, Why the Guests, What Guest He said, why those you Invited To Dinner, He says I Never Invited any body For Dinner No I says Do you mean To say that all thease things on the Table was Only Meant For us. Why it Must Have Cost Fully 2/– What we Have Eaten or a shilling at the Very least. Well I suppose we shall Make up For it During the Week by Living on Bread and water Why what's the Matter Boss You Look Bad and He Realey did He Looked as if he was Going to Have a Fit Up He jumps and Goes into the House Cursing and swearing Like mad, Well Minnie Does a Good Laugh and says I'd Better Get to work before he shoots You.

He leaves Mr. Lind and returns to Beira:

I Goes Back and says Good Night To the Boss and His Fancy

Woman, Kiss Minnie and Goes down To stop the Train as soon as she arrived, that was Not Long before she Came Along so I Puts My Box on Board and Away I Goes to Beira with My Checkue For 5£ in My Pocket and Out of Work Once Again. Well I Ought To Get on For I Do Try. at 10 o'clock we Arrived in Beira, Quarter Past 10 I stand Once More in the Point Hotel With About 7 Pounds 10/– and No Work I Don't Know What I'll shall do Now any How I Haves A Gin and Bitters and Turnes in. Good Night.

The remaining entries describe how he is advised to go to Mombasa, makes friends with "a German Chap," has some difficulty in squaring Clusserath, the hotel keeper, and finally is able to book a passage.

In this part we get the exciting uncertainty as to prospects which day to day writing alone can give. His funds are very low, but he just scrapes together enough for his passage. The inevitable gin and bitters not only before turning in, but in the morning, must have run away with pence if not shillings. At one moment he becomes very despondent:

Myself I was very Tired and Hungry and I Told Him I should wait For Him so I sat Down On on the Verandah of Martinie Henri Filled My Pipe and Has a smoke. I was feeling Just Like or Like the Man that was awaiting the Hangman's Nose To be Put Round His neck. How Long I was sitting Thinking Like this I Do Not know But I knew I Felt Damn Miserable and Lonley, Well as I said Before it is Not the first Time I Have Found in this Position But if I am Luckey Enough To Leave Beira and Get Round to Mombasa and Get Work I'll Turn Over a New leaf For the Better and show a certain Class of People What I am Made of, I'm Going To Have a Drink Now and Try and Drive these Mobid Thoughts Away.

There are a few entries at the end on board ship where he is far from comfortable:

The Admiral is a Very Dirty ship What with Cattle and Kaffirs We are Running Alive with Vermin There are 3 Portuguese Women Deck Passengers Poor Devils I Do Pity them They are Lying about the Decks Like sheep amongst The men, I think there should Be A screen Or a Proper Place separated from the men Well I cannot Help them so I'll Not think any more about them shall be Glad To Get off the ship, Good Night.

There is a philosophic vein in Russell and one can detect a certain grit and persistence in his outlook.

The diary is interesting because here we have a human

being without any equipment or diary model to copy instinctively impelled to write. Moreover, the little record is not only of psychological interest, but of literary interest. It shows how effective a narrative power can be unhampered by reading and by what we are pleased to call culture.

## WILFRID SCAWEN BLUNT

SOME of the diaries which have been kept in recent years have been rather severely criticized in the Introduction. Wilfrid Blunt's stands out as an exception. It is distinctly a good one. Two considerations prevent his record from having the highest value as a diary; it was written for publication and it was published in his lifetime, edited by himself. That he should have written with a view to publication can be accounted for by his love of controversy. This also explains his desire to publish while he could observe the effect of his remarks on readers. A diarist is never a good editor of his own diary, and as in this case the author was more intent on giving his views on public questions than on disclosing the more personal side of his life, he made his cuts to suit this purpose. Nevertheless, it is clear that there was much else in his diary than the discussion of political events, and edited though it is, we can see the man clearly enough. The chief merit of the diary rests on the fact that Wilfrid Blunt could write, and write very well—best indeed when he is not discoursing on public questions.

Son of a soldier and country gentleman, Wilfrid Blunt was born at Crabbet Park, Sussex, in 1840. He received his early education under the Jesuits, served for some years in the diplomatic service, travelled a great deal in the Near East, wrote several books and poems and made the chief interest of his life the espousal of the cause of Egyptian nationalism. He was a poet, a country gentleman, a breeder of Arab horses, painter, architect, sculptor and politician. He was a sympathizer with revolutions and a man of uncompromising views. As an amateur diplomatist he was frowned on by the official world, which considered him mischievous, but unlike many of those who occupy themselves with intrigue abroad, he was not negligible; he could not be ignored. By his knowledge and influence he had gained for himself a commanding position on Near Eastern affairs. Condemned, too, as a crank and faddist (draped as he was sometimes in Arab garments), he attracted many friends by the charm of his companionship and his literary enlightenment. We have not in Wilfrid Blunt the diarist, notebook in hand, seeking the company of celebrities in order to jot down their *bons mots*. We have a man who himself attracted the men of the day; they sought *his* company and he observed them, noted their foibles and wrote down what they said. We have not our friend the snob seeking out the aristocrats and listing their names even if he could get no word with them, but the aristocrat whose peculiarities and wide interests brought men and women of all calibres to his doorstep while he took stock of them.

Even edited, his diary is full of indiscretions; the views and conversations of men now living are noted in such a way as to excite the keenest protest. This he must have enjoyed. He may have known also that some about whom he is most indiscreet would not be sensitive enough to mind what he said. His estimates are often faulty. Like many another champion of a cause, he was taken in by some of the people who agreed with him, but he was broadminded enough not to allow political differences to interfere with personal friendships and his political views were often puzzlingly paradoxical. Some of his own forecasts are good and some which he records have been proved by subsequent events to be startlingly accurate. The controversial note is tiring and it is as difficult a diary as any to discuss without entering into the merits of his views or embarking on acute controversies of recent date.

The two volumes published cover the period from 1888 to 1914.[1] A reader may be at once amazed at the vigour and freshness with which the long entries are written. Never do we get the fragmentary jotting of the tired man who takes out his diary to make his entry the last thing before going to bed. The reason for this is interesting. His Eastern

[1] Quotations from *My Diaries*, by Wilfrid Blunt, are given with the kind consent of Messrs. Martin Secker, Ltd.

travels had accustomed him to early rising and it was in the freshness of the early morning hours that he wrote his diary, a habit which, judging by the result, is worthy of imitation. Most of us, however, even could we rise early enough, might feel disinclined to review incidents of the previous day which a night of rest and oblivion may seem to relegate into a page of the past. But Wilfrid Blunt was alive and alert, looking forward and backward, self-regardant, observant and with a desperate "itch to record." He was very social and often seems inclined to rate what he calls "excellent conversation" as a test of character and intelligence.

His personal sketches are sometimes very good, although occasionally tinged with bitterness. He shows less scorn for his political opponents than he does for those who appear to agree with him but who in his view fail him and betray the cause in question. In controversy he was fearless and he liked directing his attack boldly at the central figure—"in big-game shooting it is safest to leave the antelopes alone and go straight for the rhinoceros." Nothing delighted him more than to set every one by the ears. "My bomb has exploded with a real bang. . . . It could hardly have made a bigger noise."

Typical entries may be given in 1896 and 1906 in which he epitomizes his own position politically in an uncompromising way:

1896. We have now managed in the last six months to quarrel violently with China, Turkey, Belgium, Ashanti, France, Venezuela, America and Germany. This is a record performance and if it does not break up the British Empire nothing will. For myself I am glad of it all, for the British Empire is the great engine of evil for the weak races now existing in the world—not that we are worse than the French or Italians or Americans—indeed we are less actively destructive—but we do it over a far wider area and more successfully.

1909. There has been a debate in Parliament on the military danger from Germany and Frederick Harrison has a long letter about it in the 'Times.' I agree with him that the danger is a very real one of invasion and ruin within no great number of years only he does not draw the inference I draw namely, that we should hasten to divest ourselves of our overgrown overseas Empire and devote our naval and military resources to the defence of our own shores. We shall not do this and we shall perish as the Roman Empire perished by trying to hold too much. I am myself the extremest of all possible little Englanders and would cheerfully return to the 'spacious' days of Queen Elizabeth when we held not a foot of land outside the kingdom.

It will be impossible to make any selections from the long detailed discussions on Egyptian affairs made both while he is living out there and when he is at his home in Sussex. Nor because of their length can we give his very well told stories of incidents such as that of the boy bitten by the wolf in Egypt or the inquest on the girl who was run over in Sussex.

To give one instance, we like to find him writing as fully about his woodreeve's death as about Prime Ministers, ambassadors and authors.

My old woodreeve, Bates, at Crabbet has hanged himself in his cart shed—a man of genius in his way of life, who, beginning as a day labourer, rose to be the best judge of timber in Sussex as well as a successful farmer and churchwarden of the parish. Having completed eighty-four years of life and fifty of honest service in the Crabbet Estate and having entertained his friends the night before, he went out early in the morning to his shed and was found there dead hanging from a beam. I can imagine the old man carefully tying the noose, as his manner was, without a mistake. It was noticed by those who had been with him at dinner the night before that during the meal he had a hank of rope on his knees with which he was playing. In the morning he had got up by candlelight, asked his old wife "How are you, old girl?" and had gone out to the cart shed where he was found hanging.

The diary observations indeed are by no means confined to public events. He has many interests and is a close observer of nature. The notes of the cuckoo, the swallows flitting into his bathroom, his horses and country pursuits, plays and dinner parties, the meetings of the Crabbet Club and the books he reads are included in his record and give it the colour and personality which political dissertations generally fail to give. Nevertheless, in Wilfrid Blunt's case, his opinions on politics are so vehement and pronounced that they cannot be passed over with indifference.

He has the diarist's habit of a general reflection at the end of the year. At the close of the nineteenth century he is in a particularly violent mood and after epitomizing the condition of affairs in the world, ends :

> The whole white race is revelling openly in violence as though it had never pretended to be Christian. God's equal curse be upon them all ! So ends the famous nineteenth century in which we were proud to have been born.

> 1910. The year 1910 has been for me on the whole a happy one. Politically I still fight on and have accomplished much but it has been in what looks more and more a losing battle. I doubt if I shall see the accomplishment of any of my dreams. The cause of Eastern liberty is dark at present. In Persia it seems lost and in Turkey to be in no little danger. Without the resuscitation of the Ottoman Empire Egypt will remain in English hands till a stronger robber comes. Still we must fight on and I have done my best. What will the New Year bring ? I dare not prophesy.

> 1911. To-day a sad year ends ; the worst politically I can remember since the eighties, bloodshed, massacre and destruction everywhere, and all accepted here in England with cynical approval, our Foreign Office being accomplice with the evildoers. . . . It has been a losing battle in which I have fought long but with no result of good. I am old and weary and discouraged and would if I could slink out of the fight. I am useless in the face of an entirely hostile world.

Ill-health, as is inevitable with diarists, produces the note of depression. But, as editor, Wilfrid Blunt declares that " bodily infirmities should be hidden as far as possible from public view," so we only catch glimpses of him as he wrote in fever and sickness. In 1898 he writes :

> I spent the afternoon talking about the chances of life and death and of a world beyond. The longer I live the less I believe in any such, at least so far as my own living again goes. I feel that I have worn out my vital force and that eternity can bring me nothing but a dreamless sleep.

And in 1913 :

> A black melancholy is on me caused by a sense of my failure everywhere in life. My poetry, my Eastern politics, my Arab horse breeding, were strings to my bow and they have one after another snapped and to-day looking through my memoirs, I perceive how slackly they were written and how unworthy they are of survival. Yet the diaries are full of things too important for me to destroy and they overwhelm me with despair.

This is an interesting entry because it shows that Wilfrid Blunt thought that the exposure of political intrigues, the recital of political negotiation, the tracing of foreign policy, the indiscreet utterances of statesmen and diplomatists were the important matters which were worthy of survival. Whereas, as a matter of fact, these sorts of things very soon become stale. So far, however, as he allowed his personality and his stray passing opinions to emerge in passages which he considered no doubt of little account his diary as a human document is of unquestionable value.

The personal character studies are done sometimes in a sentence or two as when he says of Lord Dufferin that he was "too fond of paying little insincere compliments": sometimes in a controversial tone as when he writes on Gladstone's retirement:

> I suppose now he is gone there will be a general chorus of praise, but for my part I shall not join in it. He has betrayed too many good causes not to be an evil doer in my eyes and his one remaining cause, Ireland, he leaves in the lurch to-day by his retirement.

Other caustic remarks about people both dead and still living it would hardly be desirable to quote. But he often goes out of his way to give a full estimate of a character. These are long: some passages can be extracted.

> *William Morris.* He is the most wonderful man I have known, unique in this, that he had no thought of any thing or person, including himself but only for the work he had in hand. He was not selfish in the sense of seeking his own advantage or pleasure or comfort but he was too absorbed in his own thoughts to be either openly affectionate or actively kind. . . . To the rest of the world he seemed quite indifferent and he never, I am sure, returned the affection I gave him. He liked to talk to me because I knew how to talk to him and our fence of words furbished his wit, but I doubt if he would have crossed the street to speak to me. . . . The truth is he would not give an hour of his *time* to anyone, he held it to be too valuable.
>
> *Herbert Spencer.* On the whole I am disappointed with Spencer. He is so very dry, and so much wrapped up in himself, his ailments, his work, and his ideas to the exclusion, it seems to me, of individual sympathies. His mind is clear and logical, he expresses himself well, but without eloquence or such power as compels attention: not once was I able to feel myself in the presence of a *great* man, only a very well informed one, a pedagogue and able reasoner.

In yet another way he portrays character by accounts of conversation and discussions. This is specially the case in his constant entries of his intimate intercourse with his friend and cousin, George Wyndham. Although politically they were poles apart, there was deep sympathy between the two men and a reader may see them sufficiently clearly in these talks to be able to criticize them both and at the same time to gather much information as to the inner workings of the political machine.

Blunt knew many politicians and diplomatists personally. Although on friendly terms with many of them he was never impressed by their official eminence: "official greatness is made up of very small things as a mountain is made up of a tumble of small stones." Enjoyment of the social qualities of his guests did not blunt his critical faculty. Of one brilliant talker he writes: "I think he will not do anything of real value in the way of serious work, looking always for immediate applause in what he does. It is the snare of all brilliant talkers and facile writers." The incongruous and paradoxical appealed to his sense of humour. While carrying on in his usual way through members of Parliament and others his attack against the Government in 1911, he makes an offer of game to No. 10 Downing Street which is accepted. He writes:

> There is something comic in the idea of my contributing to the support of Downing Street just at present, and acting the part of Whiteley to the Prime Ministerial family.

This Diary will be politically interesting to future generations, more especially to students of Anglo-Egyptian relations: it will give some vivid first-hand pictures of public men; and it will depict a remarkably interesting personality in the diarist himself. In the personal aspect of the diary, however, we do not get the full detail. Wilfrid Blunt the diarist probably wrote about his domestic affairs perhaps with equal indiscretion and want of reserve. He certainly placed no value on reticence. But Wilfrid Blunt the editor has not allowed this part of the diary to be printed. Beyond casual references to his near relations we find no intimate entries such as are common in older diaries not written for publication. As a memoir, therefore, the volumes already published (and more may follow) will have more value than as a diary.

His Diary in Paris in 1870 is also published with the others. It is an excellent recital of events. The buoyant optimism of the young man in those days may be judged by his birthday entry:

This is my birthday of thirty, it finds me healthy, wealthy and wise, three things I never thought to be.

# INDEX

## OF DIARIES AND CHRONICLES NOTICED IN THIS VOLUME

Printed in Great Britain by Butler & Tanner Ltd., Frome and London